PERGAMON INTERNATIONAL LIBRARY
of Science, Technology, Engineering and Social Studies

*The 1000-volume original paperback library in aid of education,
industrial training and the enjoyment of leisure*

Publisher: Robert Maxwell, M.C.

Life After School

A Social Skills Curriculum

GW00703257

THE PERGAMON TEXTBOOK
INSPECTION COPY SERVICE

An inspection copy of any book published in the Pergamon International Library will gladly be sent to academic staff without obligation for their consideration for course adoption or recommendation. Copies may be retained for a period of 60 days from receipt and returned if not suitable. When a particular title is adopted or recommended for adoption for class use and the recommendation results in a sale of 12 or more copies, the inspection copy may be retained with our compliments. The Publishers will be pleased to receive suggestions for revised editions and new titles to be published in this important International Library.

Other Pergamon titles of interest

G. BARON
The Politics of School Government

G. GOULD
Learning and Language in the Classroom

C. REDDINGTON
Can Theatre Teach?

M. ROSS
The Aesthetic Imperative: Relevance and Responsibility in Arts Education
The Arts and Personal Growth

P. E. TROWER
Cognitive Perspectives in Social Skills Training

A Related Pergamon Journal

LANGUAGE & COMMUNICATION*

An Interdisciplinary Journal

Editor: Roy Harris, University of Oxford

The primary aim of the journal is to fill the need for a publicational forum
devoted to the discussion of topics and issues in communication which are of
interdisciplinary significance. It will publish contributions from researchers in
all fields relevant to the study of verbal and non-verbal communication.

Emphasis will be placed on the implications of current research for establishing
common theoretical frameworks within which findings from different areas of
study may be accommodated and interrelated.

By focusing attention on the many ways in which language is integrated
with other forms of communicational activity and interactional behaviour it is
intended to explore ways of developing a science of communication which is not
restricted by existing disciplinary boundaries.

*Free specimen copy available on request.

Life After School

A Social Skills Curriculum

by
JAMES McGUIRE and **PHILIP PRIESTLEY**

PERGAMON PRESS

OXFORD · NEW YORK · TORONTO · SYDNEY · PARIS · FRANKFURT

U.K.	Pergamon Press Ltd., Headington Hill Hall, Oxford OX3 0BW, England
U.S.A.	Pergamon Press Inc., Maxwell House, Fairview Park, Elmsford, New York 10523, U.S.A.
CANADA	Pergamon Press Canada Ltd., Suite 104, 150 Consumers Rd., Willowdale, Ontario M2J 1P9, Canada
AUSTRALIA	Pergamon Press (Aust.) Pty. Ltd., P.O. Box 544, Potts Point, N.S.W. 2011, Australia
FRANCE	Pergamon Press SARL, 24 rue des Ecoles, 75240 Paris, Cedex 05, France
FEDERAL REPUBLIC OF GERMANY	Pergamon Press GmbH, 6242 Kronberg-Taunus, Hammerweg 6, Federal Republic of Germany

First edition 1981
Reprinted 1982 (twice)

British Library Cataloguing in Publication Data

McGuire, James
Life after school.
1. Group relations training
I. Title II. Priestley, Philip
305.2'3   HM132
ISBN 0-08-025192-7 (Hardcover)
ISBN 0-08-025193-5 (Flexicover)

Library of Congress Catalog Card no: 81-82096

Printed in Great Britain by A. Wheaton & Co. Ltd., Exeter

Acknowledgments

Many people have contributed, directly and indirectly, to the preparation of this book, and we would like to thank them here.

For help in producing some of the materials, we are grateful to Erzsi Hurley, Alun Connick, James Le Feuvre, Corinne Churchill, Alison Brook, John Ewing, Renee Chanda, Marian Barrett, Sue Cowe, Andrew Pugh, Philip Enticott, and Peter Salisbury, all of the Youth Employment Officer training course at Bristol Polytechnic; to Gordon Kelsey, photographer at Bristol University; Dr Jane Grubb; Gill Cally and Rodney Ford; Mrs J. Wood; and Peter Soord, Jack Quinn, John Clennel, Jim Cowley, and Jack Binks, of the Sheffield Day Training Centre.

A number of other valuable comments and suggestions were made by Sheila Vellacott, by Val Stacey, and by Chris Toon.

For collecting some of the information used in chapter three, we would like to thank: Midi Berry and Bruce Clarke of the Swindon Work Opportunities Project; Paul Bishop of Grimsby College of Technology; Sandy Hauxwell of City and East London College; Peter Leeds of the Neasden Centre of Kilburn Polytechnic; Mary McGinty and L.A. Shorthouse of the Youth at Work Service, Cheltenham; Alan Moodie, formerly Education Officer at Haslaı Detention Centre, Gosport; Suzanna Roper, of Paddington College; Chris Walsh, of South Cheshire College of Further Education, Crewe; and all of the young people who completed questionnaires for us in these places.

Some of the exercises outlined in this book were illustrated in a BBC Continuing Education series, 'Skills for Survival', broadcast on Radio 4 during 1980. We would like to thank Simon Major, producer of the series, Jude Howells, Sarah Rowlands, and Chris Stone, programme producers, and all of the administrative staff who were involved in making the programmes. Warm thanks are also due to the tutors, youth workers, and young people who took part in the programmes: to Bruce Clarke of the Swindon Work Opportunities Project; Beverley Dann and Brian Clark of South Thames College; Stuart Eglin and Ron Nichol of Glenrothes College of Further Education; Linda Hogman of Thurrock YOP Centre, Essex; John Hopkins of City and East London College; Rose Millington and Pat Price of the Clocktower Young Adults Project, Bristol; Bridget Mitton of the Bow Centre, Sheffield; Alan Moodie of Haslar Detention Centre; Suzanna Roper of Paddington College; Gordon Rudd and Tess Weston of Liverpool Victoria Settlement; Peter Stewart of Bolton YOP Unit; and Hassan Yilmaz of the West Devon Community Service Scheme.

Finally, we owe a great debt to Mrs Rosemary Westley, of Morgan-Westley, for producing a clear camera-copy from what was a nightmare jumble of messy typing, corrections handwritten on trains, and pasted-on afterthoughts; and to Barbara Barrett and Alïx Wiles, our editors at Pergamon Press.

NOTE

Suggestions concerning sources of further materials and ideas are made at the end of each section in chapter five; all references from this and the other chapters are gathered together at the end of the book.

Contents

1 Introduction

The nostalgia felt by most adults for the untroubled days of their schooling is hard to reconcile with the elated air of most individuals when their schooldays come to an end. For the majority of young people, it would probably not be unfair to say that the last day of school is one of wholehearted celebration. Gone are the tiresome routines and seemingly endless confinements of the classroom and timetable; vanished for ever is the lowly status that adheres to the wearing of school uniform or the dependence on adults for pocket-money. If the passing of schooldays is tinged with regret, this will soon be replaced by an absorption in the pursuit of new goals keenly anticipated prior to departure from school. For the next day marks the adolescent's first entry into the adult world and the acquisition of a new kind of independence.

For many, however, the euphoria may be all too short-lived. Exit from school means confrontation with a new set of problems that have to be solved. Finding work, or coping with the strains of unemployment; managing money in limited amounts; making the most worthwhile use of time; handling changed relationships within the family; and coping with a range of other people, including the opposite sex; using, in other words, their new-found freedom to the best advantage – all require a variety of skills with which those leaving school may be only poorly equipped. Failure to solve these and other problems might have still more serious consequences: continuing unemployment; personal difficulties of many kinds; and in some cases, a resort to delinquent courses of action that can have an impact on individuals' lives over many of the ensuing years.

This book is about the position in which those who are about to leave school, or who have recently left, find themselves. Its aim is to present teachers, tutors, counsellors, youth workers, and others concerned with the

1

welfare and education of young people, with ideas and materials they can use in preparing the young for the transition from school to the wider community — or for coping with their lot once this transition has been made. Specifically, the book describes and illustrates methods of doing this, developed in recent years under the collective heading of 'social and life skills training'. These methods, drawn from a number of sources and used with a variety of groups, have the common aim of helping people to get better at solving the kinds of problems with which those leaving school are faced.

Much has been written about the adolescent years as a period of rapid and dramatic change in an individual's life. Between the early and late teenage years, there is an almost complete transformation in behaviour and experience. There are bodily changes associated with growth in general, and with the onset of puberty and sexual maturity in particular. Linked with these, there are emotional shifts — in the range of feelings experienced towards both self and others, and in the degree of control attained over them. There are intellectual changes such as the ability to grasp new concepts, and to cope with an increasing quantity of information emanating from the surrounding world. And there are social mutations, new roles to be adopted, rules to be learnt, and an expanding array of possibilities for diverse kinds of relationships. Not least of the complications is the fact that each of these developments might take place at quite different rates in different individuals. Working in concert, such alterations and others have a complex and often conflicting impact on the developing person's sense of identity.

But contemporary circumstances have combined to make the world to which the growing adolescent must adapt more awkward still. Amongst the miseries which our present economic predicament has visited upon the young, the worst may be the high level of youth unemployment which has become a recurrent, if not endemic, feature of the Western economies. Jobs, with their accompanying guarantees of at least some income and respect, can no longer be promised at the end of school: this despite a widespread rise in the career expectations of young people. Simultaneously, provision for the constructive use of leisure time is almost everywhere inadequate. More generally, there is a stark ambiguity in current definitions of the rights of the young. It is illegal for a girl to drink in a public house before she is 18; drive a car before she is 17; have sexual relations before she is 16. Yet teenagers constitute a sizeable market, and are seen as a legitimate target for the solicitings of large-scale advertising, pressuring them into patterns of consumption linked with supposedly desirable styles of life.

In addition, the social fabric to which young people must adjust has never been more complex. Not only has the unabated growth of legislation made the worlds of work or of social welfare progressively more difficult to understand, but the social environment itself is more variegated. Geographical mobility is greater, and the number of goals which it is possible (at least in theory) to pursue, is in most spheres of life larger than ever before. Even the rate at which these changes take place is accelerating; such that the experience of the members of one generation may be obsolete by the time they become parents or teachers of the next.

It is a commonly held view that school should become a more relevant introduction to the world beyond it; that more could be done to prepare adolescents for the situations that will face them after leaving, and which they may have to negotiate on their own. School, after all, contributes much to the overall process of socialisation, through which individuals are shaped as members of the society into which they are born. In this respect, schooling influences not only the academic performance of its pupils, in line with its professed aims; it also has a powerful effect on an individual's social behaviour and on his manner of dealing with others (Morrison and McIntyre, 1971; Rutter et al, 1979). Formal education clearly has the *potential* to turn out individuals able to solve their problems on their own. In the 'Great Debate' on education in the late 1970s, in addition to the 'core' subjects such as English and mathematics, aimed at imparting the fundamental skills of literacy and numeracy, a number of other subjects were considered by many to be of 'universal relevance' to children in school. These included an introduction to the 'world of work' and to the business of choosing a career, and some acquaintance with what have been called the 'adult' subjects of politics, sex education, consumer affairs, and similar fields of study (Hopkins, 1978).

A survey of recent education might detect two broad 'traditions' of practice in attempting to make school a more relevant preparation for the world outside. The first of these subsumes a batch of subjects like those just mentioned, which are intended to provide some kind of understanding of the adult world. This is the domain of *social education*. Though the aims of this have been exceedingly diverse, and the contents of proposed social education curricula have covered a very wide range, it is possible to pinpoint some central concerns (Elliott and Pring, 1975). These revolve around, amongst others:

1. The giving of information about the operation of the human world of which the school is a part; and the attempt to foster a basic understanding of it through the social science subjects of economics, politics, and sociology. This element is sometimes called 'civics' or 'citizenship'.
2. The development of a familiarity with the local community.
3. The cultivation of a sense of personal responsibility and the inculcation of ethical standards. This element, which recognises the importance of the school as an agent of socialisation, has come to be known as 'moral education'.

An inventory of the topics which have been seen as suitable for inclusion in this kind of curriculum might contain, therefore, politics, economics, sociology, psychology, anthropology, sex education, money management, law, local geography, parenting, drama, ethics, and many more. The methods used would also show greater variety than might be found in the teaching of academic subjects; and might include films, drama or roleplay exercises, group discussions, and projects in the community. In many instances, however, particularly in the teaching of the social science subjects, instruction seems to have remained the favoured mode of teaching. Only moral education has made something of a departure in devising new methods and materials. And allied in some respects to social education but with its own separate aims and methods, vocational guidance has also played a significant part in attuning those leaving schools to their prospects for the future.

A second, but quite different strand of activity which addresses itself to the individual's adjustment to the world outside school is school *counselling* (Jones, 1977). This however is designed primarily for those in specific difficulty of some kind, and is normally conducted on a one-to-one basis. The problems dealt with by counsellors have usually been of a much more personal nature, deriving perhaps from a young person's troubles at home, in relation to sex, in coping with feelings of anxiety or depression, or in making some important kind of decision. In other instances, counsellors have also been concerned with the overall personal development of children in school, and have adopted strategies for encouraging the growth of self-awareness and of an appreciation of others and one's effect upon them. To achieve these goals, the methods employed have been those commonly associated with counselling and 'group-work' — which have their ultimate origins in psychiatry — such as interviewing, discussion, psychodrama, 'encounter group' games, and confrontation (Button, 1974; Douglas, 1976). Outside schools, similar methods to these have also been employed in youth work, where it has been possible to organise groups in less formal settings such as clubs, youth centres, settlements and in special youth or community projects.

In terms of both method and content these two approaches to preparing young people for living in the 'real' world have been quite distinct. Social education has for the most part focussed on familiarising the student with the local area on the one hand, or the nature of society on the other — using the medium of direct instruction in the main. Group-work and counselling, by and large, have concentrated on the internal or psychological state of the developing adolescent, and have more frequently utilised interviewing or sensitivity-training techniques. While there is a need for both of these elements, they are also subject to some limitations. Social education often directs the attention of the learner to issues which, though important, may seem somewhat distanced from his or her everyday life; indeed some social education has deliberately eschewed everyday problems, for fear of failing to broaden the pupils' horizons. Counselling and group-work, though invaluable, have tended to locate their concerns almost entirely within the developing individual. Put together, the two seem to leave a gap in the preparation of the learner for adult life.

The gap that is left could be characterised as the meeting-point between private and public life; the domain of human activity that is intermediate between the intimate and personal on the one hand, and the structural or societal on the other. This is the arena in which individual needs come face to face with the laws and customs that govern our lives; in which one person's understanding of and ability to deal with the world comes up against reality as it applies to him or her. Much could be gained from an attempt to tackle this kind of problem explicitly; and social and life skills training has arisen out of efforts to meet this kind of need. The overall purpose of this book is to describe how such training can be adapted to fill the aforementioned kind of gap. The specific aims of the book are to:

1. Introduce social skills training and related methods of helping people to solve their problems.
2. Present a variety of exercises, pertaining to a number of problem areas, for direct use by teachers, tutors, counsellors and youth workers in the classroom and other settings.
3. Make a number of suggestions as to how users of the book can design new exercises of their own, for incorporation into their existing work or for the construction of a full-scale *social skills curriculum.*

To achieve these aims, the book is organised as follows. In the next chapter, the background to social and life skills training methods is outlined, to help clarify their nature and some of the ways in which they have been used. In chapter 3, some of the problems faced by young people who are about to leave school, or who have recently left, are looked at — in the words of young people themselves in this position. Chapter 4 describes social skills training and affiliated methods in more detail; and illustrates a number of different ways in which they can be used. Then, in chapter 5, a selection of materials and exercises is presented for direct application in work with young people. These are arranged into a number of substantive areas, each concerned with a group of problems with which individuals might be faced, or linked to the broader aims of developing self-awareness. Thus they include: self-assessment; work; leisure; interaction; sex; money; and rights. Following this in chapter 6, some additional points are made about the generation and development of new methods and materials, and their assembly into sessions or courses.

2 Social Skills Training: the background

In this book, an approach to social education is presented which is founded on a particular way of viewing the situation of individuals in the period just before and after leaving school. It defines their situation as a set of problems that have to be solved; and regards social education as a systematic attempt to help individuals *acquire the skills* of solving these problems by themselves.

In practice, of course, the successful solving of problems involves more than just skill. It might call for the possession of information relevant to the difficulty being faced; or might require that the individual hold specific attitudes or entertain certain beliefs without which his approach to solving problems will be hampered. Social education as it is currently conceived already deals with these aspects of problem-solving. But the social education curriculum could be considerably expanded were it also to incorporate methods of helping people to acquire particular kinds of skills – in short, what have come to be known as *social and life skills.*

The purpose of this chapter is to introduce social and life skills training, by looking briefly at its aims and at the areas in which it has been developed. At the same time, the chapter will also map out some of the links that already exist between this kind of training and social education.

WHAT ARE SOCIAL AND LIFE SKILLS?

Social and life skills are those kinds of skills that we use when dealing with others, which are generally important for our ability to function successfully in society – to achieve those goals which depend, in part, on the mediation of other people. By the phrase 'social skills' most people mean those kinds of behaviour which are basic to effective face-to-face communication between individuals. By 'life skills' on the other hand, most people understand some more complex kinds of behaviour that are essential to survival in society, and to the solving of such problems as finding a job or managing money. No really hard and fast distinction can be made between 'social' and 'life' skills, and in contemporary usage the two terms have become almost interchangeable. There have, in the past, however, been some differences of emphasis between work called 'social skills training' and that called 'life skills training', which are brought out later in this chapter. The present book is addressed to the whole array of abilities usually encompassed by the 'social and life skills' heading.

Exactly which kinds of skill fall within this broad definition? In fact the range extends widely, from the capacity to look other people in the eyes while you are speaking to them, to the ability to make a fairly complicated decision about money, rights, or accommodation, for example, and put it into effect. To simplify things a little, however, it may be useful to sort these skills into three large classes:

1 Self-knowledge or self-awareness skills

A knowledge of yourself and of your own limits is of immense benefit in itself and may be indispensible for solving some kinds of problems. To gain this knowledge, some skills are required; for example, the skills of assessing yourself; or finding out your own good and bad points, or strengths and weaknesses in a given area of life; the skills of understanding your own motives, appraising your own preferences, and setting your own personal goals.

2. Interactive skills

To most people, associating with others is both an end in itself, and a means of achieving other goals. Either way, a number of skills are required when dealing with others regardless of the specific situation. These include the skills of self-expression; of talking clearly; of understanding your effect on others; of interpreting other people's motives; of self-assertiveness or resisting social pressures; of listening; or of using the telephone. What most people regard as 'social skills training' is concerned with skills in this area.

3. Problem-solving skills

Going through life, especially in a society as complex as ours, there are many other specific problems to be solved. All of these call for specialised skills of one kind or another. So we also need skills like finding information; filling in forms; making decisions; thinking of alternative courses of action and choosing between them; and making plans, short- or long-term, in relation to numerous compartments of life such as work, leisure, spending habits, or the family.

It is a fairly common observation that some individuals are much more successful than others, not only in terms of securing higher incomes or acquiring more possessions — the commonly accepted indices of achievement — but also in terms of the amount they 'get out of' life. While many factors obviously contribute to these differences, at least one of them may be that those who do get more out of life are more skilled in negotiating life's twists and turns. This brings us to a vital feature of the skills surveyed above: they can be *learned*. Or perhaps more apposite to our present purposes, they can be *taught*. Just as we might learn to drive a car — just as a learner progresses in a few months from being unable to drive a car to being fully equipped to do so — so the skills of self-appraisal, social interaction, and problem-solving can also be acquired under suitable conditions of instruction.

As a matter of fact, the course of normal social and personal development involves the subtle 'teaching' of these skills. From our parents or caretakers, initially, we learn the use of language and of the various non-verbal 'signals' — gestures and facial expressions, for instance — that are accepted as conventional in our society for conveying particular messages. Parents teach their children, albeit in an unconscious and invisible way (though it may on occasion be quite explicit) to act and react as human beings in their own culture's use of that term. Later, a wider range of individuals — notably teachers, friends, leaders of clubs, or perhaps personalities seen on television — suggest in an equally tacit way how to behave in a whole spectrum of other situations met with outside the home. In each case the growing child learns by watching other people and by copying, or partially copying, what they do.

Of course, the precise nature of the learning that is going on here is very complex, and a number of different processes must be taking place. Nevertheless, the mechanisms involved are straightforward enough to make it possible to teach social and life skills by deliberate, conscious effort. This kind of effort — known as 'social and life skills training' — is the cornerstone of the approach to social education advocated in this book.

WHAT IS SOCIAL AND LIFE SKILLS TRAINING?

'Social and life skills training' then, is any organised attempt to help people acquire or develop the kinds of skills itemised above — for looking at themselves, dealing with others, or solving the problems that confront them. The overall aim of such training is to enable individuals to increase the range — and quality — of things they can do in order to get more out of life.

It may be useful to clarify first of all what this does *not* mean, and hopefully to eradicate some of the myths and misconceptions that have grown up around social skills training. Social skills training does not mean, first of all, training people to become automatons. It does not involve prescribing for individuals the ways in which they should deal with particular kinds of encounter; nor is it geared towards the production of individuals who respond in a mechanical and stereotyped fashion in interactions with others. Its aims are exactly the opposite of this: to help people expand the repertoire of their interactive skills, and so react in a more flexible manner to the demands of their social environment. The choice of whether or not to exercise a particular skill on any given occasion resides with the individual. Second, social skills training is not designed merely to induce individuals into accepting, or learning to live with, unacceptable situations or circumstances. Helping people acquire (for example) job search skills is not the same as reinforcing their acquiescence to the work ethic and their status as employees. Aiding an individual in the control of his temper is not in itself an attempt to suppress his occasionally righteous outrage. Training someone in leisure skills in an area of high unemployment is not to condone the denial of a job to her by influences apparently beyond her control. Indeed, helping individuals appreciate that the privations to which they are subject are no fault of their own may be a valuable first step in a consciousness-raising exercise.

In essence, social skills training runs a close parallel to skills training of other kinds; but as suggested above, skills alone will not enable individuals to solve their problems. The analogy with learning to drive a car, referred to above, may help to make this clear. To drive a car properly, you need not only skill — of operating the controls, and so forth — but also a certain amount of *knowledge*. In the case of driving, this knowledge is of the rules and regulations that govern motorists, embodied in the Highway Code. In addition, you will need to have appropriate *attitudes*. No-one who just does not want to will ever learn to drive. Similarly, a belief that other drivers have no right to be on the road, or an overwhelming fear of traffic jams, will stand in the way of any attempt to drive and might lead to disaster. So skills have to be seen, inescapably, as being bound up with appropriate information and attitudes.

Further, even the skills involved in driving a car are of at least two sorts. There are manipulative skills such as steering, gear-changing, and so on; and a variety of mental skills to do with anticipating events, comprehending other drivers' intentions, and making quick decisions. The successful use of social and life skills training involves all of these components together — information, attitudes, behavioural and mental skills.

The approach to social education adopted in this book rests on the assertion that all of these strands can be knitted together in a social education curriculum. Children leaving school need facts about the situations that will face them. They also require attitudes of particular kinds for dealing with sticky problems. And finally — and this is where there seem to be glaring gaps at present — they also need skills: both on the interpersonal level, and at the level of 'thinking' or 'cognition'.

At every stage, those involved in social education — whether in schools, further education colleges, youth and community work, or other settings — should be aiming to equip young people with the capacity to solve problems autonomously. This is why the notion of teaching *skills* is at the root of the methods outlined in this book. Giving individuals the facts they need to solve a problem is certainly helpful. Giving them the ability to find things out for themselves is more helpful still.

ORIGINS OF SOCIAL SKILLS TRAINING

Relative to other forms of education, social skills training is fairly new. As with any innovative development, however, it was founded on earlier work in a number of other fields. It is the product of a convergence of ideas and practices from several different directions. A brief account of some of these may illuminate the nature of some of the methods to be described in chapter 4.

The theoretical roots of social skills training methods are to be found in *social learning theory* (Bandura, 1969,1971,1973). This theory in turn evolved from behaviourist ideas about human development that were in currency during the earlier decades of the present century, centred on such concepts as stimulus, response, and reinforcement. To the social learning theorist, however, behaviour cannot be explained merely in terms of the shaping of responses by rewards and punishments, as in earlier and more rudimentary versions of behaviourist learning theory. What went on between stimulus and response had to be taken into account: the part played in learning, in other words, by the active thinking and searching of the learner himself.

Central to the social-learning account of child development is the idea of *modelling* and of learning from models. 'Most of the behaviours that people display are learned, either deliberately or inadvertently, through the influence of example' (Bandura, 1971, p.5). Were learning to take place only through the direct experience of rewards and punishments, the social learning theorists argue, the process of human growth would be exceedingly lengthy and not a little perilous. Much of what we learn, fortunately, we learn by the observation of others; and evidently, those 'models' which are present during our early and adolescent development play a key part in influencing what we learn and how thoroughly we learn it. Social learning theorists have undertaken much research in attempting to isolate those characteristics of individuals which make them effective as models; and have also expended much energy trying to understand the precise nature of the mechanisms involved in this kind of learning.

What is important for our present purposes is that this process of *observational learning* can be put to work in the direct teaching of social behaviour — to those who, for whatever reason, seem to have failed to learn such behaviour; or to those who have learned other kinds of behaviour which are damaging to themselves or those around them. Such teaching, based on the use of modelling and related processes, has proven itself to be very useful in assisting individuals with a variety of behavioural and interpersonal problems.

The most extensive applications of social skills training that have been made so far have been in the fields of psychiatry and clinical psychology. Here, the study of social skill has been part of the wider study of social interaction as a whole — the investigation of the effects individuals have upon each other, the patterns their behaviour are likely to follow in different sets of circumstances, and topics akin to these. The observation, made by many workers, that some kinds of psychiatric patients seem to *lack* those social skills which others of us take for granted — the ability for example to hold an ordinary conversation, to express oneself, or to show an interest in others — led to the suggestion that it might be possible to help these individuals by giving them training in the corresponding social skills. It has even been proposed that a lack of social skills may be partly responsible for the onset of psychiatric illness. However that may be, '. . . The social performance of all patients is disturbed in one way or another, they are unsuccessful interactors and in some cases the main symptoms are in this area . . . It follows that, whether the social deficit is causal or not, it may be possible to help mental patients by training in the area of social skills' (Argyle, 1969, p.336).

Consequently, a considerable volume of work has been reported which had the aim of giving psychiatric patients and other 'social problem' groups some training in the skills of social interaction. The patient groups involved have included both neurotics and schizophrenics, and both in-patients and out-patients. In some instances the objective of the research has been the provision of a comprehensive training programme for patients about to leave hospital (Goldstein, Sprafkin, and Gershaw, 1976). Other pieces of research have had more limited aims including:

— training patients in general social skills, and to cope with a variety of problem situations (e.g. Argyle, Bryant, and Trower, 1974; Argyle, Trower, and Bryant, 1974; Goldsmith and McFall, 1975; Marzillier, Lambert, and Kellett, 1976; Trower, Bryant, and Argyle, 1978);
— training individuals in assertiveness and independence (e.g. Eisler, Hersen, and Miller, 1973; Hersen, Eisler, and Miller, 1973);
— helping individuals to overcome social isolation (e.g. Gutride, Goldstein, and Hunter, 1973);
— training in the control of abusive verbal outbursts or 'explosive rages'

(Foy, Eisler, and Pinkston, 1975; Frederiksen, Jenkins, Foy, and Eisler, 1976);
— training alcoholics to refuse drinks effectively (Foy, Miller, Eisler, and O'Toole, 1976).

Various forms of training in assertiveness have also been used with 'normal' populations such as students, to help them conquer problems such as shyness and social anxiety (McFall and Twentyman, 1973; Twentyman and McFall, 1975), or become more relaxed and adept in the skills of dating (Curran, 1975). In addition, modelling and related exercises have been used to good effect with offender groups including juvenile delinquents (Sarason and Ganzer, 1973; Thelen, Fry, Dollinger, and Paul, 1976) and sex offenders (Crawford, 1976).

The results of these studies have been generally positive though in some cases the effects of social skills training have been somewhat limited; and social skills training has not always proven more valuable than other forms of treatment or other kinds of psychotherapy. For dealing specifically with social skill deficits, however, training which incorporates modelling and associated methods has given clear demonstrations of its usefulness.

What, in practice, have been the constituents of this kind of training? The first stage in work with psychiatric and other groups is usually *assessment* — intended to discover exactly those areas in which an individual feels inadequate or lacking in confidence, or in which his interactive skills are visibly and markedly impaired. This assessment would involve interviews with the individual patient; completion by him of some sort of questionnaire about his level of social confidence or competence; and observation by others of his actual social behaviour. The *training* which ensued would then consist of four principal elements: *instruction* or *guidance* in the kinds of skill the individual wishes to learn; *demonstration* or *modelling* of these skills by others in roleplays; *practice* of the skills by the individual himself; and the giving of *feedback* to encourage the individual and help him further improve his performance (Spence, 1980; Trower, Bryant, and Argyle, 1978). A fuller account of these methods and of how they may be used is given in chapter 4.

OCCUPATIONAL TRAINING

A major impetus in the development of social skills training came, then, from psychiatry and from attempts to help patients and other groups who had difficulty in their dealings with others. All of this work could be said to revolve around the notion of social skill *deficit*: in that the individuals given the training had to some extent failed to acquire fundamental skills which the rest of us take for granted. In another quite different field, social skills training was used to help those who already possessed the normal range of skills, to acquire additional skills for use in their work. This was in the field of occupational training.

A great many occupations involve dealing with other people as an intrinsic part of the job itself; and for many of these encounters, specific kinds of skill are required. A familiar example is the work of the personnel manager, who must interview applicants for a job and assess their suitability. The skills of interviewing — of putting people at their ease, of asking questions, of judging motivation, or of giving information — may not come naturally to many people. However, it is possible to design training packages which help potential interviewers develop these skills. Sidney and Argyle (1969) for example set up a situation in which trainee interviewers had to deal with a series of awkward interviewees — who talked too much, were very shy, or were very nervous, for example. This both helped the interviewers to see whether they could handle these encounters and enabled their trainers to coach them where they seemed to be in difficulty.

But a large number of other skills are also susceptible to improvement using social skills training. Exercises have been devised in many industries for training people in such diverse skills as salesmanship; the art of negotiation; team leading and group problem solving; briefing, persuading, or motivating others; supervision; and public relations.

An illustration of this variant of social skills training is the work carried out in the Air Transport and Travel Industry Training Board (Morgan, Rackham, and Hudson, 1974a,b; Rackham and Morgan, 1977). This work was addressed to the needs of a variety of staff not solely in the air industry but also from elsewhere. The staff groups included managers, their advisers, personnel officers, and supervisors. The main aim of the work was to develop a short, intensive training course (under the title DIS — Developing Interactive Skills) which would provide a basis for the future improvement of their social skills by the course members. The skills covered in the course included accurate self-perception; interviewing and fact-finding; listening and communication; dealing with grievances and matters of discipline; and briefing and persuading others. The exercises used in the course were founded on observation and feedback. Using a set of pre-arranged categories for analysing the trainees' behaviour — which was of necessity very prescriptive since the component skills for each task were analysed in advance — the course organisers gave the trainees immediate and detailed feedback on how they had behaved in a variety of exercises which called the above skills into play. Evaluation of these courses suggested that they were very useful to trainees for their future development of these 'professional' social skills.

Thus, exercises which help individuals just to anticipate what will happen in various encounters, to assess their own ability to handle them, and where necessary to practise skills for handling them better, have demonstrated their usefulness with groups who already possess most of the 'basic' social skills. Latterly, training modules of this type have also been devised and implemented for a number of other occupational groups, including nurses (Goldstein and Goedhart, 1973) and other health service staff (Ellis, 1980), teachers (Brown, 1975), and bar staff (Flegg, 1979).

Apart from exploring the uses of social skills training, however, occupational — and particularly management — training has also influenced the development of life skills training through the forging of links between the ideas of skill development and those of *problem-solving*. The notion that people can be trained to solve problems and make complex decisions has been current in this field for some time (Adair, 1971; de Bono, 1970; Jackson, 1975; Whitfield, 1975). Models of the process of problem-solving — guidelines for tackling problems in a systematic, step-by-step manner — played a seminal part in the evolution of the idea that individuals could be trained to cope not only with the minutiae of social interaction, but also with the many other difficulties presented by everyday life. This merger between the methods of social skills training and the ideas of problem-solving was known, on the other side of the Atlantic where it occurred, as *life skills training*.

SOCIAL DISADVANTAGE AND LIFE SKILLS

During the 1960s in North America, a growing awareness of the extent of social disadvantage in the midst of apparently universal affluence led to a substantial channelling of funds and of effort into compensatory education programmes. The fate of the many 'Newstart' projects, and their general failure to redress the limited life chances of minority ethnic groups, is now well known. The majority of these programmes revolved around provision of extra resources for education in socially deprived areas; however, the bulk of this provision was aimed, perhaps not unnaturally, at the teaching of the standard academic subjects. A number of projects, though, sought to supplement the school curriculum with additional material concerned with the self-development of school students, with preparation for the world of work, and other related topics. From these projects there emerged a sizeable amount of material aimed at the nurturing of what were to be called 'life skills'.

Perhaps the earliest of these programmes to deal explicitly with the concept of life skills was that formulated by two psychologists, Winthrop Adkins and Sydney Rosenberg, in their proposals for a youth training project in New York City in 1965 (Conger, 1973). This initially focussed mainly on employment, and on those aspects of self-image which might influence success or failure in securing a job and coping with problems at work. In subsequent developments, these authors produced a series of multi-media units concerned with the skills involved in finding and keeping a job, and elaborated a *Life Skills Syllabus* (Adkins, n.d.) covering such topics as 'Developing one's self and relating to others' and 'Managing a career'. The approach developed by Adkins was highly structured, comprising a series of sessions each of which was organised according to the same formula, and backed up by an array of audio-visual aids including videotaped roleplays, audio-cassettes, and printed material (Lee, 1980). Due to limitations of funding, however, the further preparation of these life skills programmes was somewhat curtailed.

The largest-scale life skills programme yet developed — which took its inspiration from the work of Adkins and Rosenberg — was that run from 1969 onwards under the aegis of the Saskatchewan Newstart project in Prince Albert, Saskatchewan. This project was one of a number set up by the Canadian government during the mid-1960s in various provinces, aimed at '. . . developing new training and counselling methods for use with disadvantaged adults' (Lee, 1980). A 'Life Skills' division was set up within the project, which took as its remit the preparation of life skills teaching materials, and their systematic evaluation over a three-year period.

The target population for this project was socially disadvantaged adults. These were seen as adults earning low incomes, perhaps suffering long periods of unemployment, or if employed only intermittently so. Their educational attainments were poor, and their lives were characterised by instability, 'low levels of participation in the society surrounding them' (Himsl, 1973, p.13), and the not infrequent manifestation of a number of other difficulties such as marital breakdown, alcoholism, drug use, and impoverished personal relationships. To the Saskatchewan Newstart project staff, the disadvantaged appeared to encounter these misfortunes at least in part because they lacked 'life skills'.

What are 'life skills'? 'Life skills, precisely defined, means problem-solving behaviours appropriately and responsibly used in the management of personal affairs' (Himsl, 1973, p.13). The guiding idea of the project, therefore, was the training of the disadvantaged in a small number of 'problem solving behaviours' which would be applicable in a very large number of situations they would meet within everyday life. To transmit these abilities, the project staff designed a life skills *course* which was mounted repeatedly over a number of years with groups of disadvantaged adults.

A large quantity of material was specially developed for the running of these courses; including a substantial volume of printed material supported by slides, films, charts, videotapes and cassettes. A *Life Skills Coaching Manual* was prepared, consisting of 61 lessons covering five categories of content: *Self, Family, Leisure, Community,* and *Job.* The lessons were so arranged as to concentrate first of all on the analysis and development of a basic skill, and then to move on to the deployment of the skill in a number of different areas. The specific topics covered ranged from relatively simple items such as 'Seeing oneself on video' and 'Listening to others' to more complex and ambitious problem areas such as 'Getting out of a money trap' or 'Raising a family alone'. In addition to this wealth of material, sufficient in itself for the running of a four-month full-time life skills course, the project also produced shorter manuals for work with adolescents and with offender groups.

To run the courses, a number of life skills instructors or *coaches* were specially trained on an intensive, eight-week course. Considerable care was taken in the selection of these coaches, who were then given training in teaching and problem-solving; human relations; the use of social skills methods; and the use of all the material contained in the *Coaching Manual* itself (Curtiss & Friedman, 1973).

A total of 295 individuals took the life skills courses between 1970 and 1972; their responses to the course were extensively monitored and evaluated, using a variety of questionnaires, psychological tests and follow-up interviews. The results of this evaluation were very positive. Before- and after-course comparisions of the attitudes, feelings and behaviour of life skills trainees suggested that they benefited substantially from attendance on the course: in their views of themselves, in their dealings with others, and in their overall ability to cope. These findings were in marked contrast to those obtained from a 'control' group, who had been on a parallel course of 'basic education' only, and amongst whom no significant changes in any of the life skills indicators could be found. Two question-marks hang, however, over the real effectiveness of the Saskatchewan courses. First, it cannot be said whether or not the benefits which accrued to trainees as a result of the course persisted over a longer period. Interviews with members of one group twelve months later suggested the existence of a post-course 'slump' in morale after three months had elapsed from the course; following this however, their morale had steadily improved again (Warren and Lamrock, 1973). But what the longer-term effects of the courses were we shall never know, as the evaluation was interrupted by the cessation of funds. Second, there is also some doubt as to whether the trainees were genuinely better at solving specific problems which came their way. It has been suggested that in many of the lessons insufficient time was allowed for thorough practice of the skills supposedly being taught (Lee, 1980).

We have dwelt on this Canadian project at some length because it is the most comprehensive piece of work yet undertaken on the development and evaluation of life skills techniques. Also, the materials it produced have been widely used elsewhere in North America, and have provided a stimulus to the advent and dissemination of life skills teaching in the UK.

RECENT DEVELOPMENTS

While all of these innovations had been taking place in spheres outside social education — and indeed at a considerable remove from schools themselves — a number of projects within the purview of social education (as most people understand it) had already been following similar lines. The Cambridge Moral Education project developed materials for preparing young people to make decisions in a variety of dilemmas that might confront them (McPhail, Ungoed-Thomas, and Chapman, 1972). The Schools Council also sponsored other experiments in social education which incorporated some training in communication skills and directed the attention of pupils to particular difficult situations they might face (e.g. Rennie, Lunzer, and Williams, 1974). Workers in various disciplines pursued the use of simulation and roleplaying methods for teaching subjects in a lively, participative way (Taylor and Walford, 1978). In another project, secondary school pupils were given a series of exercises in self-assessment, designed to enrich their self-image and level of self-awareness by compiling a *Record of Personal Experience* (Stansbury, 1980).

But most significantly for the development of life skills training in the UK, large-scale government-funded programmes aimed at the young and unemployed sought to incorporate the teaching of life skills into an overall package aimed at improving the individual's potential employability. *Wider Opportunities Courses* (WOC) and, subsequently, the *Youth Opportunities Programme* were intended to ease the employment situation amongst the young, to help them get jobs where possible, and to equip them for and keep them attuned to the world of work where prospects of employment were actually more distant. A life skills element was injected into these schemes, focussed predominantly on issues related to work, such as assessing job preferences, acquiring job search skills, or handling relationships at work. Wider Opportunities Courses were installed in some of the government's own industrial Skill Centres, where small teams of job instructors were retrained for the task of running courses which would give trainees the chance to try their hands at a variety of work skills. A proportion of the sessions were also to be devoted to life skills. The Youth Opportunities Programme, a successor to the Job Creation Projects of the mid-seventies, was on a much larger scale. Here, funds were made available to local government bodies and other agencies for the running of job placement schemes and part-time training programmes for unemployed youths. The provision of these funds was conditional upon the inclusion in any proposed scheme of a mandatory life skills element for the young trainees. For the most part, this element has been supplied by Further Education and Technical Colleges, by requiring trainees to attend there, typically on a one-day-a-week basis. The unemployed on this and on affiliated programmes — said to number some 225,000 –

must constitute the single largest body of individuals ever given any form of life skills training. But in contrast to the Saskatchewan project, the Manpower Services Commission (the government body responsible for funding and directing the programmes) funnelled few resources into the preparation and testing of teaching materials for the life skills sessions that were to be run. A short instructional manual (M.S.C., 1979) represents the sum total of the guidance that has been made available to tutors of life skills. As might be expected under these circumstances, many tutors charged with the task of life skills teaching have tended to fall back on more traditional forms of social education, moral education, and liberal studies.

The arrival of these programmes did however act as a stimulus to workers in adjacent areas who were interested in life skills teaching. Recent years have witnessed something of a proliferation of training materials, small-scale projects, and hybrid ideas in education, youth work, social work and psychiatry. Most of these have combined social skills training, problem-solving, traditional social education, or community action in varying amounts, and the boundaries between all of these ingredients have become progressively more blurred. A number of training manuals have been published; some firmly in the tradition of behavioural psychology (Falloon, Lindley, and McDonald, 1974; Spence, 1980), others with a closer resemblance to the Saskatchewan approach (Ellis and Barnes, 1979). Sets of programme materials have been marketed (e.g. Cheston, 1979; Hopson and Scally, 1980; Scally and Hopson, 1979; Scottish Community Education Centre, 1979) and resource-packs for work on particular problems have been produced by a number of agencies including Community Service Volunteers, the ILEA Learning Materials Service, and the National Youth Bureau. Information 'banks' have been compiled, and elements of life skills training have been integrated into work in community development (Gibson, 1979).

At the same time, other projects have surveyed the work being done and have offered conceptual 'models' of the directions it has taken (Lee, 1980; Stanton, Clark, Stradling, and Watts, 1980).

Over the same period, research projects in Britain and the USA have extended the applicability of social and life skills methods to a mixture of other groups. In a long-term research project at the Hahnemann Medical College in Philadelphia, George Spivack and his co-workers (Spivack, Platt, and Shure, 1976) have investigated the nature and importance of what they term *interpersonal cognitive problem-solving skills*. These are viewed as a series of interconnected intellectual abilities with which individuals deal with difficulties involving other people — such skills as generating alternative solutions to problems or appreciating the likely consequences of one's actions. Spivack and his colleagues have developed and evaluated sets of training programmes for imparting these skills to various groups, including children of different ages; psychiatric patients; mothers of young children; and maladjusted adolescents and adults.

In Britain, social and life skills training courses have been developed and established for offenders, in a number of prison and probation settings. The prison courses, known as 'release courses', are run by specially trained prison staff, and are geared towards equipping prisoners with skills they need for solving their problems after discharge (Priestley, McGuire, Flegg, Welham, Hemsley, and Barnitt, 1981). Analogous courses have also been run outside prison, in Day Training Centres, hostels and other settings. Results obtained from the monitoring and evaluation of these courses suggest that they have both short- and long-term benefits for the offenders who take part in them, in terms of finding work, controlling violence, and keeping out of trouble. Elsewhere, these authors have cast the use of social skills training techniques within a broad-based problem-solving framework (Priestley, McGuire, Flegg, Hemsley, and Welham, 1978). The materials included in the present book are derived from this approach to social and life skills training.

The foregoing, then, are the principal trends that can be detected in the growth of interest in social skills training methods over the last fifteen years or so. Drawn partly from work in psychiatry, allied to practice in occupational training, merged with ideas from the field of compensatory education, social and life skills training as it stands at present is a synthesis of methods from areas with separate concerns and traditions of their own. However, given the bewildering array of problems with which young people are currently beset, it may be that an eclectic approach will have advantages when helping to solve them — and more important, when teaching individuals to solve their problems by themselves.

SOCIAL SKILLS TRAINING: REMEDIAL EDUCATION?

Possibly due to its long-standing links with psychiatry, and more recently with youth employment programmes, social skills training is associated in many people's minds with remedial education. It is seen, therefore, as being aimed predominantly at the less able individual: the one who fails to achieve much from an academic point of view, who seems doomed to unskilled work and periodic unemployment, and perhaps delinquent behaviour. That social skills methods can be used as part of remedial work is certainly true; but it would be unfortunate if they were seen as being viable *only* with less able groups. Two assumptions that flow from this may be worth challenging. First, we cannot conclude automatically that 'less able' people must lack the ability to solve their problems by themselves. They may in fact be wholly capable of handling all the difficulties life has to thrust upon them. Though not achieving much in school, they may nevertheless stand to gain little or nothing from a course on social skills and problem-solving. Second, the converse of this is equally true. The apparently more able individual, who shows outward signs of success according to the accepted criteria, may in some instances *lack* the ability to solve personal problems, to deal with other people, to negotiate intricacies that he or she is confronted with. The possession or lack of these kinds of skill is only poorly correlated with other more familiar measures of a person's ability.

The general point which emerges from this is that, whatever an individual's level of performance in other respects, there will often be other goals he or she would like to achieve, which pose some difficulty or which seem out of reach. And even if already fairly competent and socially skilled, the more able person might want to learn how to deal with yet more complex situations. In addition to their applications in work with the disadvantaged, social skills methods have also been used in the training of managers and other professionals normally assumed to be of above-average ability. There is nothing intrinsic to the methods, therefore, which makes them more suitable for use in one setting rather than another, or with one ability band rather than another.

The pivotal principle on which the flexibility of these methods depends is that the starting-point of any social skills training exercise must be the perceptions of the individuals who take part in it. The unifying aim of the methods to be described in this book is the provision of opportunities for individuals *first*, to identify and explore problems that are of importance to them, *second*, to do something constructive about these problems where possible, and *third*, to acquire the necessary skills for solving these problems again should they arise. Given that life skills methods should be harnessed to meet the needs and problems defined by young people themselves, the next chapter takes an excursion into the world as it appears to them.

3 The Problems

Mention the phrase 'personal problems' to most people, and their likely reaction will be to wince with embarrassment and discomfort. The notion of talking openly about such problems, and of engaging others in an attempt to do something about them, is still for most of us slightly taboo; and this after several decades of the rapid spread of 'psychotherapy' in a variety of popular forms. This reluctance stems from a number of sources. One is the defensiveness which many individuals have learnt is the best way to cope with situations they find awkward or threatening. Another is the perfectly justifiable wish many people have simply to preserve their privacy. And in the minds of many, there is probably a disturbing equation between talk of 'personal problems' and the kind of items they associate with the agony columns of the daily press. Common to all these reasons is the widespread conception of a 'personal problem' as having its roots in some complex interpersonal entanglement, involving people's feelings, their self-esteem, and their long-term relationships with one another: something to be shared only with one's closer friends and kept strictly secret from the rest.

While most of us experience difficulties of this kind at some time in our lives, there are a great many other situations we have to deal with which are not like this, but which are still in some sense problematic. They may arise from the fact that some occurrence is new or unfamiliar to us; that we approach some encounter in the wrong frame of mind; or that we lack the information or skills necessary for dealing with a specific situation that crops up. The social skills approach to social education addresses itself to problems of this kind; problems which, as suggested above, manifest themselves at the meeting-point of the public and personal spheres of life. While this can never, of course, exclude discussion of external features of society on the one hand (the domain of traditional 'social education'), nor of internal or interpersonal collisions on the other (the domain of counselling and groupwork), it focusses most closely on the difficulties which emerge when individuals try to achieve personal goals in a social setting. During adolescence particularly, individuals have to face a number of new developments for which they may be inadequately prepared — for example with information as to how some rule applies to them, or with confidence in dealing with others, or with skills appropriate to encounters they will have to see themselves through. Social skills training, in a sense, concentrates on trying to make the unfamiliar more familiar: on helping people to approach a problem that is new to them armed with the information, feelings and abilities necessary for solving it to their own satisfaction and benefit, as well as that of others.

What exactly are the problems to which these kinds of methods can be applied? In this chapter we survey some of them, based on the views of young people themselves. In the course of doing so, we will illustrate a number of methods which can be used to help individuals identify and explore their own 'personal problems'.

Experienced teachers, youth workers, and parents may feel that they already know a great deal about the problems with which the young are pre-occupied. After all, they were young once themselves, were they not? Whatever their age, however, people will always be more highly motivated to do something about problems or issues which *they* have defined. Engaging individuals in the demarcation of their own problems and goals serves to build up their energy for release in appropriate action later on. A recommended starting-point for a social skills session or curriculum, therefore, is the *assessment* of problems, by asking people questions, or getting them to ask themselves questions, about the situation they see themselves in.

There are several ways in which such questions can be asked; four of them are described below, and illustrated in terms of the replies they evoked from a number of young people recently departed from school.

BRAINSTORMING

Attempts to solve problems are often frustrated when individuals wander into one particular kind of trap: they become pre-occupied with one possible course of action to the exclusion of all others. Arguments for and against this course of action present themselves; its relative merits and defects are balanced against each other; further pros and cons emerge — and so on until individuals are 'hooked' on what was originally only one out of a large field of possibilities. Meanwhile, alternative courses of action — potentially just as fruitful — remain undeveloped or are almost completely ignored.

Research has shown that an alternative route to problem-solving can be more efficient: if individuals begin by spending part of the time simply pouring out ideas related to the problem in question (Stein, 1975). In other words, rather than isolating one proposed solution and scrutinising it in depth, we concentrate first on just inventing things we *might* do to solve our problem, and worry about their likely efficacy afterwards. The phase in which we devote our energy to the generation of possible solutions has come to be known as *brainstorming*.

Brainstorming was devised by Alex Osborn (1953) as a means of helping individuals and groups to formulate alternative courses of action when solving problems. While initially, brainstorming was intended to help amass possible *solutions* to problems, it can also be used prior to this: in helping individuals to identify and explore their problems in the first place.

As a means of helping members of a group to assemble a list of their problems, brainstorming can be a very lively exercise. In fact to a casual observer it might seem like little more than an excuse for disorganised shouting. But there are rules underlying it, all designed to enhance its value as a method of generating ideas. It may be worthwhile telling a group what these rules are before you embark on a brainstorming session. First and foremost, the overall purpose of the exercise is to produce ideas in *quantity*: to get hold of as many suggestions as possible that might have a bearing on the issue under discussion. Second, to make this work as well as possible, there are three subsidiary rules:

1. SUSPEND JUDGMENT: all ideas are regarded as being worthwhile during a brainstorm; none should be rejected. Criticism and evaluation of each idea can come later.
2. FREEWHEEL: people should feel free to produce even the wierdest of ideas. In the long run they may turn out to be very important.
3. CROSS-FERTILISE: you should also be willing to combine your own ideas with those of others; if someone else says something that suggests another idea to you, you should immediately shout it out.

In practice, you may have to insist on another rule: that members of a group should try to shout out their ideas one at a time; for the brainstorming session will be of little use unless you record its proceedings in some way. This can be done on a tape-recorder, or better, on a blackboard or large sheet of paper. Some trainees on a YOP scheme at a Further Education college in London were asked to brainstorm on their 'problems'. The results are shown in the box below.

Money	Drugs	Parents	Sex	Sister	Brothers	People
Discrimination	Boys	Punks	Teds	Rastas	Soulheads	
Skinheads	Niggers	Jobs	Police	War	Life	Houses
Friends	Birth Control		Racism		Lack of Money	
Food	Clothes	Inflation	Work	Teachers	Schools	
Colleges	Society	Government		Plastic Surgery		
Doctors	Nurses	Patients	Pensioners	Boss	V.D.	

This brainstorming exercise, which took approximately five minutes amidst a great deal of laughter and occasional periods of silence, in fact produced a fair number of suggestions concerning problems which the members of this group were facing. Following this introductory stab at identifying some of their most salient concerns, subsequent 'brainstorms' could have been conducted in which selected items from the first list (e.g. 'money', 'parents', 'jobs', or 'police') were explored in more depth. For the present however, the results of this exercise have enabled us to take a preliminary glimpse at some of the more manifest problems of young people recently departed from school. Of course, brainstorming as illustrated here is a group exercise, which does not permit us to look closely at the problems of any one individual. It is also very loosely structured and might be unsuitable for appraising the frequency or relative importance of various problems to different individuals or different groups. To accomplish the latter we would need to use more structured exercises; where possible asking young people to write down their views in some ordered way. Two approaches to doing this, and results obtained from using them, are outlined below.

'QUESTIONNAIRE' METHODS

According to their appointed purpose, questionnaires can be designed in many different ways, and the phrasing of items can be varied to suit the nature of the topic with which they are concerned. Questions can be *open-ended* — allowing respondents as much freedom as possible in the manner of their replies; or *forced-choice* — asking them to choose from amongst a pre-arranged set of alternatives. Individuals can be asked to rank items in order of importance; or to make judgments on issues by giving ratings or marks out of 10. In many instances however, the most direct kind of item — the open-ended question — is the most valuable, in that it allows individuals to express their replies entirely in their own words.

For example, information about the problems faced by young people before and after leaving school can be gathered by asking a question like this:

"We are interested in the problems you are facing at the moment. What do you think are the most important problems you have to deal with? Can you list them below in the space provided."

The response of one unemployed 17-year-old boy to this question was:

Giving up smoking.
Smartening my appearance.
Getting 100% fit.
Perking up my attitude towards life.

While a 17-year-old schoolgirl said:

Finding a job.
Learning at school.
Mixing with other people.
And a 19-year-old man in a Detention Centre replied:
To find a job as a semi-skilled mechanic.
To find permanent accommodation.
To pay off my motorbike monthly.
These are the views of individuals; it is also interesting to find out how frequently various problems are mentioned amongst a larger group of young people. We distributed a questionnaire, which incorporated this item, to 221 young people on the Youth Opportunities Programme in different parts of the country. For a series of reasons of course, many people are hesitant to reply to a question of this sort when it forms part of a larger questionnaire. They may for example feel, despite assurances to the contrary, that their replies will not remain confidential or anonymous; they may feel pretty dismissive about the idea of filling in forms and their peers may reinforce their reluctance further; or they may just not be literate enough or articulate enough to define their problems in this way. Nevertheless, many are willing to report on the main problems facing them. In this group, there were 88 males and 132 females (one respondent giving no indications of his or her sex). Their average age was just over 17, and 82% of the group had left school within the previous two years.

In the table on page 26, the numbers of respondents who mentioned problems in major categories are set out, giving a picture of the relative frequency with which different kinds of difficulty were experienced by members of this group.

Perhaps not surprisingly, the most frequently cited problem is work; closely followed by a cluster of associated problems deriving from the lack of a satisfactory income. A number of other problems were each mentioned by one person only; these are listed in the box below.

Problems mentioned by one person only

Becoming an adult	Attitude to life
Keeping my temper	Making decisions
Police	Feelings of depression
Concentrating	Shotbolt
Thinking about problems	Needing a push
Becoming too independent	Age
Not free to do what I want	Pollution
Employers' prejudices	Stress
Coping	Contraception
Sexual problems	Not have a zoo near here

Problem area	No. of people mentioning problem	Percentage of group
WORK Getting a job, being unemployed, travelling to work	121	54.7
MONEY Not having enough; getting by; managing money	90	40.7
HOME Parents and family	39	17.6
OTHER PEOPLE In general, the opposite sex, friends, supervisors	33	14.9
TIME Leisure and boredom, managing time, boredom at work	16	7.2
HEALTH and APPEARANCE	12	5.4
COLLEGE PROBLEMS Adjusting, coping with work	11	4.9
BEING AWAY FROM HOME	10	4.5
ACCOMMODATION	10	4.5
The future in general	8	3.6
Getting up in the morning	8	3.6
Having bad exam results, not being clever	7	3.2
Smoking and drinking	6	2.7
Filling in forms like this	5	2.3
Confidence	2	0.9
Keeping out of trouble	2	0.9
Adapting to the UK	2	0.9

It seems fairly likely that in any group of young people about to leave school, a pre-eminent concern will be with finding work, both for the provision of an income and for the general sense of purpose that the possession of a job seems to give to people. Those who see in today's young the vanguard of a new anti-work ethic will be sadly disappointed by findings of this kind. The concern of this group with money does not derive from some deeply-felt material acquisitiveness, but from the simple fact that their incomes are amongst the lowest in society. In fact when asked what they would consider to be a fair week's wage, the pecuniary ambitions of these young people are remarkably modest: they sought, on average, only £50.00 a week.

An alternative means of asking a similar kind of question to the above, but one which can supply a more accurate estimate of the relative importance of each problem, is that in which individuals are asked to mark problems on a scale according to their degree of severity, or the amount of confidence the individual feels when dealing with each problem in turn.

RATING SCALES

Questions formulated like this are known as *rating scales,* and in essence they ask individuals to attempt to quantify their views on some issue or problem by placing themselves or the problem on some kind of scale, usually of five, six, or seven points. People might be asked, for instance, how difficult they found it to get a job in their local area, on a scale of difficulty as follows:

Very difficult   3   2   1   1   2   3   Not at all difficult

The principle underlying this is self-evident to most people though it is advisable to explain the idea as clearly as possible, perhaps giving some examples, to avoid possible misunderstandings. Using a scale like this one — which it should be pointed out has no centre point in order to eliminate the 'don't knows' — one 17-year-old girl, out of school five months previously, rated a selection of problems as follows:

	Very difficult						Not at all difficult
Writing job applications	3	②	1	1	2	3	
Filling in forms	3	2	1	1	②	3	
Being interviewed for a job	3	②	1	1	2	3	
Getting a job	③	2	1	1	2	3	
Keeping a job	3	2	1	1	2	③	
Using the telephone	3	2	1	1	2	③	
Getting your rights	3	②	1	1	2	3	
Managing money	3	2	①	1	2	3	
Getting information you need	3	②	1	1	2	3	
Talking to people	3	2	1	①	2	3	
Getting on with parents	3	2	1	1	②	3	
Getting along with friends	3	2	1	1	2	③	
Getting along with the opposite sex	3	2	1	①	2	3	
Meeting strangers	③	2	1	1	2	3	
Finding things to do in your spare time	3	2	1	1	2	③	
Saying what you think	3	②	1	1	2	3	
Being part of a group	3	②	1	1	2	3	
Looking the way you want	3	2	1	①	2	3	
Coping with feelings of depression	③	2	1	1	2	3	
Controlling your temper	3	2	①	1	2	3	
Feeling confident in yourself	3	②	1	1	2	3	
Making decisions	③	2	1	1	2	3	

The points on each scale which this girl marked (by putting a ring round them) have been joined together in a continuous line to show a kind of 'profile' of her problems. While this will not of course be comprehensive, it does give a general picture of the main areas which, by her own testimony, she finds difficult to handle; and also of other areas in which she feels much more confident and capable. This closer acquaintance with the girl's problems might then enable the teacher or youth worker to organise some exercises designed to give her some practice, and boost her confidence, in some of the areas she finds demanding. So far, we have looked at three different kinds of exercises which can be used for assessment of problems with individuals or groups. Brainstorming encouraged a group to take an initial step in listing issues of concern to them. An open-ended questionnaire item asked individuals to make a note of their own personal priorities. And the use of rating scales permitted a closer analysis of the actual degree of 'severity' of a selected list of problems as experienced by each individual. A further step in this progression, allowing for the most thorough appraisal of individuals' problems, can be taken through the use of the *interview*.

INTERVIEWING

The most familiar kind of interview to most people is that involved in selecting someone for a job, although many other encounters which are not normally called 'interviews' in fact follow roughly the same kind of format. Broadly speaking, the overriding purpose of most kinds of interviews is to enable one person — like a personnel officer, DHSS clerk, or doctor — to collect information about another for the purpose of making some kind of decision about him or her. There are less formal kinds of interview, however, which can have other kinds of aims. These might range from encouraging people to get to know one another better to giving them the opportunity to exchange facts or opinions on some topic of mutual interest. Interviews can also be used to help people pinpoint and consider in depth the problems that are of concern to them.

While most individuals will be unlikely, in a face-to-face interview, to respond too well to the cold question 'What are your problems?', a fruitful interview can be initiated by asking people first of all to complete a questionnaire or rating scale of the kind portrayed above. A useful additional tool for this purpose is the *problem checklist* (described in more detail in chapter 5 below). This consists of a list of problems which individuals might encounter; they are asked to specify exactly which items on the list are of importance to them. Their responses, if they agree to reveal them, can then be used as the starting-point of an interview designed to help them look at their problems in greater depth.

Having completed a short checklist of this kind, Steve — an unemployed 17-year-old attending a Further Education college on a Youth Opportunities Scheme — was interviewed about his problems by Philip Priestley. The interview focussed first of all on Steve's problems in managing money.

Steve: Another one that I've put down as a severe problem is . . . I owe people money. That's because when I spend all my money on Friday nights, during the week I just sort of generally borrow money off people. When I get paid on Friday nights again I just pay them back the money I owe them and the rest I spend. Then I start borrowing again then I pay it back then I spend it. It just goes round in a vicious circle really.

Philip: Do you owe anybody any money now?

Steve: Yeah. I owe one of my friends £2 because he bought me a ticket to see some group, which I didn't go to see in the end. I owe my dad £3 and that's about it. That's £5 . . . I only get £20. £20 from the college. Give £7 of that to my mum, that leaves you with thirteen and I owe five and that leaves me with eight. Then it's all gone.

Philip: If it's a problem to you, why do you think you spend all your money on Friday? Do you not think 'If I could keep a little back . . .'? . . . You must be aware that you're spending it all.

Steve: Yeah, but when I do get my money I always say like 'This time I'm determined I'm going to save some'. But when you bring it up to the pub or wherever you're going you know, you just spend it. You sort of lose conscious of what you're doing. When you've got through about £4, £5, you'll be reasonably tipsy like, and you just want more and more drink, so you buy and you buy and you buy, buy your friends a drink and all that. Plus I play pool. Just keep on playing pool all night. I play on the fruit machines. It's stupid, but I just can't help it. I just spend all my money.

Steve is caught in what he himself labels a 'vicious circle' of spending, borrowing, and spending again. In other areas too he seems to have some difficulties in self-control.

Philip: What else did you put down as problems?

Steve: Can't control my temper.

Philip: What does that mean?

Steve: Well when people sort of hit me or something like that, I don't just lose my temper, I go over the edge. And when I fight, I don't fight for, you know, just to prove a point, I fight to really hurt the person. I just lose all conscious of what I'm doing. I just sort of, go straight for the kill, like.

Philip: Can you give me an example of something like that, where you lost your cool?

Steve: Well, a bloke sort of punched me in the mouth when I was in a pub and . . .

Philip: Why did he do that?

Steve: Well I don't know, he just started you know. What was it? FA cup day and I had a Man. United red and white scarf and he wanted a . . . who was it they were playing? Well I don't know who they was playing but anyway . . . that's right it was Arsenal that won. When Arsenal won I was in the corner of the pub saying 'Sod it, they shouldn't have won it' and all this, you know. And a bloke sort of just turned round, I weren't even talking to him, and he just punched me in the mouth and he split the inside of my mouth. I should have had stitches, you know, but couldn't be bothered to do it. And I lost my temper and the barman and the bloke that punched me sort of, they both got together and they brought me outside, threw me out in the road and the bloke that punched me, he stayed out there and the barman went back in, and the bloke that punched me had a bottle in his hand and he smashed it and went for me. And I kicked it out of his hand and I just lost my temper 'cos it seemed like he was really trying to hurt me and so I just lost my temper, I just started sticking in to him. I just lost all conscious of what I'm doing.

Philip: Are there any other circumstances, apart from people hitting you, where you lose your temper?

Steve: Eh . . . no not really, no. But I just lose my temper when people do aggravate me and hit me. That's the only time.

Philip: Do you think that's a bad thing?

Steve: Yeah, because one day I could kill a bloke, just because of my temper.

Philip: Do you think there's anything you could do to control your temper?

Steve: Well, you've got to have it inside yourself really, haven't you? If you can control it you can control it, if you can't, you can't.

Unfortunately, Steve seems to think there is little he can do to gain more control over his violent temper. Nevertheless, the interview has explored the circumstances in which he loses self-control and might lead to his recognition of an impulsiveness or lack of self-control which seems also to extend to his failure to manage money very successfully.

This interview was not difficult to carry out as Steve is fairly forthcoming about his problems and finds it easy to talk candidly about them. In other instances, or for other individuals, interviews of this kind might prove less valuable. However, if individuals are hesitant to talk to the teacher or youth worker about their problems, they might nevertheless be willing to talk to each other. What have come to be known as *peer interviews* can then be introduced: in which group members ask each other questions of some pre-arranged kind (and some possible topics for this purpose are also suggested in chapter 5 below). The essence of this kind of interview is that it aims to stimulate *self-assessment*. Its purpose is not to gather information about someone, so much as to induce them to look at their difficulties, to turn them over in their minds, and to contemplate what they might do about them. In the above extract, for example, Steve identified incidents in which he had lost his temper; in fact isolated the specific kinds of events which gave rise to his violent outbursts. In addition, he acknowledged that this was a problem he would like to do something about. Subsequent work with Steve might then be addressed to the ways in which he could achieve this goal — not an easy task by any means. However, interviews of this sort with those who are willing to participate in them can be of substantial benefit to interviewer and interviewee alike.

PROBLEM-SOLVING AND SOCIAL SKILLS

A great many problems have been mentioned by the young people quoted above; covering a considerable range from the everyday and practical to the more sensitive areas of emotion and interpersonal conflict. Problems with work, money, family, friends, sex, rights, depression, violence, have all arisen with varying degrees of frequency. These sorts of problems — described in this way by groups of young people just before or not long after leaving school — are the ones to which this book is addressed.

It should be pointed out, of course, that this book is not an inventory of solutions to these problems. The exercises set out here are intended to provide a basic structure within which individuals who wish to do so can be helped to acquire the information, attitudes and skills they need for solving their problems by their own efforts. Inevitably, the materials included in the book do not deal with all of the kinds of problems delineated above. They have been grouped together in terms of what seem to be some common areas of difficulty — such as work, social interaction, or rights. Nonetheless, new methods and materials tailored to the needs of individuals with problems other than these can be created without a great deal of effort.

Finally, the methods sketched out here are in no sense designed to be prescriptive of the kinds of problems young people should have, or of the sorts of things they should think or do about them. On the contrary, they are in themselves completely void of content. Their purpose is to act as catalysts to self-directed change. They should be conceived of as open, empty containers into which individuals can insert thoughts and actions of their own; they are nothing more than vehicles or aids to learning which individuals should employ in whatever manner they think fit. The eventual outcome of any session or exercise will depend, therefore, on those taking part in it and on the exact problems and goals which they have in mind.

4 Social Skills Methods and how to use them

The exercises in this book are designed to stimulate self-knowledge and self-awareness; to improve interpersonal skills; and to help people to learn how to solve problems more effectively. These are very broad aims, not unlike those of education in general, and very close to those of social education in particular. They are also complex aims which cannot be attained through any single teaching strategy.

Some of the mechanisms of social learning were outlined in chapter 2. In this chapter, a number of techniques for putting them into effect will be discussed and illustrated under four main headings:

1. Information and its uses;
2. Pencil and paper methods;
3. Interviews and discussion; and
4. Variations on the theme of role play.

And in the problem-centred programmes which follow (in chapter 5), to which this chapter is an introduction, examples will be given of how to combine some of these elements in social skills training packages.

However, the emphasis on method and technique in social skills work should not be thought to imply *either* that this is a difficult way of working with young people, *or* that it is a mechanical process, turning out mindless robots programmed to act in pre-determined ways. The methods — even the less familiar ones — are essentially simple, and if used properly are fun to do. When they succeed, the outcome, far from being some sort of puppet dancing to other people's tunes, should be a more self-aware, self-possessed, alert and active person. In fact the approach described in this book can be distinguished sharply from traditional academic education on the one hand by its emphasis on the individual him- or herself as a proper subject of study; and from more recent efforts at therapy or behaviour modification on the other by its insistence that students, trainees, or group members can acquire greater control over their own thoughts, feelings and actions by processes which are rational, conscious, and self-willed. It is, in the fullest sense of the word, a self-help approach.

INFORMATION

Information of various kinds plays a vital role in social skills training, but in ways which differ from the learning of facts in standard curriculum subjects. In social skills training, information serves to promote *understanding* about oneself, about others, and about the contingencies of everyday life; and it is needed in order to make *problem-solving* more effective.

In terms of *understanding* themselves and others, the most valuable kind of information that individuals can possess is that which is self-generated. Self-realisation of this sort is sometimes described by counsellors as 'insight', but many of the exercises in this book are designed to bring about personal learning in ways that do not require the tutor to be a skilled therapist, or to engage in activities that look like group or individual therapy. The exercises are intended as far as possible to be both self-explanatory in their aims and straightforward in their application; and since they are also concerned with the development of participants' skills, they more often take the form of 'learning by doing' than of 'teaching by telling'.

Even so, there are times when direct information about human behaviour, about values, about ways of looking at or thinking about oneself, needs to be provided by the person who is running a training session. This does not nec-essitate that teachers and tutors become experts in social psychology. A basic grasp of some of the principal concepts of social skills training can form the foundation of direct teaching in this area. Just pointing out that social behaviour is learned behaviour; that individuals can comprehend and then change the way they respond to social situations; and that they can assume a greater degree of control over their own destinies, can be a good starting-point for the exercises that follow. Specific exercises themselves need to be explained to individuals in terms that relate to these overall aims. So while many exercises may be enjoyable and educational in their own right, their importance from a 'training' point of view is that they should contribute to more socially skilled performances. Exercises will function best, therefore, when presented within a clear framework, for example of improving job search skills; getting on better with other people; managing money; or know-ing your rights. Ideally, every exercise should be introduced in a way which couples it explicitly with clear aims like these.

Information about behaviour, and about self in relation to others, assumes another shape in social skills training, and that is as *feedback;*

responses from the environment to what one is, says, or does. The tutor's job in this respect is to provide channels along which this information can flow to the person concerned, and to monitor and control its character so that it is helpful and constructive rather than hurtful or destructive. Some methods of doing this are described in more detail in the sections on group discussion and on roleplay later in this chapter.

Lastly, people need information about the world around them in order to help them *solve problems* for themselves. One part of this consists of information about information itself: about where to look for certain facts, or where to go for certain kinds of advice, for example. Another part has to do with the nature of officialdom and of the many organisations which play a part in our lives; who they are, what they do, and the procedures involved in approaching them successfully — a knowledge, in other words, of basic rights in relation to law, housing, money, consumer affairs, and similar topics. Unfortunately, a lot of this information may be locked away in inaccessible filing cabinets, or worse, embedded in the impenetrable prose of official leaflets and other publications. Making this information more readily available and more easy to understand is a challenging task. Some of it can of course be conveyed directly by traditional methods of instruction; some of it is best delivered in talks by outside speakers or by the showing of slides or films; some can be provided in the form of libraries or packs of relevant materials; and some is more effectively obtained through planned visits to appropriate sources of supply. All of these means of information-giving might be employed in a social skills curriculum. In some of the topic areas of chapter 5, suggestions are made concerning the kinds of information that might prove useful, the locations in which it might be found, and the methods by which it can be relayed to participants in a social skills course.

But the exercises in this book lay stress on an additional strategy with regard to the transfer of information: the acquisition and development by learners of the *skills* of securing information for themselves. An accent is placed, therefore, on exercises which encourage individuals to find things out from each other and from suitable sources in the community. An example of this principle in action is the *learning exchange* exercise on page 134, which seeks to exploit the storehouse of knowledge and experience that resides in the minds of even the most ordinary group of students. Extending this, other exercises such as those of *information search* on page 175 set group members specific tasks like the collecting of facts or the surveying of opinions germane to some chosen issue. On a still larger scale, suggestions for *projects,* which may incorporate the finding and handling of information, are made at various points in the text. Like the rest of the material in this book however, these should be seen as illustrative hints rather than prescriptions; you will be able to think of topics and exercises more carefully fashioned to the needs of those with whom you are working.

PENCIL AND PAPER EXERCISES

To most individuals concerned directly or indirectly with education, the notion of a pencil and paper exercise will be most likely to conjure up images of essays, exams, and psychological tests; and, apart from their uses in note-taking as an aid to memory, pencil and paper methods probably are associated more widely with assessment than with anything else. This can hardly be unexpected, given the number and variety of 'mental tests' currently available, which can be used to appraise characteristics as diverse as motor ability, intelligence, personality, moral values or sense of humour. For helping people to acquire social skills or the ability to solve their problems, however, the majority of these measures would be quite unsuitable. Many of them are also copyright and can be administered only by specially trained and authorised personnel. Even the instruments which can be used in the assessment of social skills have for the most part been devised with specific target groups in mind.

The pencil and paper exercises included in this book are quite distinct in purpose and content from most of the products of the 'mental measurement' tradition. They are, to begin with, meant to be self-administering and self-scoring — or sufficiently self-evident in outcome as to require no scoring at all. Equally important, none of them should be seen as a finished and polished article to be used just as it is. Our advice is that exercises should, whenever possible, be adapted, changed or substituted with others of your own invention which fit more closely the needs and problems of the groups with whom you happen to be working.

Pencil and paper methods can serve several purposes in social and life skills training, which are discussed more fully below. In format they can also conform to a number of different 'styles'. One way of defining their range is in terms of how 'structured' they are, on an imaginary continuum of varying degrees of structure. At the *unstructured* end are some elementary devices for stimulating or eliciting people's thoughts as far as possible in their own words. These sometimes take the shape of questions or instructions such as:

> Describe yourself in your own words.
>
> What do you want out of life?
>
> Make a list of the difficulties you face when you leave school.
>
> What do you do in your spare time?

In a way, essay questions are the most extreme versions of this kind of item because they prompt individuals to produce a quantity of ideas, without dictating too precisely how they should organise them. Thus one of the virtues of the open-ended question is that it can tap directly what is going on inside the head of the respondent, as free as possible from contamination by the views of the person who is asking the question.

A quite different kind of open-ended method consists of showing someone a drawing or photograph which has been deliberately prepared so as to be ambiguous in content. The individual is then asked to describe what he or she thinks the picture represents, or what is happening in it. This is sometimes known as a 'projective' test, in that a person's response will be influenced largely by his or her own thoughts, wishes, and feelings; and it is frequently used by psychotherapists to help them assess the motives of their clients. In social skills training, methods similar to this can be used to assist young people in identifying some of the assumptions they make about other people or about social interaction, or to help them assess their own ability to judge other people. For this purpose, such simple material as ordinary snapshots can be used. For an example of how this can be applied, the reader is referred to the 'first impressions' exercise on page 108 in the section on 'work'.

One of the disadvantages of unstructured methods is that many people find them difficult, and some people impossible, to complete properly. They either say nothing, or so little that it has no meaning for them. *Semi-structured* pencil-and-paper methods give more guidance to respondents by asking them, for example, to specify name or address, age, schools attended, examination passes. Another way of structuring replies is to ask someone to complete an unfinished sentence:

> I am good at . . . .
>
> I like . . . .
>
> I am worried about . . . .
>
> I would like to . . . .
>
> Politicians are . . . .

Sentence completion, as this is called, directs the attention of the person doing it towards some aspect of him or herself, but leaves lots of scope for individuality in replying.

Finally there are more highly *structured* exercises which take three basic forms: checklists, questionnaires, and rating scales. 'Checklists' as their title indicates consist of lists of items on which respondents are invited to 'tick' or 'check' those which apply to them. For example:

PROBLEMS AT WORK

☐ Getting there on time.

☐ Getting on with workmates.

☐ Accepting orders.

☐ Taking responsibility.

☐ Taking time off.

☐ Working hard.

If any of these is a problem for you
put a tick in the box beside it.

There are many ready-made checklists in existence, both general and specific, and it is not difficult to devise others for topics in which you are interested.

'Questionnaires' by way of contrast are more likely to be concerned with some of the less tangible aspects of people's lives; with their opinions or values or attitudes. They tend to take the form of statements with which you are asked to agree or disagree, e.g.:

	Agree	*Disagree*
1. I am worried about the state of the world.		
2. The Prime Minister is doing a good job.		
3. Licensing laws should be abolished.		

A common feature of questionnaires is that they force the person who completes them to make a choice of one kind or another, rather than allowing him or her to have no opinion or to remain undecided. This may be done, as above, by insisting that you agree or disagree with a statement; or by providing more than one statement, one of which *must* be selected. For example:

☐ Violence is caused by circumstances over which individuals have no control.

☐ Individuals who resort to violence are responsible for their own behaviour.

TICK THE STATEMENT YOU AGREE WITH MORE.

More than two choices may be given, but the principle is the same, and when the questionnaire is completed, all the items chosen by the individual can be added together to produce a 'score', which might have to do with attitudes to law and order, to moral issues, optimism-pessimism and so on.

But 'agree-disagree' responses are obviously very crude indicators of what someone thinks about an issue. To take the job of measuring attitudes or beliefs a stage further — as was illustrated in chapter 3 — resort can be made to the *rating scale*. For instance, it is often valuable to gauge shades of opinion that fall somewhere between the two extremes of complete endorsement and total rejection. So you might ask the question:

How good a job do you think the Prime Minister is doing?
Mark the point on the scale which indicates your view.

The Prime Minister is doing:

| A very good job | |_____|_____|_____|_____| | A very bad job |

Alternatively, points on a scale could be replaced by words or by numbers:

I feel nervous about talking to strangers —

| *Always* | *Often* | *Occasionally* | *Seldom* | *Never* |

or,

How confident are you about going for an interview?

| Very confident | 3 | 2 | 1 | 1 | 2 | 3 | Not at all confident |

Some of the uses of rating scales are discussed below.

Beyond rating scales and questionnaires there is an additional degree of structure in pencil-and-paper methods, which is the realm of psychometric testing proper. Intelligence, personality and aptitude tests are to be found here, but the majority of them lie outside the scope of everyday educational practice, and their relevance to social skills work is more distant.

The aims of pencil-and-paper methods

Pencil-and-paper methods have three principal functions in social skills sessions; they can be used as an aid to description and *self-description;* as a way of *measuring* attitudes and behaviour; and as a *stimulus* to personal thought and group discussion and action.

(a) Description and self-description

Socially skilled behaviour cannot be taught like tricks to performing animals; it demands a certain level of self-awareness, a reasonably accurate perception of other people and of the situations in which they are encountered, a stock of knowledge about the world, a grasp of the basic rules that govern social interaction, and above all a desire to do whatever appears appropriate in given situations. Strange as it may seem, a lot of people have never taken the time and trouble to think systematically and constructively about the sorts of people they are. Open-ended and semi-structured pencil-and-paper methods can provide a starting-point for such a process of self scrutiny. Several of the exercises later in the book are designed to initiate this by helping individuals to look at some of their personal attributes, their strengths and weaknesses, their attitudes, their behaviour and experience, their likes and dislikes.

(b) Measurement

Open-ended methods like sentence competion or interview responses provide information which is sometimes referred to as 'soft'. 'Harder' data can be obtained from questions and items cast in a way that makes it possible to *count,* to *rate,* and to *rank.* Counting can be done in two ways. Checklist or survey responses can be added up to form scores which may be interesting in their own right, and even more interesting when compared with the scores of other people, both individually and collectively as averages or group norms. Behaviour, on the other hand, can be counted more directly by recording the number of times something occurs within a given period; say the number of cigarettes smoked in a day or a week or a month; the number of times someone loses his or her temper; the amount of time spent in looking for work; the number of attempts to start social conversations with comparative strangers. All of these can be recorded on simply designed forms, logs or diaries. (See for instance the Leisure diary on page 130.)

Ratings, whether of the numerical or the verbal kind, permit more exact comparisons to be made between individuals. It may be objected that marking a point on a line is just as subjective as plucking a word out of the air to describe a feeling or an attitude; which is true. But in the last analysis, nearly all so-called 'objective' measures depend on the self-report of the subject. And in a social skills context the uses of comparison serve simpler ends than those of scientific research. Looking at a neighbour's completed exercise is an opportunity for discussion and debate. Comparing the scores for a whole group can be even more stimulating. Comparison also makes it possible for an individual to monitor behaviour and attitudes, and any changes which may be taking place in them, by filling in the same piece of pencil-and-paper material at dated intervals over a period of time. Even if the ratings *are* utterly subjective it is unlikely that the nature of the subjectivity will change from one completion of items to another. So ratings make it possible to monitor personal progress and also the effectiveness of the social skills training sessions themselves.

(c) Stimulus

The third function of pencil-and-paper methods in social skills training is to stimulate participants to think more deeply about themselves and their lives and their problems; to discuss with others some of the things they are finding out; and to take some action.

Thinking and talking about yourself has not always been encouraged by conventional pedagogies, partly due to the morbid associations of the idea of introspection, and partly to avoid pandering to the conceit of individuals. But the kind of self-knowledge required for the development of better social skills is neither morbid nor conceited; it is simply a prelude to effective action. Learning *how* to think about yourself and to analyse social situations and personal problems – the acquisition of thinking skills – is also important in its own right.

Using pencil-and-paper methods

Provided some simple rules are followed, pencil-and-paper methods should not prove too difficult to administer and use fruitfully with groups of students or trainees.

To begin with you should be clear about the purpose of the exercise you are introducing so that you can explain it properly to the people who are taking part in it. It may be helpful, especially with slightly unfamiliar material, to write out in advance of the session the aims of the exercise and to use that as the basis of what you say to your group. For example:

> 'We are going to do an exercise now for looking at the reasons why
> people go to work; or why they don't go to work. I want you to form
> two groups; one on this side of the room, and the other over there.
> One of the groups is going to think of ten good reasons for going to
> work; and the other will have to think of ten good reasons for not going
> to work. And when you've done that we're going to use the results to
> find out how strongly motivated everybody is to go to work.'

Then, as in this example, you should be able to make clear the mechanics of what is going to happen, so that none of the participants gets it wrong. (Easier said than done this; someone usually gets it wrong.) And finally you should have some ideas about how you are going to help people make sense of the exercise when they have completed it. This may involve drawing their attention to some feature or other of their replies; providing them with some categories with which to analyse their answers; or arranging for pairs and small groups to look more closely at the results.

One of the most obvious obstacles to the use of pencil-and-paper methods is lack of basic literacy skills. In groups where more than one in five of the members have marked difficulty with reading or writing, then some of these exercises would prove very hard going indeed. In groups where literacy skills are not absent but of a generally low order, the problem may be overcome by reading out questionnaire and other items so that the group members need only identify the correct number on the sheet and fill in a word, or check off the appropriate point on a scale. In mixed ability groups, the faster readers and writers are not usually averse to sharing their skills with slower members; and staff members can also help individuals without drawing too much attention to their difficulties.

Care should also be taken not to bore group members with an over-enthusiastic application of pencil-and-paper techniques; they are an important part of a balanced social skills programme; but only a part. If five or ten minutes are spent filling in a form or checking items on a list then the remainder of a forty minute session should be taken up with activities of a different nature; with discussion, with role play, with project work, giving information and so forth.

Another problem which sometimes occurs is that specific pencil-and-paper exercises are resisted by participants because they are too difficult to do, are written in language they do not fully understand, or are not really relevant to their personal concerns. The answer is either to find one that is more relevant, or failing that, to devise your own. If you are clear about its purpose, it is not all that hard to put together a workable checklist, or questionnaire or rating form. There are some fairly obvious pitfalls in the construction of such devices, such as phrasing questions or instructions in a way that predicts too closely the reply, or which make it obvious that there is a 'correct' answer which is being sought.

With practice these problems can be avoided, and in any case, unworkable questions draw attention to themselves in a way which invites immediate revision.

The principle of do-it-yourself test construction can also be extended to the people who are themselves taking part in a social skills programme. Groups of young people are perfectly capable of constructing productive pencil-and-paper exercises for looking at themselves and their problems. Thinking about how to collect information may be as instructive an activity as applying the finished product; and it is always interesting to compare the categories and constructs which young people themselves use when doing this.

Self-help of this sort can be extended to the idea of students keeping a record of the work they are doing in social skills sessions in a 'personal file'. This is similar in conception to the 'records of personal achievement' adopted in some schools (Burgess and Adams, 1980); we have found that many young people respond positively to doing this, not in relation to their work on the syllabus, but on themselves. A personal file might contain a variety of items; completed questionnaires and inventories; self-descriptions; write-ups of interviews conducted by colleagues; information about specific problems and how to set about solving them; monitoring and evaluation sheets charting progress, or lack of it, towards specific targets such as getting a job; leaflets; letters; project reports etc. Such self-portraits can be fascinating and fruitful for the individuals who compile them.

Last, but not least, filling in forms and completing questionnaires is in itself a skill which some people lack, to their own obvious disadvantage. Virtually any contact with formal organisations involves the filling in of pieces of paper of one sort or another. Familiarity with the various questions and how to answer them properly can reduce anxiety and improve people's ability to get past the first barrier which often stands across their path towards a desirable goal, whether it is a job or a supplementary benefit payment.

INTERVIEW AND DISCUSSION METHODS

A lot of behaviour to which the term 'social skills' refers is in fact *verbal* behaviour. So it is not surprising that social skills training places great emphasis on verbal exchanges between the individuals who take part in it. It is an emphasis which forms a bridge between the more reflective self-assessment of pencil-and-paper methods and the more active role-play methods described later in this chapter.

The most familiar type of discussion that goes on in classrooms is between people sitting next to each other; teachers have been trying to stamp it out for years. Social skills trainers, far from frowning on this practice, positively encourage it, but in the guise of 'peer interviews', which go well beyond the limits of a friendly but surreptitious chat. A peer interview is focussed on a topic or task, is limited in time and leads to some sort of conclusion; a report back to a larger group, a decision, a set of items agreed. Apart from the outcomes, peer interviews provide valuable practice in the arts of inter-viewing and being interviewed. Also anathema to supporters of the 'silent classroom' is the 'buzz group' which is formed by asking two or more people sitting in one row to talk with the two sitting immediately behind or in front of them. Again, the purpose of the 'buzz' will vary, but basically it is just a larger forum for discussion, only not so large that the voice of the individual is lost.

Other small groups can be formed, on a self-selected basis, to discuss issues of particular interest to their members, to prepare positions for larger group exercises, or to design and carry out projects over longer periods.

Larger group discussion is also important, but sometimes more difficult to achieve in view of the widespread reluctance to speak in front of what appears to constitute an audience.

Whatever form it takes, group discussion in social skills training is important in a number of ways:

1. *Self-expression*

Contributing to discussion of any kind provides practice in self expression. This entails thinking about issues, marshalling facts, the use of logic in argument, speaking clearly. Many young people lack sufficient confidence to make a point publicly. The relaxed atmosphere of small group discussion encourages even the shyest member to say something, and having spoken once, confidence to do so again is created.

2. *Conversational skills*

Presenting a point of view and listening to that of others is the basis of conversation. Where conversational skills are very poor, individual tuition and instruction in the relevant arts of responding, use of posture and gesture, expression, tone of voice, verbal and non-verbal following and the like may be necessary. After that, group discussion provides opportunities in abundance for practising and perfecting them.

3. *Learning about self*

Exposure of one's views, opinions and experiences to others leads as often as not to greater realisations about oneself; to a deepening of the insights which may have been provoked by pencil-and-paper self-assessment exercises.

4. *Learning about others*

Prolonged discussion with others, particularly when it is about the issues raised in social skills sessions, can hardly fail to promote a better understanding of what makes them tick, of the values they hold, of the way they think, speak and act. Such an understanding is a pre-condition of socially skilled performance.

5. *Giving and getting feedback*

One of the most important mechanisms in social learning is that of 'feedback' — the response which a person's behaviour receives from the social environment. This may be positive, in which case it acts as a reward and encouragement for the retention and development of the behaviour in question, or it may be negative, which tends to act in the opposite direction. Positive feedback may take the form of praise, tangible rewards or personal satisfaction; negative feedback may be lack of attention, failure, or critical or hostile comment or other reactions. Working in groups facilitates the receipt of copious quantities of feedback from others, and also creates opportunities for giving it back to them. And because, in social skills training, this is made explicit, it need not be difficult to discern as it sometimes is in social situations; nor need it be wounding and unpalatable.

6. *Exchanging information*

Much of the content of ordinary conversation is information of one kind or another. Some of it is trivial and inconsequential; some of it highly personal. But when the talk turns to matters of substance in the real world any group of individuals turns out to be a veritable repository of knowledge and experience. These are assets of great value in any social skills training programme which should be tapped and exploited at every possible opportunity. In the classic model of education, information is derived from an authoritative source, from a text or a trained teacher. In social skills work useful information is likely to be widely diffused amongst those taking part.

7. *Grasping concepts*

Increasing use is being made of small group discussion in higher and further education to enable students to grasp concepts. It has been found that concepts and ideas presented in lectures, books or films can be more firmly fixed in students' minds by guided discussion (Abercrombie, 1969). These need not, of course, be of an abstract mathematical or philosophic nature; the principle applies to humbler concepts such as tackling problems in a more systematic way than normal, or understanding some of the factors that influence the way that people behave.

8. *Working with others*

The educational emphasis on individual performance has obscured to some extent the fact that for most people living is a co-operative venture, requiring coordination of effort, sensitivity to others and the ability to work alongside them without too much friction. Working on common tasks in social skills sessions; analysing behaviour, generating alternative solutions to problems, planning and executing projects for instance, can be valuable for its own sake, quite apart from the specific content of the task.

9. *Group support*

Lastly, good groups act as agencies of mutual aid and support for their members. The nature of this support will vary from group to group, and from time to time within a group, but its best expression lies in the pleasure that members take in each other's company, in their general willingness to work on each other's problems, and in the atmosphere of tolerance and respect and good humour that is generated when things are going well.

It is not suggested that all these benefits will automatically accrue to every individual who takes part in small group discussion. Clearly, success depends on many factors, some of them beyond the control of the tutor or teacher or group leader, but in most cases the majority of people gain tangible benefits from participation in groups.

Running groups

As with other social skills methods, teachers and tutors who wish to use group discussion should first of all rid themselves of the notion that it represents 'treatment' for the sick or the deviant. All of these are learning methods with broad applications from remedial education to management training. And the underlying principles, those of social learning, are implicit in normal socialisation. All that social skills training does is to make them *explicit.*

Group discussion then is not an amateur version of group therapy, it is a sustained conversation about a particular topic, which may be as practical as pocket money and bus routes, or as potentially abstract as parents' and children's rights in families. Provided there is a clear task, a timetable, and some clearly understood conventions about their conduct, small groups ought to run themselves. The group leader's job is to create the framework within which this can happen, and to sort out any problems that arise.

Preparing for a discussion may involve gathering information pertinent to the topic in hand and presenting it in a suitably lively way; showing a short film; arranging a speaker or a visit; distributing leaflets; organising a structured role-play; posing a problem; or filling in any of the many pencil-and-paper exercises which are available. After that, the structure of the group or groups will depend on what is being attempted; individuals can feed back to the whole group the results of a written exercise; pairs can be formed to discuss issues and report their findings after ten minutes or so; small groups can be set to plan a project.

The biggest problems in groups have to do with members who say nothing at all on the one hand, and on the other, members who monopolise the proceedings. There are no easy answers to either of these problems. Often a group itself will act to restrain the dominant contributor or to encourage contributions from silent members. If not, the group leader may need to re-arrange the membership of a group or give explicit instructions that the views of everyone should be taken into account.

ROLE PLAY

Many of the methods described so far in this chapter — pencil-and-paper; discussion, and information-giving — are likely to be fairly familiar to most people who work in education. Role play on the other hand still appears to be a slightly exotic activity, a disguised form of therapy perhaps, demanding an extrovert and dramatic mode of teaching.

It is true that role play can, on occasions, be both therapeutic and dramatic, but it need be neither when it appears in a social skills session. If a parallel is drawn between acquiring mechanical or physical skills and social skills; between say, learning how to ride a bicycle and how to cope with stressful confrontations at work or at home; then practice is the key to success. If people wish to improve some aspect of their social skills then they must be provided with opportunities for trying out new behaviour. And since the behaviour is to do with mundane issues like claiming benefits, being interviewed for a job, talking to officials, parents and friends in everyday situations, no-one need feel embarrassed or out of depth when rehearsing it in front of colleagues. There is of course a natural reluctance to take part in *anything* which smacks of theatricals, but the audience in a role play may consist of one other person, who happens to have a part in the role play as well. As group members become accustomed to the initially strange idea of role play they will be happy about performing in front of progressively larger, and more critical, collections of their peers.

So teachers and tutors need not feel hesitant about using role play in their sessions; it can be a good laugh for everyone involved, and still be a valuable learning experience. Its major uses in social skills work are:
(a) *To examine behaviour,* and especially one's own, in a critical way;
(b) *To help generate alternative ways of behaving;*
(c) *To allow practice and rehearsal* of new or improving skills.

Examining behaviour

Complex social skills, like manual or mechanical ones, can be broken down into smaller components which can be learned separately and then re-combined in a competent performance of the skill in question. Role play can help individuals to analyse their own behaviour so as to pinpoint some of the things they are doing badly, or even omitting to do at all. This is especially true of some non-verbal aspects of behaviour which are more obvious to observers, or which become immediately apparent through the medium of video tape recording. Watching yourself on video, if one is available, is educational in a sense that transcends any merely technical analysis of behaviour. Very few people possess really accurate perceptions of the way they are seen by others; hence the disbelief with which they greet the first sight of themselves on a television screen. When they have recovered from the shock — and it rarely survives two or three exposures to the medium — most people readily perceive things about themselves and the face they present to the world that they would like to change or improve: their expressions for example, or posture, gesture, voice tone, or mannerisms of speech.

In the absence of video, and it is valuable but not essential for social skills training, behaviour can be analysed in other ways. The first is by reflection and discussion; the telephone skills exercise on page 106 starts with such an analysis of the component skills of a good telephone call. Another is for an observer, or observers, to watch a role-play and to spot deficits in the performance of the person concerned. And pencil-and-paper formats can be used both by observers, and by the individual looking back at his or her own behaviour; counting the number of times someone smiled, or swore, or lost his temper; rating the quality of various parts of the performance; breaking down the whole into some of its smaller constituent parts. One exercise for looking at behaviour in more complex situations is to invite pairs or small groups to prepare and present a brief role play lasting not more than two or three minutes which portrays a 'critical incident' in which one of the players has been involved in the past, or which it is thought might present difficulties in the future. It should be clear to the spectators what the nature of the problem is; if it is not, the role-play needs revising until it is.

So role-play behaviour can be examined by observation, by discussion and by reflection.

Generating alternative ways of behaving

Let's take the case of a person who finds it hard to apologise, even when firmly in the wrong. Let us assume that he or she has prepared and presented a role-play version of a 'critical incident' in which, having turned up late for an important date for no good reason, the necessary apology is not forthcoming.

The next step then, would be for other members of the group to discuss the incident and how they would have handled it better; suggesting alternative ways of behaving, appropriate forms of words to use, and so on. In some cases, the suggestions alone are enough to help the person with the problem to go away and act differently in the future. More often though, it is not as easy as that.

One of the primary mechanisms of social learning is the observation and imitation of the behaviour of others; a process known as 'modelling'. A 'model' performance need not of course, be exemplary in a perfectionist way, like a 'model' answer to an examination question; it need only be an ordinarily competent way of coping; in this case with making an adequate and acceptable apology to somebody. Several members of a group could model different, but equally successful ways of making an apology, none of them necessarily the 'right' way. The upshot of such a session is that the person on the receiving end, the person with the apologising problem, will have seen and heard a variety of alternative ways of acting. These may be retained as mental notes for future use, or they may form the basis of rehearsal and practice exercises.

Rehearsal and practice

Having looked at a piece of social behaviour; having identified some difficulties and deficits associated with it; and generated some alternative ways of dealing with it; the next step is to try doing it differently until the problem is overcome or the behaviour is improved to a satisfactory degree. This can be done in several ways.

The first consists of 'imaginal rehearsal', which involves running through, in the mind's eye as it were, the anticipated event which is thought of as difficult. Imagining future events is a common enough feature of most people's mental life but it can assume the form of anxious worrying about what might go wrong. Imaginal rehearsal does not ignore the sticky bits, but concentrates on mentally rehearsing how to get them right. Thus, someone summoned to an important interview would imagine the scene in the office where it is to take place; the greetings, the preliminaries, the nature of the questions, some good replies, awkward moments, asking questions, and retreating from the room in good order. It is not possible to work out in exact detail every last thing that will happen in reality, but the constructive use of imagination can go far towards reducing the natural anxiety that accompanies social ordeals like job or disciplinary interviews.

An allied technique for defusing anxiety is known as 'successive approximation'. This means devising a series of role-plays which become progressively more lifelike. An interview training programme for example might start with two students interviewing each other in a fairly relaxed and informal fashion. Interview panels composed of peers might follow, with or without the added dimension of audio or video tape recording. Next, a teacher or a tutor unfamiliar to the students could conduct more formal and realistic interviews, and finally unknown outsiders such as a youth employment officer or a personnel officer from a local firm could be called on to bring the series as close as possible to the real thing. In this way the performer is required to cope with successively more realistic and demanding situations, but none of the steps is too difficult compared with the one that preceded it.

Successive approximation and straightforward rehearsal should be followed by a further phase of 'practice' in the real world. This is sometimes called 'homework' by social skills trainers, which may be a rather unfortunate term to adopt with young people just out of school; but whatever the name, the aim is the same, namely to encourage individuals to try out what they have been learning, at home, with friends, in contacts with officials and their agencies. A chronically shy person, for instance, might set a target of talking to at least two strangers within a week. Tasks of this nature are vital if classroom learning is not to remain just that.

Running role-play sessions

The commonsense and down-to-earth uses of role-play that have been described in this section should not present too many difficulties for the teacher or tutor or group leader who is clear about the aims of social skills work, can communicate them to group members, and can create an atmosphere which will enable most of them to take part. But, like any other method, it will work with some people and not with others, and on some occasions but not others. The worst that can happen is that invitations to take part in a role-play will meet with blank refusals from everyone in the room.

A strategy for avoiding such scenes is to introduce people gently to the practice of role-play by *structuring* what you ask them to do. For example, in the course of a discussion about how to handle aggressive people, the session leader might ask one group member:

Session leader:	'What would you say to someone who pushed in front of you in a queue where you'd been waiting for a long time?'
Group member:	'Well, it would depend on how big they were; if they looked really mean, I wouldn't say anything. But if it was just someone ordinary I'd say "Excuse me I was here first; the back of the queue is over there." '

At this point the tutor could ask for other possible responses to queue jumpers, *or* say to the first respondent:

Session leader:	'Could you just turn to the person sitting next to you and show us *how* you would say something like that.'

A demonstration ensues, other group members make their contributions and comments, and show how *they* would cope with someone pushing in front of them; and there is a role-play session in full swing. Whereas an announcement that: 'We are now going to role-play dealing with queue jumpers. Can I have two volunteers to come to the front?' might fall on apparently deaf ears.

Asking pairs or groups to prepare 'critical incidents' is another way of getting into role-play without too much fuss (Priestley et al., 1978). And yet another is to provide participants with a starting-point for their dramatic efforts and run what are known as *structured role-plays*. Prepared, written briefings can be given to those who are to play the roles: e.g.

A. You lent your friend two pounds last week to go to a concert, on condition it was paid back the next week; but it wasn't. You are short of money yourself this week and could do with the money. Your friend can be a bit funny sometimes so you are not quite sure how to approach asking for your two pounds.

B. You have a friend who lends you small amounts of money from time to time, and you return the compliment other times. The last time your friend borrowed money from you, you didn't get it back for three weeks; but you weren't worried. You borrowed two pounds last week but are a bit short again this week. If your friend could manage it, another couple of pounds would be welcome.

Each of the characters in this incident receives one of these briefings, and is allowed a few moments to read and digest it. You then ask them to continue with the encounter to see what will transpire.

By structuring the beginning of the role-play you have posed a problem in an area of interest to your group members and provided the role-takers with enough information to relieve them of any creative agonies. All they have to do is to get on with the action. Briefings like these can be made increasingly elaborate, both about the characters involved and about the circumstances in which they are to interact with each other. As detail is added to the structure of the role-play it turns imperceptibly into what is better described as a 'simulation'.

Simulations are more complex versions of role-play which attempt to re-create not just isolated incidents, but larger social environments. War-games and business games are probably the most widely known examples of the genre, but they are increasingly used in social studies to impart information, knowledge of procedures, and a variety of skills such as decision making, communicating, working with others, negotiating and so on. The simulated television news on page 140 does many of these things, and also illustrates the point that in simulations it is not always necessary for the participants to 'act' a part; they are too busy performing a task to worry about being on show. There are many ready-made simulations available

(Davison and Gordon, 1978), and as with pencil-and-paper exercises, new ones can be invented without too much difficulty.

It must be stressed that all these variations on the theme of role-play are not intended to be ends in themselves; their focus at all times should be on the needs, the problems and aspirations of the people with whom you are working. They are methods to be placed, in other words, at the disposal of their consumers.

Further Sources

For those who would like to find out more about the methods described in this chapter, the following should prove useful:

General: M. Argyle (1969), *Social Interaction,* Tavistock; and P. Priestley, J. McGuire, D. Flegg, V. Hemsley and D. Welham (1978), *Social Skills and Personal Problem Solving,* Tavistock.

On information-giving: L.C. Taylor (1972), *Resources for Learning,* Penguin Books; L. Cohen and L. Manion (1977), *A Guide to Teaching Practice,* Methuen; D. Lawton and B. Dufour (1973), *The New Social Studies,* Heinemann. On the use of audio-visual aids see: National Audio-visual Aids Centre (1980), *The Audio-Visual Handbook,* Kogan Page; and *Audio-Visual Resources in Social Education,* available from the Youth Service Information Centre, 37 Belvoir Street, Leicester LE1 6SL.

On pencil and paper methods, see the book by Priestley et al., cited above; and also: M.B. Youngman (1978), *Designing and Analysing Questionnaires,* Nottingham University School of Education; and P. Priestley and J. McGuire (1981a), *Forms and Tests — an introduction,* Basic Skills Unit, 18 Brooklands Avenue, Cambridge CB2 2HN.

On interview and discussion methods: E.A. Munro, R.J. Manthei, and J.J. Small (1979), *Counselling: a skills approach,* Methuen; M.L.J. Abercrombie (1970), *Aims and Techniques of Group Teaching,* Society for Research in Higher Education; A. Brown (1979), *Groupwork,* Heinemann; and P. Priestley and J. McGuire (1981b), *Learning to Help: basic skills exercises,* Tavistock.

On roleplay methods: M. Chesler and R. Fox (1966), *Role-playing Methods in the Classroom,* Science Research Associates Inc.; S. Spence (1980), *Social Skills Training with Children and Adolescents: a Counsellor's Manual,* National Foundation for Educational Research; and A.P. Goldstein, R.P. Sprafkin, N.J. Gershaw and P. Klein, *The Adolescent: Social Skills Training through Structured Learning* — a chapter in G. Cartledge and J.F. Milburn (eds, 1980), *Teaching Social Skills to Children,* Pergamon Press.

On simulations: K. Jones (1980), *Simulations — a handbook for teachers,* Kogan Page; J.L. Taylor and R. Walford (1978), *Learning and the Simulation Game,* Open University Press; and A. Davison and P. Gordon (1978), *Games and Simulations in Action,* Woburn Press.

Some accounts of the use of social and life skills methods with young people will be found in *Social Education in informal settings: case studies of practice within the Youth Opportunities Programme,* obtainable from the Youth Opportunities Development Unit, National Youth Bureau, 17-23 Albion Street, Leicester LE1 6GD.

5 Programme Materials

USING THE MATERIALS

Some ideas and practical exercises for use in social and life skills teaching are presented in the sections that follow. They are organised under a number of topic headings: self-assessment, interaction, work, leisure, money, rights, and sex.

The order in which these appear should not be thought to represent a suggested curriculum, neither in terms of the topics under consideration nor of the sequencing of individual exercises. Above all, none of the exercises should be seen as a finished product to be applied in a precisely prescribed fashion. Some, in any case, would only last for part of a standard teaching session, and must be combined with others if maximum advantage is to be extracted from them. Comments on how some exercises might be combined are made in chapter 6.

It may be helpful if we make some general suggestions on the use of these materials, based on our own experience and on that of other teachers. Firstly a word about literacy. To some tutors, teachers, or youth workers, the material here will appear to contain a high proportion of tasks that require literacy skills of an order not possessed by their particular student groups. Filling in forms, completing questionnaires, compiling lists, even making marks on simple rating scales may be beyond the capacities of the young people with whom they work. But *most* young people *can* read and write; the crucial question, more often, is whether or not they are motivated to use their skills. For the fraction who cannot read or write a word even if they want to, there is no reason why most if not all of these pencil-and-paper exercises should not be adapted for use in verbal form; providing a basis, for example, for interviews between workers and students or between students

52

themselves. Cassette and video recorders come into their own in these circumstances; spoken versions of questionnaires can be pre-recorded and used both individually and on a group basis to overcome the hurdle of illiteracy. Just reading out the items and giving straightforward assistance with the answers can be equally effective. Alternatively, tutors might like to invent non-literary (pictorial or activity-based) versions of questionnaire, checklist, or rating scale methods — this is not impossible and the results would be useful to a great many other people in education, further education and youth work.

A second important point is that none of the exercises is meant to be an end in itself. An exercise is successful only to the extent that it provokes some further thought, discussion or action *beyond* itself. The teacher's job is to ensure that this is what happens as often as possible, for as many participants as possible. So filling in a piece of paper, listening to a speaker, working in a small group, performing a brief roleplay, collecting information or taking part in a simulation should all be seen as a prelude to learning something about oneself, about others, about the outside world, and about ways of acting upon and interacting with the environment. The art of social and life skills work, as with most forms of education, lies in adapting your own ideas and those of others to the needs of your students. You should feel free, therefore, to improvise on any or all of the materials in this book; many of them are improvisations already.

Finally, the suggestions included here obviously consititute only a part of a possible life skills or 'survival skills' curriculum. Each of them could be augmented or further extended, and many other areas — such as family problems, moral values, alcohol, drugs, violence, interacting with police, finding accommodation, health and hygiene, minority group problems, or making decisions about politics — have not been covered at all. The fields of education and youth work are open to innovation in the teaching of these subjects.

SELF-ASSESSMENT

Introduction

There is a puzzling disjunction between theory and practice in education as it exists today. While in theory, the process of education begins with individuals themselves, in practice the goal of education seems to be to tell the individual about as many things as possible *other than* him or herself. In social and life skills training, these priorities are reversed. Because the main aim of this training is to give individuals more control over the course of their own lives, the point of departure has to be the individual's state of self-knowledge. We begin this section, therefore, with some exercises that can be used to help young people increase their level of awareness of themselves.

The materials and suggestions on the following pages are intended for use in aiding young people in the business of self-exploration or self-assessment. This means looking at likes and dislikes; strengths and weaknesses; skills and deficits; attitudes and feelings; in the past, present, and proposed future. Self-knowledge may include anything from measurements of your own height and weight to clear insight into your own motives and aspirations. Similarly, self-knowledge can be attained by a great diversity of methods; those appended here are only a sample of the directions that might be taken.

Some of the exercises described here involve asking people to write things down; but as suggested above these could be modified for purely conversational use. Others are based directly on the use of interview or discussion. All of them can — and should — be used as a starting-point for talking to others; one of the prime sources of our 'sense of self' is other people.

The first batch of exercises here are for direct use in self-description:

1. A self-description questionnaire;

2. Sentence completion: 'I am . . .';

3. Sentence completion: 'If . . .';

4. 'How will I know you?' — describing your appearance;

5. Self-characterisation.

These represent a number of different approaches to the task of describing oneself, which vary in their degree of structure. For some purposes, it can also be interesting to ask young people to describe themselves in terms of diagrams rather than just words. Two exercises for doing this are:

6. 'Lifelines': sketching your autobiography;

7. The 'self-and-others' chart; mapping interpersonal relationships.

Hearing what other people have to say about themselves can also be a valuable aid to self-discovery; two suggestions for stimulating this are:

8. 'Top tunes' — looking at your past in terms of music;

9. Peer interviews — getting to know yourself through others.

Finally, to act as a basis for subsequent exercises in life skills, two other exercises are included for the purpose of trying to help individuals sort out their priorities:

10. A Problem Checklist; and

11. A Checklist of Personal Goals.

The order in which exercises are presented here should in no way, of course, dictate how they are used in practice.

Self-description form

When applying for jobs, driving licences, passports, supplementary benefits, marriage licences, memberships of clubs — and even when entering some kinds of competitions — people have to supply a number of what are known as 'personal details'. Apart from name, age, and address, the actual information asked for varies according to the purpose of the inquiry. But it can be useful, not only for the purpose of filling in forms, but also in a more general way, to think of how you might describe yourself as fully as possible. There are clearly many ways in which this can be done; the self-description form below lists just a few of the possible categories. This can be given to individuals as a means of initiating the process of self-assessment using some questions they will almost certainly be familiar with, and perhaps others to which they don't know the answers:

Name ....

Date of birth .... Present age ....

Height .... Weight .... Colour of hair ....

Colour of eyes ....

Measurements: Chest .... Waist ....

                Hips .... Inside leg ....

Marital status .... Sex ....

Present occupation ....

Education: Schools attended: (1) ....

                             (2) ....

                             (3) ....

Previous jobs if any: (1) ....

                             (2) ....

                             (3) ....

Address ....

....

Type of accommodation ....

Hobbies and interests ....

....

Sentence completion: 'I am . . .'

A self-description form like that depicted on the previous page is one way of asking people for information about themselves. Usually, however, information that is gathered in this way tends to be used for other people's purposes. It can nevertheless, be useful to people themselves; but a more entertaining way of asking people to describe themselves is to ask them to do so by completing a sentence: 'I am . . .'.

Try asking young people to do this. Begin, for example, by asking them to complete the sentence five times; setting a time-limit of between two and five minutes. The exercise can be structured a little by giving them a piece of paper marked:

I am . . . .

I am . . . .

I am . . . .

I am . . . .

I am· . . . .

If individuals are sufficiently interested in the exercise, they can carry on completing sentences ten, fifteen, twenty or more times.

It is usually intriguing, and often very amusing, to ask people to read out some of the things they have written down; if they feel relaxed about doing this, it can add a lot to the atmosphere of a group, and also help people to get to know themselves and each other a little better.

After doing an exercise like this, it can also be valuable to 'analyse' what people have said — or rather suggest to them ways in which they might think about what they have said. Three possible ways of doing this are:

(a) Asking people how many times they managed to complete the 'I am' sentence and how easy or difficult they found it to do so. This might direct attention towards how relaxed or inhibited they feel about describing themselves, how articulate they are in defining themselves, and so on.

(b) The kinds of things people say can be classed as *positive* or *negative;* and the balance between the two might tell them something about their self-concept, their self-confidence and self-esteem.

(c) It can also be interesting to see to what extent the sorts of things individuals say place them in a relationship to other people. Do they refer to the groups to which they belong, or describe themselves in terms that make no reference to other people? The relative numbers of statements of these two kinds might also help them to define themselves more clearly.

Sentence completion: 'If . . .'

Sentence completion has many applications in enabling people to describe themselves. For instance, they might be asked to complete sentences such as 'I am good at . . .' or 'I feel good when . . .'; 'I used to be . . .' or 'I would like to be . . .'; 'I hate myself when . . .' or 'I lose my temper when . . .' and so on. The number of sentence-beginnings that can be used in this way is virtually limitless.

A particularly engaging version of this exercise consists of asking people to complete sentences that refer to imaginary events or situations. This in a way asks them to project themselves; and in doing so, can help them to gain a fuller picture of themselves which might have the by-product of boosting their confidence. Once again, the outcomes of this exercise can provide a valuable basis for interviews or discussion.

Some of the possible 'hypotheticals' that might be used are given below.

If I were prime minister I would . . .

If I were a millionaire I would . . .

If I were a big-time criminal I would . . .

If I were ten years older (or younger) I would . . .

If I could change our area I would . . .

If I could swop places with somebody else it would be . . .

If I could move to somewhere else it would be . . .

If I could be born again I would be . . .

If I were a film star, the kind of film I'd be in would be . . .

If I were an author, the kind of book I'd write would be . . .

If I owned a restaurant, it would be a . . .

If I could choose any job I wanted, I'd be a . . .

If I were world champion of something, I'd like it to be . . .

If there's one thing I wish people wouldn't do, it's . . .

If there's one way people could be improved, it's . . .

If . . .

'How will I know you?'

This exercise is primarily a mechanism for getting individuals to think about their personal appearance and how they would describe themselves to others. But it can also lead on to wider discussion of the ways in which appearance is important (if it is), or how it can be improved (if that is on the minds of those taking part). In addition, the exercise can be useful in helping members of a group to get to know one another better.

All it entails is asking individuals to imagine that they are in a particular predicament: they have arranged (by phone or letter) to meet someone they haven't met before, and have to tell them what they look like so that they will be recognised at the time of the meeting. Each participant is required, then, to produce a brief verbal sketch of him or herself.

You can do this directly by just asking people to describe themselves to other members of the group. Alternatively, ask them to write down a short self-description (if doing so verbally seems embarrassing). If written descriptions are produced, the game can be further enriched by asking people to drop them into a tray, mixing them up, and then asking individuals to pick one and see whether they recognise the writer. The accuracy of the sketches, the dominant features which emerge in them, individuals' attitudes towards their looks, the importance of dress, etc, should all provide valuable themes for discussion.

Self-characterisation

'Self-characterisation' is a device for enabling people to describe themselves from the outside as it were, as if in part they were someone else. This method of self-assessment was invented by Kelly (1955; see Bannister and Fransella, 1971), and consists of inviting individuals to describe themselves in the third person. They are asked to write a character sketch of themselves as it might be written by a very close friend; beginning with their own name, for example,

'Harry Brown is . . .'

The friend has an intimate understanding of Harry Brown, and can make a realistic appraisal of both his strengths and his weaknesses. The character sketches which result from this exercise can be quite revealing to individuals, helping them to clarify the priorities they have in mind when looking at themselves and to see, as Kelly put it, the way they structure their own world. Self-descriptions obtained in this way can form the basis of inter-views, peer interviews, or group discussion.

'Lifelines'

Sketching your own life story

This pencil-and-paper exercise is intended to act as a vehicle for the appraisal, by young people, of the course of their lives so far. It provides a kind of stimulus for the writing of an 'autobiography' — however crude, inaccurate, or incomplete that may turn out to be. By doing this, individuals may be able to pinpoint turning points or detect patterns in their lives, which yield insights into the position they are in now and the kind of person they have turned out to be. The outcome, hopefully, would be a better perspective on an individual's past life — which might be valuable in helping them to make plans for the future.

The exercise consists of giving people a piece of paper (preferably of at least A4 size) and asking them to draw a line which represents their life, from birth up to the present moment. They can draw the line all at once, or bit by bit as they think about different things that have happened to them. If it seems helpful, a time-scale can be written on the bottom or along the side of the sheet to use as a kind of guide. What they are asked to do then is to write down — or symbolise in some way — anything whatever that they consider has been of importance in their lives. This might include a list of places they have lived, schools they have attended, jobs they have had, or changes in their state of material well-being. It might focus on other people who have played a part in their lives such as family, friends, teachers, or workmates. Or it might reflect personal concerns such as their feelings, motives, or religious or political beliefs.

If people are willing to do this, they can be allowed anything up to half an hour to draw their lifeline and fill it in — with some groups even longer will be needed. Then, again if they are willing, they could compare their lifelines in pairs or in small groups; read them out to the group as a whole; or even sign them and pin them up on the wall.

Some of the points that are worth discussing include:

— the key events people describe

— changes of direction in the line and what they represent

— whether one particular period has emerged as most eventful

— any dominant themes or patterns which appear

— how they feel about the exercise overall.

Finally, the exercise can, if people wish, be extended — by projecting their lifelines into the future, and attempting a bit of fortune-telling.

Self-and-others chart

The idea of charting relationships between oneself and others is based on exercises used by Ziller (1973) and Button (1974). In these exercises, people are asked to map out their personal relationships in the form of a diagram, by using circles to represent themselves and others. They have to place the circles at various distances apart which correspond, in some way, to their feelings about the people involved. Obviously, the way in which people do this could be affected by many factors — such as their emotional attachments to the people concerned; their working relationships with them; their importance in other terms e.g. their authority, status, or sex; and according to whether the relationships are depicted in actual or ideal terms.

The exercise can be carried out in different ways. One circle —'me' or 'self' — always stands for the individual compiling the chart. In one version of the task, individuals are given a sheet of paper with circles in pre-arranged positions, and asked to insert the names of others in the circles provided. In another version, people are asked to draw circles denoting others anywhere they like. You can make this easier by supplying individuals with a large sheet of paper (with a circle in the centre marked 'me') and a number of other circles labelled with a variety of relationship names, as suggested below. Alternatively, ask people to make up their own circles depicting the individuals that are important to them.

All of these issues — who is chosen, where they are placed, how the relationship is conceived — are then worthwhile discussing.

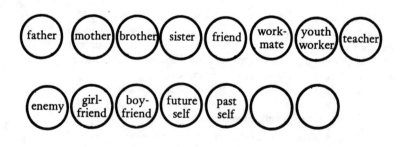

Top Ten Tunes

Talking about personal feelings or emotions — about love or hate, anxiety or depression — is taboo for many people except in very intimate or extreme situations. Everyday speech respects these reticences through the use of a variety of evasions and euphemisms for coping with emotionally-loaded topics. But art, literature, and music provide alternative universes of discourse for feelings that are otherwise denied or permitted only limited expression.

Teachers and others have made extensive use of literary forms to address some of these topics, but no matter how provocative a piece of verse or prose might be, the figures and events it refers to remain fictional, and discussion of them usually retains a comfortable distance from real life.

Music, on the other hand, often makes a much more direct appeal to the emotions; and can provide a peg on which to hang a discussion of personal feelings.

Ask group members to think of pieces of music (which will most often turn out to be pop songs), which they associate with particular places, people, periods or events in their lives — and to make a list of some of them together with a word or two which will convey the feeling that hearing the music evokes in them.

Although some people find this impossible to do, perhaps because they don't like music or can't remember tunes from the past, most can identify a number of tunes or records which have some kind of emotional significance for them.

Discussing these songs and the feelings that accompany them can provide a non-threatening vehicle through which individuals can share some views on emotionally important subjects.

For those who have difficulty in getting started on this exercise, it may be useful to display a list of 'Golden Oldies', or even to play a tape of excerpts from some of them and ask what group members were doing when they were current.

Peer interviews

Getting to know yourself through others

To most people the word 'interview' conjures up a fairly formal, rigorous and perhaps even frightening event; which is associated closely with the feeling of being judged by others. But in broader terms, an interview can be defined as nothing more than a 'purposeful conversation'. More important though, interviews are not necessarily meetings between people who differ in status, as is the case in most interviews for jobs. An interview can, in contrast, be merely an opportunity for two people to find out more about each other. This kind of interview is called a peer interview. The peers in this case are any two people who have something in common — like their age, their membership of a group, or their problems in some respect.

In addition, peer interviews also provide people with a chance to find out more about themselves. Just as, during growth, we build up a picture of ourselves at least partly through what others say, so in a peer interview we learn about ourselves by the comparisons that knowledge of other people makes possible. Many conversations between friends stimulate such a process of comparison and reflection. Peer interviews capitalise on this process, by setting out to:

1. Give people opportunities to find out more about others;

2. Stimulate thinking about themselves as a result — and so enhance self-awareness.

Since they are interviews as such, they can also be used to give people practice in the interpersonal skills of asking questions, listening, and summarising what others have said.

A 'peer interview' exercise can be carried out by asking people to form into pairs or trios. Suggest a topic to them, and ask them to find someone they would like to talk to about it. Allocate a fixed amount of time for the interviews (between 5 and 15 minutes will probably do) and then ask for some feedback on what they have been saying.

Possible interview topics might be:

- a good day you've had

- a bad day you've had

- something you like/hate doing

- somebody you admire/despise

- your family or friends

- one change you would make in . . .

- something really good that happened to you

- something you would like to happen

- personal goals — for the next 6 months or 5 years

- favourite: pastimes, groups, TV programmes, sports performers, places, people, foods, etc.

Checklists of problems and personal goals

Asked to say what their problems are or to define their personal goals, many young people will find it difficult to articulate the things that are on their minds. Prompted by a list of specimen problems or possible goals, on the other hand, they can find it much easier to identify things they would like to change about their lives. The checklists on the following pages are for helping them to do this.

The problem checklist

As its name implies, a checklist is a series of items which individuals have to classify in some way by putting ticks or crosses in appropriate boxes. In some checklists, they have to deal with all the items by sorting them out into different categories; in other checklists, they simply have to choose some items and reject others. In each case, they record their decisions by putting a mark in a box.

The 'problem checklist' on the next two pages is of the former kind. It presents people with a list of problems they might have, and asks them to mark these off one at a time into one of three categories: major problem, minor problem, or no problem. The idea of doing this is common to many different checklists that have been used (see Anastasi, 1976); but the essence of a good checklist is that the items it contains are likely to be recognised by individuals as difficulties they might have. You should not hesitate, therefore, to make up a checklist of your own — based on your estimate of what will be on the minds of the young people you are working with — or even ask them to compile one for you. Alternative or additional items to the ones listed here are not difficult to invent.

The idea behind a checklist is that first, it should help people crystallise their ideas about the problems they have got; and that second, their responses to it should be used as a basis for interviews, counselling, or group discussion. After a checklist like that on the next two pages has been introduced and completed, therefore, responses to it should be developed in this way.

The checklist of personal goals

Checklists can be adapted to many different purposes, and the second one illustrated here contains a list of possible goals which individuals might like to achieve. In this instance, they tick the goals in which they are interested and leave the rest blank; and again, their responses provide a basis for interview or discussion. Finally, it should be borne in mind that both checklists can be adapted verbally for use by non-literates.

Problem Checklist

Opposite each item on the left, please put a mark showing whether this is a major problem, a minor problem, or no problem for you.

	Major problem	Minor problem	No problem
1. Can't get a job of any kind			
2. Can't get a job I'd really like			
3. Can't keep a job			
4. Don't know where to look for jobs			
5. Find it hard to get on with people at work			
6. Don't have anywhere to live			
7. Unhappy with my present accommodation			
8. My rent is too high			
9. I have to leave the place I'm living			
10. Want to leave home but I'm not allowed to			
11. I'm having difficulties at home			
12. Don't get along with my parents			
13. Can't get up in the morning			
14. I'm short of money			
15. Can't manage money			
16. Can't save any money			
17. I owe people money			
18. People owe me money			
19. I don't know enough about my rights			

	Major problem	Minor problem	No problem
20. Making claims at the DHSS			
21. Being in trouble with the police			
22. Always being late			
23. Drinking too much			
24. There's nothing I'm good at			
25. Don't feel very confident in myself			
26. I'm very easily embarrassed			
27. I haven't got any decent clothes to wear			
28. Haven't any close friends			
29. Feeling bored			
30. Having nothing to do in my spare time			
31. Can't control my temper			
32. I give in to people too easily			
33. I don't get along with the opposite sex			
34. Feelings of loneliness			
35. Feelings of depression			
36. I don't feel very fit			
37. I don't feel very healthy			
38. I can't make decisions			
39. People don't understand me			
40. I don't understand other people			

Personal goals

If any of the items in the following list are things you would like to do, put a tick or a cross in the box beside them.

I would like to:

1.	☐	Get a job
2.	☐	Find out more about how the law protects me at work
3.	☐	Be more tolerant towards my workmates
4.	☐	Go on a training course
5.	☐	Find somewhere to live on my own
6.	☐	Move to a new area
7.	☐	Make a complete change in my life
8.	☐	Keep my life more or less as it is
9.	☐	Get better at managing money
10.	☐	Find out about ways to save
11.	☐	Save £100
12.	☐	Be independent as far as money is concerned
13.	☐	Learn how to resist sales pressure
14.	☐	Find out more about my welfare rights
15.	☐	Know what goes on in supplementary benefits tribunals
16.	☐	Understand what my rights are if I'm arrested
17.	☐	Understand how courts work
18.	☐	Learn how to control my temper
19.	☐	Learn how to control my drinking
20.	☐	Be more self-confident
21.	☐	Be less dependent on other people
22.	☐	Get on better with my parents
23.	☐	Know what effect I have on other people
24.	☐	Feel more relaxed
25.	☐	Get better at making decisions

Self-assessment — sources of further ideas

The exercises that have been described in this section have all been concerned with the assessment of the social and personal development of young people rather than with assessment from the more familiar academic standpoint. However, it has recently been suggested in a number of quarters that schools should concern themselves with the assessment and development of their pupils on a much broader base than they have done before. A number of schemes have attempted to foster assessments of this kind; some of them are described in *Outcomes of Education*, edited by T. Burgess and E. Adams (Macmillan, 1980).

A variety of suggestions and measures for assessing various aspects of the self will be found in the following books: R.B. Burns (1979) *The Self Concept. Theory, measurement, development, and behaviour*, Longmans; L. Button (1974), *Developmental Group Work with Adolescents*, University of London Press; and R.C. Ziller (1973), *The Social Self*, Pergamon Press. A number of other exercises that are useful for looking at attitudes to self can be found in L. Hudson (1966) *Contrary Imaginations* and (1968) *Frames of Mind*, both published by Penguin books.

For a guide to the construction and uses of simple questionnaires, see M.B. Youngman (1978) *Designing and Analysing Questionnaires*, Nottingham University School of Education.

A number of games that can be very valuable for self-assessment are described in *So You Think You Can Play Games?* produced by the Panmure House Staff Team, Lochend Close, Canongate, Edinburgh.

The 'self-characterisation' exercise described here is illustrated more fully in *Inquiring Man* by D. Bannister and F. Fransella, Penguin, 1971.

INTERACTING WITH OTHERS

Introduction

Departure from school signals a kind of transition in the social experience of young people. One set of acquaintances is exchanged for another; the faces of teachers and fellow pupils are replaced by those of the college, workplace, or dole queue. A larger number of encounters have to be managed, and with a greater variety of people, such as new friends, supervisors, workmates, officials of this or that organisation, and a range of others met with in the course of pursuing various goals. Perhaps more important, there is a change in the *kind* or *quality* of the personal transactions young people make. Others expect different things of them; they are understood to have become 'responsible'; and they themselves want to treat others and to be treated by others in a new way.

The materials and suggestions in this section of the book are concerned with individuals' social attitudes and with the skills they use when dealing with others. Subsequent sections of the book present exercises for developing social and life skills in specific problem areas such as work and rights; here, the focus is upon basic or general skills which operate in most social encounters, and which affect our ability not only to solve our problems through others, but also to form meaningful and satisfactory relationships with them. The exercises here extend from an examination of how people see themselves and others, to the deployment of roleplay in helping young people to acquire quite complex social skills like assertiveness, resisting pressure, or self-control under provocation.

Exercises are organised as follows:

1. Communication; judging others and communicating with them.
   (a)   mapping personal space;
   (b)   judging and conveying emotion: facial expressions;
   (c)   judging and conveying emotion: postures;
   (d)   talking and listening.
2. Self-perception and the perception of others.
3. Assessing social skills.
4. Uses of roleplay:
   (a)   simple roleplays;
   (b)   modelling exercises;
   (c)   structured roleplays.
5. Group problem-solving exercises.
6. Social 'games'.

'Communication' exercises

Although the mere physical presence of another person seems to affect the way people behave, most forms of social interaction are dependent on some kind of direct communication. Communication is the basis of all social skill. Human beings communicate by a variety of means — some intentional, some not. When two individuals hold a conversation, they exchange signals in a number of different 'channels' at once. Their speech conveys a message not only by means of the words they use, but also via the modulation of their voices. They express some of their feelings by virtue of the positions in which they stand, the gestures they use, and the way they look at each other. Even if they have never met before, each will have formed an impression of the other based on his or her manner of dress, general demeanour, and overall appearance. Ordinary, everyday conversation contains whole sets of signals — vocal, facial, gestural, and postural — subtly put together to form an integrated whole.

The exercises included here are designed to help young people appreciate some of these features of communication, and if possible put them to better use. But to be socially skilled means to be competent in two complementary aspects of the communication process. It means being able to put *your* message across to others; and it means being able to interpret — as accurately as possible — the message *they* are putting across to you. The suggestions below can be used to look at both of these facets of communication skill.

Before embarking on any of these exercises with individuals or groups, it can be useful to have a general discussion on communication. One way to initiate this is to have a brainstorm on all the possible methods by which people can communicate with one another. Another is to ask for two volunteers to sit down facing each other and hold a conversation, watched by other members of the group. The 'observers' can then be invited to describe some of the things the speakers are saying and doing. This can be made more vivid, if video is available, by re-playing the action for the speakers themselves. Many people are surprised by the things that they do — or fail to do — when talking to others; and the realisation can provide a valuable stimulus to ensuing exercises.

Mapping personal space

Most people have around them a kind of air-bubble which they like to think of as their own. Under normal circumstances, of course, they are not even aware that it's there — until it is encroached upon by someone they would rather keep at a distance. Social psychologists call this bubble 'personal space' (Argyle, 1975); it is a kind of invisible extension of the body into the surrounding atmosphere. Only those, such as close friends, who have been given special permission, can freely enter this space. If others do so, it may be seen as some kind of threat.

The size of 'personal space' varies from one person to another and from one culture to another; and this exercise is designed to enable individuals to measure their personal space and so become aware of a factor which, possibly without their knowledge, influences their behaviour towards others.

In the simplest version of this exercise, two people are asked to stand facing each other across a room. One is then invited to walk slowly towards the other. All the stationary individual has to do is to say 'stop' when he or she starts to feel uncomfortable. If a measuring tape or large piece of paper is available, it can be used to measure the outer limits of that individual's 'personal space'.

This exercise can be repeated with a number of individuals to look for variations in personal space. It may be advisable to avoid telling participants the purpose of the exercise until after they have tried it, as this might influence what they do — they can be asked to leave the room while the idea is explained to others. A 'scientific' dimension can be added by looking for differences between groups, e.g. between males and females, or tall and short people — in average size of the space. You can even investigate whether someone's personal space alters according to who is approaching them. A 'balanced experiment' might consist of:

a boy walking towards a boy
a girl walking towards a girl
a boy walking towards a girl
a girl walking towards a boy

Of course, the 'scientific' element in all this is slightly suspect, but it can add spice to the proceedings.

A more thorough appraisal of personal space can be undertaken by 'mapping' someone's space from different directions. An individual can be approached, in turn, from the front, the back, and both sides, thus giving an all-round picture of the dimensions of his or her personal space. The whole exercise can then be discussed, considering differences between people, how participants feel when strangers stand too close to them, who *is* allowed to stand near them, and other similar points.

Judging and conveying feelings: facial expressions

One of the principal means by which people convey their feelings to each other is through their facial expressions. Despite the almost infinite variety in the shape and size of the human face, its expressions exhibit sufficient uniformity for a smile or a grimace to be recognisable as such anywhere in the world.

The exercise on the next two pages is aimed primarily at helping young people to assess their own ability to judge the feelings of others from their facial expressions. But for those who have difficulty in using appropriate expressions to convey feelings themselves, the exercise can also provide a basis for training in communication skills.

Facial expressions manifest considerable variety and subtlety; the eyes, mouth, cheeks, nose and brow can, by the slightest movements in combination with each other, signify literally thousands of different emotional states. It has been suggested, however, on the strength of extensive research, that there are only six basic emotional expressions — for anger, fear, happiness, sadness, surprise, and disgust (Knapp, 1980). The exercise below concentrates on the use of these six key facial expressions.

The exercise itself if a kind of multiple-choice 'test'. Opposite each photograph on the next two pages is a list of four things that the person in the photograph might have been thinking or saying. In each case, the person was actually thinking one of the things on the list. The job of those doing the 'test' is to pick the correct item. The 'answers' are given at the foot of the page.

As presented here, this exercise is designed to illustrate one way of assessing someone's ability to 'read' the expressions of others. It can be used direct, or modified in a number of ways. For example, the list of possible answers can be discarded and the photographs used 'openly'; young people can be prompted with the photographs or with the statements and then asked to model the expressions for their peers; or photographs of group members themselves can be used. Other moods or feelings can be included, such as excitement, boredom, depression, amusement, bossiness, submissiveness, and many more. And in addition, the modelling aspect of the exercise can be extended to provide training for any individuals who find it difficult to express their feelings — using mirrors, video, or other means.

Finally, the whole of this exercise should be discussed, highlighting such questions as: how do you recognise different moods? Are some feelings easier to identify than others? How well do you have to know someone before you can tell how they're feeling? Can the same expression mean different things for different people?

(The correct choices are: Photograph 1: (b) — anger; 2: (d) — surprise; 3: (a) — sadness; 4:(c) — fear; 5: (d) — happiness; and 6: (b) — disgust.)

What are they saying?

Look at the photographs below. Beside each one is a list of things that the person in the photograph might be thinking or saying. Taking each photograph in turn, which of the four things do you think the person is saying?

1

This person is saying —

(a) *"I'm sorry I'm late."*

(b) *"Oh shut up you!"*

(c) *"I'm starving — and it's hours till tea-time!"*

(d) *"I hate to see people making fools of themselves."*

2

This person is saying —

(a) *"That's the worst joke I've ever heard in my life."*

(b) *"Could you lend me a fiver till next week?"*

(c) *"You're useless, you are!"*

(d) *"What a nice surprise!"*

3

This person is saying —

(a) *"It's a pity they had to move away, I really miss them."*

(b) *"I think you did that deliberately!"*

(c) *"Hello Jo! How are you?"*

(d) *"So what do you expect me to do about it?"*

4

This person is saying —

(a) *"That just isn't funny."*

(b) *"Don't ever talk to me like that again!"*

(c) *"This place gives me the creeps."*

(d) *"What are you doing tonight?"*

5

This person is saying —

(a) *"Don't worry about things so much."*

(b) *"Who cares?"*

(c) *"You'll be telling me next you did all the work yourself!"*

(d) *"Just think — three whole weeks of freedom!"*

6

This person is saying —

(a) *"That's the nicest thing anybody's ever said to me."*

(b) *"Just the thought of it makes my stomach turn."*

(c) *"Sorry — we're all sold out."*

(d) *"Sorry — could you say that again?"*

Judging and conveying feelings: postures

This exercise is similar in its aims and methods to the preceding exercise on judging facial expressions. This time, however, the focus of attention is on body posture. This is also an important signal of an individual's emotional state, and as with facial expression, there are many permutations and combinations of bodily movements and positions which convey as many different feelings and moods. It has been suggested (see Argyle, 1975) that while the face expresses the *kind* of emotion someone is experiencing, the bodily posture conveys the *intensity* of feeling being experienced. Nevertheless, some postures do seem to be associated with particular feelings; and this exercise illustrates how you might enable young people to carry out a further self-assessment of their ability to judge the feelings of others.

In the scientific study of postural communication, stick-figure drawings have been used, in order to eliminate the 'contaminating' effects of facial expressions. A series of stick-figures of this kind is illustrated in the book by Argyle (1975).

As in the previous exercise, individuals are asked here to decide which of four possible feelings is being expressed by the person in the photograph. Even more in this exercise than in the last, it might be useful to use the photographs as prompts, and to ask volunteers to model the postures for the rest of the group to identify. Once again, many other feelings can be added to the list; and the exercise can be used in reverse, as it were, to help individuals get better at *making* appropriate bodily signals as well as recognising them in others.

This exercise and the two previous ones — on 'mapping personal space' and 'judging facial expressions' — are all concerned with what is known as non-verbal communication or NVC. Exercises can also be devised for exploring other dimensions of this, such as gestures, gaze, and touch; some other examples are given by Priestley et al. (1978) and by Spence (1980), and a great deal of background information is available in the books by Argyle (1975) and Knapp (1980). It is worthwhile discussing all of these with young people; perhaps extending the discussion to consider other non-verbal signals like hair-styles, make-up, and clothes.

(The correct answers here are: Photograph 1: (d) — puzzled; 2: (b) — determined; 3: (a) — turning something down; 4: (c) — shy; 5: (c) — pleased with himself; 6: (b) — angry.)

Which of the four things opposite each photograph do you think the person in the photograph is feeling or doing?

1

This person is feeling —

(a) annoyed,

(b) worried,

(c) bored,

(d) puzzled.

2

This person is feeling —

(a) anxious,

(b) determined,

(c) defeated,

(d) relaxed.

3

This person is —

(a)   turning something down,

(b)   being friendly,

(c)   saying goodbye,

(d)   telling someone off.

4

This person is feeling —

(a)   irritated,

(b)   amused,

(c)   shy,

(d)   outgoing.

5

This person is feeling —

(a)   ashamed of himself,

(b)   depressed,

(c)   pleased with himself,

(d)   rejected.

6

This person is feeling —

(a)   friendly,

(b)   angry,

(c)   sorry,

(d)   mixed up.

Talking and listening

However important non-verbal signals may be in transmitting feelings and attitudes, the most effective medium of communication between individuals is speech. Whilst in skilled communication many different kinds of signal are acting in concert, there can be no doubt that the most serious single failure that can occur is in the use of the spoken word. Similarly, the ability to express oneself in words is one of the most valuable assets any individual can possess. Although social skills training is not designed to do the job of language teaching or of speech therapy, exercises can be carried out which contribute to an individual's confident, fluent, and expressive use of language.

Talking

The ability to speak well need not be founded on the possession of a large and impressive vocabulary. It simply means being able to put your own ideas into your own words, in a form that other people can understand. Some young people nevertheless find this very difficult and are very lacking in confidence when it comes to talking to others.

A basic mechanism in helping individuals (who would like to do so) to talk more, and with greater confidence, lies in just giving them suitable opportunities and encouragement. The chance to talk to others should be built into any social skills course in the shape of frequent informal group discussions; and more widely, in a freedom to air views which is more or less continuous.

But it is also worthwhile to run an exercise in which individuals are specifically asked to *give a talk*, however short, on something they know about, something in which they are interested, or something on which they have views. Over a series of sessions, each member of a group can be asked in turn to prepare and give a brief talk to the other group members.

Apart from the content of the talk itself — which might be geared to some other topic in a course — the 'audience' can also be asked to comment on the speaker's confidence and skill while giving it. Individuals can be asked to rate each other's performance, in terms of some important features of speech — e.g. clarity; overall volume and speed of delivery; how well the talk flowed (were there any abrupt silences, did the speaker have to rush at the end); and the expressiveness of the speaker's voice. Additional feedback can be given if the talks are recorded on video and played back for the speakers themselves.

Listening

Equally important in the business of communicating verbally is the ability to listen. Clearly, listening is an essential part of social interaction; yet some individuals find social interaction difficult because they often fail to listen to what others are saying.

Effective listening really consists of two different types of skill: there is the cognitive or intellectual skill of absorbing and otherwise dealing with what someone has said; and there is the social skill of showing interest and giving appropriate cues to people while they are speaking.

Most people possess the first kind of skill, but still occasionally miss what another person has said, because they are pre-occupied, distracted, or find what is being said uninteresting or unpalatable. In a way, good listening depends on 'prompting' yourself to concentrate on what a speaker is saying. Listening skills of this kind can be developed using exercises in which one individual reads a passage — say from a newspaper — to another or to a group. The listener's job is to summarise what has been said. It is then possible to see how closely they listened; how good they were at sorting out the main points from the background detail; or what sorts of things they found distracting. The results could then be used if necessary to help them improve their listening skill — for example, by increasing their resistance to distraction, or by suggesting they try to extract a small number of points from a talk rather than try to remember it all. With practice, it is possible to become a better listener. A variation on this theme will be found in the 'whispers' exercise on page 125.

Coordinating skills: holding a conversation

The social skills of listening are really part of the more complex process of holding a conversation. In most conversations, people give each other permission to talk at different points (according to what is being said, their relative status, and so on), and they signal their involvement in the conversation by the use of facial expressions, eye contact, movements of the head, and various 'following' or 'listening' noises such as 'yes' or 'mm'. Individuals who fail to follow these rules find their popularity rapidly diminishing. Skilled conversation also requires that each individual recognise when it is his turn to talk; that he come in 'one cue'; and of course, that he be able to speak coherently when the moment arrives.

Conversational skills — talking, listening, and exchanging appropriate signals which will keep the conversation going — can be assessed and practised in a number of social skills exercises. For instance, two individuals can be asked to think briefly about a topic and then to talk to each other about it — in front of their peers, a video-camera, or both. Observers (which might include the talkers themselves if the event is recorded) can then evaluate their conversational skills. You can direct their attention, for this purpose, to the various components of the skill; and ask them to report back afterwards on the performance of the two speakers. If it makes observation easier, the group can be divided in two, and one half allocated to observe each participant. The feedback so obtained can subsequently be used to help individuals improve their conversation skills in sessions devoted to practice.

'Practice' exercises can be organised in two ways. First, if individuals are having difficulty with one aspect of conversational skill — say the use of eye contact — then sessions can be run in which they focus on this particular problem. Then, just as when learning to drive a car one has to *prompt* oneself to look in the rear-view mirror, use the indicators, and the like, so in acquiring some elementary social skills one has to begin by consciously *making* oneself do something; which after sufficient practice becomes automatic.

Second, if individuals are having problems with whole pieces of conversation, exercises can be run in which they take separate parts of a conversation one at a time. They might for example look at a number of complex conversational skills, e.g.

(a) beginning a conversation
(b) sustaining the conversation
(c) controlling content (keeping to the subject, or changing it)
(d) ending the conversation.

In this case, it may be helpful to suggest to individuals a variety of ways in which they can accomplish each of these tasks. Using brainstorming or group discussion, a list of possible things to say or do e.g. to start a conversation, can be obtained from other group members; who might then be invited to portray or *model* some of these strategies in brief roleplays, for the benefit of those who find starting conversations a problem. (The use of modelling to approach skill deficits of this kind is dealt with more fully below.)

Combinations of methods such as the giving of instructions, modelling, practice, and feedback have been shown to be effective in improving the conversation skills of both children (Whitehill, Hersen, and Bellack, 1980) and adolescents (Lindsay, Symonds, and Sweet, 1979).

Self-perception and the perception of others

The images people have of themselves, and the impressions they form of each other, will obviously play an important part in influencing what passes between them. This series of exercises is intended to help young people learn more about how they see themselves, how they see others, and how others see them.

The basic tool for exploring this is the *perception questionnaire* shown on the next page. This consists of a series of rating scales, each of which represents a dimension that people might use to describe themselves or others. Taking each scale in turn, they have to say where they think they stand between two adjectives which are opposites of each other.

Some of the uses of rating scales were described in chapter 4. In the simplest version of this exercise, the perception questionnaire is used to help individuals build up a picture of themselves. Having explained the idea of a rating scale, you then ask participants to run through the questionnaire describing themselves on each dimension: 'me as I am' or 'me as I see myself'. Having circled the point where they think they stand on each scale, you can then ask them to join up their ratings to make a kind of 'profile'. Although this may not contain many surprises in itself, it is usually interesting to see how different individuals' profiles compare with one another. This can lead to a discussion of why people rated themselves in a particular way; how important are the differences between them; whether they agree with each other's self-ratings, and so forth.

This kind of exercise can be extended and used in various other ways which are described below. Young people can find out how they are seen by others; discover discrepancies between their pictures of themselves and the way they look to their friends; think about the ways in which they change over time; and talk about which attributes of themselves and others are important to them in forming relationships.

All parts of this exercise are open to modification, according to the needs of those using it and what they think will be of interest to the groups with whom they are working. You can, in particular, assemble new sets of adjectives to use in the rating scales, or ask young people to suggest their own.

Perception questionnaire

The pairs of adjectives below are arranged into a set of *rating scales.* Between each pair of opposites there is a 6-point scale. Taking each scale in turn, put a ring round the point on it where you think you stand.

For example — if you think you are a very *kind* person you should mark the 'kind — unkind' scale like this:

Kind (1) 2   3   4   5   6   Unkind

On the other hand if you think you are very *unkind* you should mark the scale:

Kind   1   2   3   4   5 (6) Unkind

If you think you are *a little* kind but not very kind you should mark the scale:

Kind   1   2 (3) 4   5   6   Unkind

Kind	1	(2)	3	4	5	6	Unkind
Reliable	1	(2)	3	4	5	6	Unreliable
Easy to talk to	(1)	2	3	4	5	6	Hard to talk to
Hard-working	1	2	(3)	4	5	6	Lazy
Clever	(1)	2	3	4	5	6	Stupid
Very good-looking	1	2	(3)	4	5	6	Not good-looking
Talkative	1	(2)	3	4	5	6	Quiet
Shy	1	2	3	4	5	(6)	Outgoing
Happy	1	(2)	3	4	5	6	Unhappy
Relaxed and easy-going	1	2	(3)	4	5	6	Tense and worried
Honest	(1)	2	3	4	5	6	Dishonest
Always the same	1	2	(3)	4	5	6	Moody and changeable
Fun-loving	1	2	3	(4)	5	6	Serious
Friendly	(1)	2	3	4	5	6	Unfriendly
Independent of others	1	2	(3)	4	5	6	Dependent on others
Well-organised	1	(2)	3	4	5	6	Mixed-up

Using a perception questionnaire

Apart from asking people to rate themselves on a perception questionnaire in the fairly straightforward way described above, there are several other exercises that can be run using scales of this kind.

1. Rating each other

Each person can be asked to rate someone else and then a comparison made between their ratings of the person and the person's own. Even this can be done in several different ways. In the simplest, one person rates another, for example 'So-and-so as I see her'; or completes a new set of self-ratings, for example 'Me as So-and-so sees me'. In a more complex version, one person rates another the way they think that person would rate him- or herself — 'So-and-so as he sees himself'. Any or all of the resultant profiles can then be set beside people's original sets of self-ratings. While some people find this kind of exercise difficult, for others it can prove very revealing of the gaps that exist between their picture of themselves and the picture others have of them.

2. Ratings over time

If you are working with the same group of young people over a period of several weeks or months, it is possible to obtain a rough measure of changes in their self-image by repeating the perception questionnaire at different points in time e.g. at the beginning, in the middle, and at the end of a course.

Alternatively, you can ask them to rate themselves at different periods from the standpoint of the present — 'Me as I used to be'; 'Me in five years time'; 'Me as I would really like to be'; 'Me when I'm old'. A combination of one of these and a questionnaire completed 'Me as I am now' might help isolate changes which people would like to make, and which you can build upon in a social skills course.

3. Ratings of different 'selves'

Most people recognise that they behave slightly differently in different circumstances; some change so dramatically that no two reports of them are the same. By asking people to rate themselves as they think they are in different settings, variations in their reactions and in their self-image can be explored in great depth. Some of the 'selves' that can be described in this way include:

Me at home	Me at the weekend
Me in school/at college	Me on a Saturday night
Me at work	Me on a Monday morning
Me on the dole	Me on holiday
Me as a son/daughter	Me at my best/worst
Me as a brother/sister	Me in a good mood/bad mood
Me with friends/with strangers	Me as my boyfriend/girlfriend sees me

Not unnaturally, young people will only be willing to try a small number of all the foregoing exercises — say two or three at the most; so you have to decide in advance which would be most useful for any particular individual or group.

A 'group perception' exercise

An extra dimension can be added to the exercises described above through the introduction of *group ratings*. For this purpose, a group with any more than a dozen members might prove rather unwieldy.

All that is required for this exercise is that each person in a group should first of all complete a perception questionnaire 'As I see myself', or 'As others see me' or 'As the group sees me'. Then, each individual in turn is rated by everyone else in the group; the easiest way to do this is to focus on one group member at a time, have everyone do ratings on him or her, and then collect together the ratings made of each person.

Each person can then be given the ratings produced by their peers and asked to average them out, so producing a composite 'group profile' of him- or herself — a portrait of how they are seen by the rest of their group. This can obviously take some time and may require a number of sessions before everyone has finally obtained an 'average' of his or her ratings.

The exercise can however be rich in revelations, and discussions should bring out any discrepancies — large or small — between individuals' perceptions of themselves and others' perceptions of them. While some people turn out to be remarkably accurate in their appraisal of their social 'image', others can be very wide of the mark. The nature of the specific differences which emerge as well as the skills involved in 'putting yourself across' can both be fruitful areas of discussion.

Two precautions ought however to be taken if you decide to use this exercise. First, in some instances people can be confronted with rather unsavoury comments on themselves, and it is important to ensure that this will not cause unnecessary distress; and second, it might be wiser to have group impressions done anonymously — to avoid potential animosity between particular group members. Both of these difficulties can be at least partly avoided by making it clear in advance what this exercise involves, so that only those willing — and hopefully able — to cope with possible criticisms will take part.

Assessing social skills

A number of methods can be used to assess the social competence of young people or to help them assess their own. You can interview them about any difficulties they may have; you can ask them to interview each other in pairs and then report back to their group; or you can set up roleplays for the purpose of directly observing their behaviour. A useful prelude to all of these, however, is to ask them to complete a short pencil-and-paper exercise in which they estimate their own social skills on a series of rating scales. This is a fairly common practice in social skills training and there are now a number of specially designed questionnaires and inventories in existence.

One implement for doing this is illustrated on the next page. This *social skills survey* consists of a list of skills involved in communicating and interacting with others. Those using it are asked to rate themselves according to their level of competence on each skill in turn (though they can also use it to rate each other's skills). The ratings have to be made on a five-point scale, as follows:

1 = this is something I am NEVER good at

2 = this is something I am SELDOM good at

3 = this is something I am SOMETIMES good at

4 = this is something I am USUALLY good at

5 = this is something I am ALWAYS good at

(If you think a scale like this would be too difficult for some individuals to use, it can be replaced by a 3-point scale, e.g. 1 = never good at, 2 = sometimes good at, 3 = always good at.)

Before giving out the survey, it will probably be worthwhile to have a short discussion about social skills and to talk about the idea of being skilled in dealing with others. Next, you should run through the ratings so that it's clear to everyone what they mean; perhaps writing them out on a large sheet or blackboard.

The completed survey can then be taken as a kind of 'baseline' measure of someone's self-defined strengths and weaknesses in social interaction. Its most important use is to help young people to identify skills they would like to improve; so it can be used in a very direct way to lead on to roleplays and other training exercises. In addition, it should also pinpoint skills which individuals are more confident about, and which they might be willing to demonstrate to others. Finally, it can serve as a 'marker' for the purpose of monitoring an individual's progress in developing social competence and confidence.

The list of skills here should not be regarded as definitive; you should add or subtract items as you see fit.

Social skills survey

How good are you at using each of the social skills in this list? Put a ring round one of the numbers on the right according to how good you think you are at using each skill. Use the numbers as follows:

1 = this is something I am NEVER good at
2 = this is something I am SELDOM good at
3 = this is something I am SOMETIMES good at
4 = this is something I am USUALLY good at
5 = this is something I am ALWAYS good at

1.	Starting a conversation	1	2	3	4	5
2.	Keeping a conversation going	1	2	3	4	5
3.	Listening to people	1	2	3	4	5
4.	Saying thanks	1	2	3	4	5
5.	Using the telephone	1	2	3	4	5
6.	Apologising if I've done something wrong	1	2	3	4	5
7.	Giving people compliments	1	2	3	4	5
8.	Telling jokes	1	2	3	4	5
9.	Asking questions	1	2	3	4	5
10.	Showing people I like them	1	2	3	4	5
11.	Showing people if I'm annoyed with them	1	2	3	4	5
12.	Asking people for favours	1	2	3	4	5
13.	Asking people to return things they've borrowed	1	2	3	4	5
14.	Making complaints in a shop	1	2	3	4	5
15.	Resisting pressure from others	1	2	3	4	5
16.	Talking to people in positions of authority	1	2	3	4	5
17.	Holding my own in an argument	1	2	3	4	5
18.	Controlling my temper	1	2	3	4	5
19.	Talking about myself	1	2	3	4	5
20.	Talking to people I don't know well	1	2	3	4	5
21.	Talking to members of the opposite sex	1	2	3	4	5
22.	Showing sympathy to someone who has a problem	1	2	3	4	5
23.	Being interviewed at the social security office	1	2	3	4	5
24.	Being interviewed for a job	1	2	3	4	5
25.	Ending a conversation	1	2	3	4	5

Uses of roleplay

Using some combination of methods — such as the Skill Survey presented on page 86 or a similar instrument devised especially for the purpose; interviews or peer interviews; and group discussion — it should be possible to help young people identify encounters they find hard to handle, or pinpoint social skills they would like to acquire or improve.

Actually to achieve the latter, however, they will almost certainly have to engage in another activity through which they can test out and practise the skills in which they are interested. They will have to *roleplay* the events which they wish to cope with more effectively.

Roleplay is one of the key methods of social and life skills training. A roleplay is a make-believe representation of some real-life event, carried out in order to help participants get better at managing the event itself. This being the case, roleplays are almost as heterogeneous as the events of which they are analogues. They may vary greatly in complexity — from the re-enaction of a telephone call involving two people to the simulated production of a television programme involving two dozen. And although all roleplays are artificially constructed, they can also differ widely in their degree of realism. While some 'survival-game' roleplays will depict happenings — such as moon landings, shipwrecks, or the making of big business decisions — quite distant from most people's experience, others — such as simulated job interviews or shopping expeditions — could almost be mistaken for their counterparts in everyday life.

The general aims of roleplay are always however the same; it is designed to help individuals identify and examine happenings which they find difficult to deal with; explore alternative possibilities for action; and rehearse and practise skills for future use when dealing with other people. These aims and some of the ways in which they can be attained have already been discussed in chapter 4. The aim of the pages which follow is to suggest ideas as to how roleplay can be used, and to provide some basic materials which can be further developed to suit the needs of particular individuals and groups.

Exercises are arranged, roughly, in order of complexity (though how complex a roleplay session might turn out to be can't really be decided exactly in advance).

Simple roleplays

Whereas in psychodrama and related therapeutic procedures, the substance of roleplay tends to be individuals' internal, emotional conflicts, in social skills training the focus of activity is more likely to be quite commonplace, everyday interpersonal encounters. (Oddly enough, J.L. Moreno, who devised psychodrama, originally intended it as a skills training exercise for delinquent girls.) This is not to say that feelings and attitudes do not play a part in such everyday events; on the contrary, problems in dealing with other people very often arise from individuals' anxiety about social situations, or from their misunderstanding of what goes on in them.

However, it is possible to help individuals to cope with feelings – to alleviate their anxiety, for example – through the use of roleplay, while at the same time training them in the exercise of a skill. When roleplay is used properly, the development of skills and of relaxation and confidence in using them go hand in hand.

Roleplay can be used first of all on a fairly simple level – concentrating, to begin with, on situations that will be familiar to young people, and which involve only two, three or four 'actors' at a time. Used in this way, roleplay has two aims:

1. To help those who are unable to do so to get better at dealing with a range of quite ordinary encounters with others;
2. For those who already know how to deal with these situations, to introduce roleplay as a method that can be used to help them learn to cope with more complex events.

By and large, the most difficult roleplay to run with the members of any group may well be the very first. At that point, their reluctance to stand up and play-act in front of their peers will be at its maximum. Overcoming this initial hurdle could be very important in deciding whether the group will use roleplay for any other purpose.

To help groups 'limber up' for doing roleplays, it can be useful to begin the session with a game of some kind. To run the roleplay itself, volunteers can be asked for; the more extrovert members of a group will usually respond to this. Alternatively, asking people to say how they would deal with some situation, and then to demonstrate how, can help get a roleplay session off the ground. The showing of a pre-recorded roleplay on video can also help to induce group members to have a go at it themselves. Some suggestions for simple roleplays are given below; where necessary, additional background details should be invented to assist those taking part.

1. Two friends, who haven't seen each other for some time, meet in the street one day by chance. They say hello and start a conversation.
2. Two friends are looking in a shop window. Someone else arrives who knows only one of them. The person who knows both has to introduce the others.
3. A group of three friends are sitting in a cafe or pub. Another person comes in and has to join the group.
4. Someone knocks on the door of a friend's house to see if the friend is in; one of the friend's parents opens the door.

5. Walking along the street, someone has to ask a policeman for directions to the bus station.

6. Three people are having a conversation; one of them has to go. The other two don't want this person to leave.

7. Several people are waiting in a queue to buy tickets for a rock concert. Another person walks to the front of the queue.

8. One person has to ask another if she can borrow his stereo cassette deck for a party.

9. Someone is watching TV in a room (at home, in a club, or at college) when two others come in and start talking.

10. In a cafe (or pub), someone went up to get a drink and returned to find that his seat had been taken, or that someone was reading his newspaper.

11. ·A trainee would like a day off work to visit a friend in hospital some distance away. He or she has to ask the supervisor about it.

12. Having said that they would be home by eleven, someone arrives home much later to find his or her parents waiting up.

13. Someone is asked to babysit for relatives, but has to refuse because he or she has already arranged to go out that evening.

14. One person has to apologise to another for something, e.g. being late, saying something rude, having borrowed something and failed to return it, etc.

15. In a queue, somebody turns round and wrongly accuses another of pushing.

16. Having left a scarf on a bus, someone has to go to the lost property office to see if she can get it back.

17. Two friends meet; one of them has been away the previous day to an interview for a job she really wanted but didn't get. The other asks how things went.

18. Someone is sitting at home when there is a knock at the door; he opens it to find a door-to-door salesman.

19. Having bought something in a shop, a customer is given change which is one pound short.

20. A group of two (or three) friends are talking about another friend when suddenly he or she appears; it is obvious whom they have been talking about.

When people have taken part in one of these roleplays, you can then ask other members of the group to say how good they were, and whether the outcome might have been different if they had behaved in a different way.

If the roleplay has been videotaped it should be played back for the benefit of participants. The whole encounter can then be discussed; and followed possibly with other roleplays in which individuals demonstrate alternative ways of handling it successfully.

Modelling exercises

If roleplays of some common social situations have been carried out, it may emerge that some members of a group have never had to deal with these situations, or that they feel anxious or diffident about how to deal with them. In this case, other members of the group may be able to show them how to manage the encounters in question through *modelling*.

Modelling consists of the roleplayed demonstration of a social skill or response, *by* someone who is competent in its execution, *for* someone who is not. It can be carried out 'live' (face to face), or recorded on video. There are two distinct ways in which modelling can be used in social skills training:

1. To illustrate to someone a specific kind or pattern of performance that is needed for a particular situation, where little flexibility is allowed e.g. making an appearance in court, being interview at the DHSS;
2. To illustrate a range of different responses that could be made in a situation which calls for flexibility — but in which the learner's past behaviour has been rigid or stereotyped, e.g. coping with threats of violence, talking to members of the opposite sex.

In the first kind of modelling, individuals learn from others almost by direct imitation — though of course their own version of a skill is bound to be in some ways different from the model's. In the second, a more subtle kind of learning is going on; individuals are helped to realise that there is more than one way of reacting to a situation in which their typical response is ineffective or even counter-productive.

Working with a group, you can try out modelling exercises after having identified some skills which members of the group would like to acquire. Other group members who possess the skills in question demonstrate their use in appropriate roleplays. Next, those who are interested in developing the skills take the part of the models and the same roleplay is repeated. This should be followed by some discussion designed to bring out the main features of the skill, and to give feedback to those who are trying it out. Such a sequence may need to be run through several times until learners feel more confident about the use of the skill (a process which may form part of several successive roleplay sessions). Finally, individuals can be encouraged to set real-life targets for the exercise of their skill.

The extended use of modelling exercises can be made easier by the compilation of a library of video *modelling tapes*, which contain good examples of the execution of particular skills.

Some skills that can be demonstrated in a modelling session include:

Beginning or ending conversations
Using the telephone
Asking someone to dance
Making a complaint in a shop
Thanking someone for a favour
Politely refusing something, e.g. a drink, a lift, a request of some kind
Showing anger without overdoing it.

Of course, any of the skills listed in the Skill Survey or amongst the simple roleplays listed above can also be used as the basis of a modelling exercise.

It is worth noting that, for modelling to be most effective, the model should share certain characteristics (for example, age or background) with those who are trying to learn. Individuals learn best from those whom they perceive to be similar to themselves, and whose performance they can see themselves matching if they make the necessary effort. If in some instances teachers, tutors, or youth workers have to act as models, it may help to have one other group member who will 'take over' the part soon afterwards.

Structured roleplays

If the participants in a role play find it difficult to get started, or cannot keep the momentum going; or if you want to look at encounters in which people have more complex sets of expectations, then it is possible to run roleplays in which individuals are given more elaborate instructions about who they are supposed to be and what they would like to happen. An exercise like this is called a *structured roleplay*.

Of course, all roleplays have some kind of structure, in that people are allocated parts to play beforehand; even if they are told only, for example, that one is to be a policeman and the other an unemployed youth. But in structured roleplays so called, the actors are given much fuller background pictures of their roles, aims, and expectations.

Suggestions for structured roleplays will be found at various points in this book. Each can be pruned down or expanded as users see fit. To run a structured roleplay, write or type out the directions for each participant on a separate piece of paper. Alternatively, take the actors outside or into another room and brief them verbally. It can sometimes be useful to let them use name-plates or other props to help them and their audience remember who they are and to ease their adoption of roles. Then, ask the role-players to act out the situation for a few minutes (perhaps avoiding the use of the word 'roleplay'). If possible, the performance should be video-recorded so that the actors can see themselves afterwards.

A session incorporating roleplays like this might consist of:

(a) a short introduction to the topic involved;

(b) giving out the roleplay briefs and running the roleplay;
(c) discussion of the roleplay and of how else it might have gone, including comments from observers and playback of any videotape;
(d) further roleplays of alternative strategies that could have been used;
(e) where necessary, practice by participants of new skills etc, and setting of goals for 'real' behaviour.

Finally, it is not difficult to make up structured roleplays yourself, or even ask young people to create their own.

Structured roleplay: 1

Dave and Alison have been going out for a couple of months. They live in different parts of the same town and neither of them is on the phone. Just lately, Dave has been a bit late on three occasions in a row for meetings with Alison. One evening, because of a series of mishaps (late buses, losing his key, etc) Dave is so late arriving at their meeting-place that Alison has gone. He goes round to her house but no-one is in.

DAVE really likes Alison and wants to continue going out with her. He plans to go round and see her the following evening.

ALISON likes Dave but is fed up with his habit of lateness. She thinks that he might be going out with her because he hasn't got anybody else. Someone else asked her out recently and she's thinking of going.

At lunchtime the next day, they run into each other by chance in the centre of town.

(This can be roleplayed both as suggested here and with the roles reversed.)

Structured roleplay: 2

Jane is unemployed and is claiming supplementary benefit; she hasn't had a job since leaving school. She has two brothers and two sisters, her father is an unskilled labourer and her mother has no job. She doesn't get on too well with her parents. She pays them something each week for her keep. One Friday, her Giro arrives £10 short. She goes to the DHSS but they say they can't rectify the problem until the following week.

JANE wants to go out that evening and can only afford to do so if she can put off paying her mother until the following week.

JANE'S MOTHER needs her daughter's weekly contribution to the household as they are quite hard up and every penny counts.

Jane gets back from the DHSS at 4.30 in the afternoon.

Group problem solving

There are many problems that occur in everyday life to which people find solutions by the fairly rapid and comparatively undramatic method of asking others. Those who have never dealt with a particular situation before, for example, are likely to consult those who have; people regularly turn to each other for information, for guidance in making decisions, and for practical help in getting things done. Such informal 'counselling' forms quite a large part of the exchanges that take place between people; and it not uncommonly has to deal with problems of a quite serious nature.

In any group of young people there will probably be a certain amount of this kind of helping going on. But it is also possible to build upon it and make it more explicit by organising a *group problem-solving exercise;* a kind of group discussion in which individuals pool suggestions and work together on a quandary with which one of them is faced.

Group problem-solving can be arranged in a number of ways. It can, first of all, be addressed to a set of standard situations which young people might encounter. For example, you might compile a list of problems and present them to group members in the form of fictional case-studies of individuals whom they have to advise. They can then form 'working parties' to consider each problem and return after a fixed period to make suggestions and recommendations. The solutions arrived at by each working party can then be compared and debated. This can be used to look not only at interpersonal problems but also at practical issues e.g. to do with money or rights.

Secondly, group problem-solving can be focussed on the self-defined problems of group members, in a way which permits them if they wish to preserve their anonymity. Ask individuals to write down on a piece of paper a sketch of one problem with which they are faced (or are perhaps, trying to help someone else with). The papers are then collected, jumbled together, and picked out of a tray by group members (if they pick up their own they should of course put it back). Individuals are then asked to comment and propose solutions to each other's problems. A further layer of anonymity can be added to this by asking people to write suggestions on their piece of paper, then re-distributing the papers and asking for comments on both the original problems and the suggested solutions. If the whole group also discusses some or all of the problems, a large number of points should have emerged by the end of the problem-solving exercise, which will hopefully prove useful to those whose problems the group deals with.

Social 'games'

Most games revolve around some kind of social interaction; in fact it is possible to look upon games *as one form* of social interaction carried on according to special sets of rules. While in some games the 'interactive' element is of pretty limited importance, in others it is the *raison d'etre* of the game itself. There are many games of the latter kind which can be built into a social and life skills course.

The educational value of games has long been recognised, and they can be used to teach almost any subject. The main reason for including them in a life skills course, however, would be merely to help people in a group relax and enjoy each other's company. If they are doing this, interaction between them will be much more fluid and they will work together much more productively. But a lot of games – including many that have been specially devised for courses on personal development or on problem-solving – also have useful by-products; for example, of directing the attention of players towards some aspect of their relationships, or of helping them to get to know themselves better.

A number of games and of game-like exercises are included in different sections of this book. Several games are described below, and many more can be found in the books listed at the end of this section.

The ball game

This could be described as an 'icebreaker' game, i.e. it helps people to get to know one another and loosens up their inhibitions slightly if they have only recently met. You would therefore use it early in a course (though probably not at the very beginning).

The purpose of this game is to help members of a group remember each other's names. Arrange people's chairs in a circle so that everyone can see everyone else. Next, ask them to write their names on a piece of paper and fold it so that it will act as a 'name-plate' on their desks or on the floor in front of them. You then take a small, light ball – a ping-pong ball will do – and show how the game is played by throwing it to someone in the group, at the same time saying his or her name. The recipient then has to throw the ball to someone else. Naturally, only *gentle* throws are allowed. If you continue this for a few minutes, people in a group learn each other's names with surprising speed, and enjoy themselves at the same time. You can then try it briefly with the nameplates removed.

The blind walk

This game falls into a category of what are sometimes called 'trust' games or exercises. Ask the group to form into pairs (with one trio if there is an odd number overall). One member of each pair is then blindfolded; and for a period of perhaps ten minutes has to be guided everywhere by the other. At various stages the guides can stop their charges and ask them where they think they are; and see if they can recognise objects by touching them. At the end of the 'blind walk', the whole group should re-assemble; and you can then ask those who were blindfolded whether they managed to keep their blindfolds on; where they think they were led; how it felt to be dependent on other senses than vision; and what were their reactions to having to rely on someone else for their safety.

Killer

This is a well-known party game which calls on people to watch each other very closely. The group should be seated so that all can see one another. By drawing lots (e.g. by putting pieces of paper into a hat, one with a 'K' on it), one person becomes the 'killer'. The 'killer' must keep his identity secret, and can 'kill' other players by winking at them. Of course, if he is seen doing this, or if someone works out his identity, he loses his own life. Those who make false accusations suffer the penalty of death themselves. Winking at people under these circumstances requires considerable subtlety!

Find the leader

This game, described by the Panmure House Staff Team (1979), also calls for great subtlety on the part of the person appointed as 'leader'. The group should again be seated in a circle, and one person is asked to leave the room. In their absence, one person is chosen to be the leader of the group; whatever they do must be imitated by the other group members. The absentee then returns and has to discover who the rest of the group are following. The leader can make any kind of movement — standing, sitting, gesturing, dancing or whatever — but obviously making sounds would give her identity away. When the leader has been tracked down — which takes some people much longer than others — the 'leader' of this particular episode becomes the next 'victim'.

Analogies

This game is slightly different from the preceding ones in being abstract and conceptual rather than activity-based. One individual in a group has to think of some person, who should be either another member of the group or someone known to all the members. The rest of the group have then to work out whom the individual has in mind. They do this by asking questions which bring out some characteristic of the person by analogy with something else. So someone might ask, 'If this person was a song, what kind of song would he or she be?' Different people ask different questions of this sort until enough is known for someone to work out the identity of the unknown person. Whoever succeeds in doing this goes next in thinking of a 'mystery' person.

Interacting with others — sources

Background

If you would like to find out more about the background to social skills training, the following books should prove useful:

M. Argyle (1969), *Social Interaction,* Tavistock Publications, especially ch.10.

A.P. Goldstein, R.P. Sprafkin and N.J. Gershaw (1976), *Skill Training for Community Living,* Pergamon Press.

E. Lakin Phillips (1978), *The Social Skills Basis of Psychopathology,* Grune & Stratton.

P. Trower, B. Bryant and M. Argyle (1978), *Social Skills and Mental Health,* Methuen.

And for a collection of illustrative case studies, which describe the use of social skills training and other methods with a wide range of problems, see:

J.D. Krumboltz and C.E. Thoresen (1976), *Counselling Methods,* Holt, Rinehart & Winston.

On non-verbal communication

M. Argyle (1975), *Bodily Communication,* Methuen.

M.L. Knapp (1980), *Essentials of Non-Verbal Communication,* Holt, Rinehart & Winston.

Assessing social skills

The social skills survey presented here is based on ideas in the book by Goldstein, Sprafkin and Gershaw, cited above. However, there are many similar instruments for assessing different aspects or areas of social skill. If you would like to pursue any of these further, see the following books and articles:

for a *social anxiety* scale: D. Watson and R. Friend, 'Measurement of Social-Evaluative Anxiety' in the *Journal of Consulting and Clinical Psychology* (1969), vol.33, pp.448-57.

for an *assertiveness* scale: S.A. Rathus, 'A 30-item schedule for assessing assertive behaviour' in *Behaviour Therapy* (1973), vol.4, pp.398-406.

for an *anger* inventory: R. Novaco (1975), *Anger Control,* Lexington Books.

for a *shyness* survey: P.G. Zimbardo (1977), *Shyness,* Addison-Wesley.

A variety of methods for assessing social skills are also described in the book by Trower, Bryant and Argyle, mentioned above; and also in a manual by S. Spence (1980), *Social Skills Training with Children and Adolescents. A Counsellor's Manual,* published by the National Foundation for Educational Research.

Roleplaying

For background information about uses of roleplay, see J.V. Flowers and C.D. Booraem, 'Simulation and Role Playing Methods', a chapter in *Helping People Change*, F.H. Kanfer and A.P. Goldstein (eds) Pergamon Press, 1980. For more practical 'how to do it' books, see:
M. Chesler and R. Fox (1966), *Role-Playing Methods in the Classroom*, Science Research Associates, Inc., Chicago.
R. Lewis and J. Mee (1980), *Using Role Play, an introductory guide*, published by the Basic Skills Unit, 18 Brooklands Avenue, Cambridge CB2 2HN.

Modelling

If you would like to know more about the principles on which modelling is based, see either of:
M.A. Perry and M.J. Furukawa, 'Modeling Methods', a chapter in K.H. Kanfer and A.P. Goldstein (eds) *Helping People Change*, Pergamon Press, 1980.
D.C. Rimm and J.C. Masters (1979), *Behavior Therapy, Techniques and Empirical Findings*, Academic Press — especially ch.4.

Games

A great variety of games will be found in:
D. Brandes and H. Phillips (1978), *The Gamester's Handbook*, Hutchinson.
So You Think You Can Play Games? by the Panmure House Staff Team, Lochend Close, Canongate, Edinburgh.
P.G. Zimbardo (1977), *Shyness*, Addison-Wesley.

JOB SEARCH

Getting and keeping a job is the number one concern of most young people leaving school or further education. In one sense the whole of education is concerned with preparing people for the work they will do when they come of age. But in more recent years there has been a growing interest in careers education and vocational guidance as integral parts of the curriculum in their own right.

In its most elementary forms, careers education supplies information to school and college leavers about the nature of the job market, pre-entry qualifications, training opportunities, vacancies and so on. The information can be made available in a variety of forms: leaflets and pamphlets produced by firms and employers and by commercial and other agencies; talks; visits; films, etc. The use to which individuals can put this sometimes bewildering volume of facts varies enormously, and in recent years increasing attention has been paid to this aspect of job search by vocational and careers counsellors.

Besides a knowledge of the job market, another vital prerequisite for the successful job seeker is self-knowledge. An informed awareness of oneself; of strengths and weaknesses; of interests, experience, skills and aptitudes; makes for better decision-making at this crucial stage of people's lives. A great many methods have been developed for helping individuals acquire greater self-knowledge in these areas and many of them are systematically used by careers specialists both in and out of school and further education.

A third dimension to careers education which has become more prominent as job opportunities for young people have contracted, is that of improving the skills which are needed in job search — such as answering advertisements; writing letters; making telephone calls; performing well at interviews; relating to other people at work. This may be loosely termed the 'social skills' dimension of careers guidance and it provides a bridge between information about the outside world and self-knowledge.

The exercises in this section relate to all three areas: to self-knowledge and self-awareness; to securing and using information about the job market; and to the skills of job search itself.

Following a list of suggestions for stimulating interest in the business of job search and related problems, the first exercise here is for finding out about why people want to work, or not, as the case may be. Our experience of using this 'force-field' analysis is that young people are often more positively motivated to work than their elders; including teachers, counsellors and social workers. 'Writing job descriptions' and 'analysing jobs' are vehicles for examining the demands which specific occupations make on those who do them, and can be extended so that individuals measure themselves against those demands to see how far they fit.

Next, the 'Job Prospects survey' is concerned with helping young people to find out about the job market. Two exercises have been included for helping students make decisions about jobs; 'Making career decisions' and 'My job goals'.

The rest of the section is devoted to the business of job search itself: using the telephone to find out about jobs or to make interview appointments; an exercise which looks at the importance of personal appearance in forming our impressions of others; a number of interview-based activities which are designed to increase self-knowledge as well as competence in self-presentation; and some role-play prompts which look forward to problems that might be encountered at work, if the job search is successful.

Finally there is a list of games that might be used in a series of sessions on work; and outlines of two simulations: one on a 'Dispute' at work, and one on 'Job Search' as a whole, which can be used to pull together many of the separate exercises that make up this programme.

Stimulating interest

Although most young people are keenly interested in finding work, the assumption should not be made that they are all that keen to engage in discussion and other learning activities connected with the business of job search, the mechanics of which may appear to them to be boring or reminiscent of school lessons. It may be necessary to stimulate their interest in the subject with a lively speaker, or a film, or a brainstorm or sentence completion exercise on some aspect of work and the problem of finding it.

Some possible speakers

Personnel officer; job centre manager; youth employment officer; YOP scheme organizer; people working in different occupations e.g. nurse, hairdresser, building trades, secretary, salesman, designer, retailing (some of these might with advantage be young people in their first or second jobs, and if possible they should be graduates of the class or course to which the students being addressed belong); supplementary benefits official; representatives of organizations like Claimant's Union or Child Poverty Action Group; union officials and members; proprietors of small businesses; Small Business Advisory Service; solicitor specialising in unfair dismissal cases; a retired person with a long and varied work experience.

Good speakers on these and other topics are worth their weight in gold to a course organizer, and should stimulate plenty of questions and discussion. The benefits of a speaker can often be increased by preparing students in advance, thinking about some of the issues that are likely to be raised and formulating possible questions and discussion points to raise during the session.

If you have video equipment it can also be useful to tape brief talks (not more than ten minutes) by visiting speakers, and to build up a tape library of informative and entertaining items related to job search — or to any other topics of concern to students.

Responsibility for suggesting speakers, and even arranging for them to visit, can be given to individuals or small groups of course members.

Some brainstorm topics

Brainstorming, which was described on page 22, is a good starting-point for any activity, provided of course that it is not abused by over-use.

Places to find jobs — Work — Best job in the world — Worst job in the world
Unemployment — Employers — Trades unions — Wages
Deductions — Good things about work — Bad things about work
Reasons for not getting jobs — Training schemes — People to ask about jobs
Outside jobs — Jobs with people — Low paid jobs — High paid jobs
Adventurous jobs — Dangerous jobs — Why people work — Job satisfaction
Microchips and work — Conveyor belts — Women's work — Men's work

Some sentences to complete

Just as simple, and equally productive as a starter to thinking and talking about work and related topics, is sentence completion:

People who don't get jobs are . . . .

Unemployment is . . . .

I can't get a job because . . . .

Most of the jobs in this area are . . . .

My ideal job is . . . .

I wouldn't like to work in a . . . .

If you work hard you . . . .

I expect to spend most of my life working as a . . . .

Employers are . . . .

Union members are . . . .

I would enjoy working as . . . .

People at work hate . . . .

The government ought to . . . .

It is not difficult to invent sentence starters of your own that will stimulate your students.

'To work or not to work' — assessing motivation

Although most studies show that unemployed people would prefer to be in work, and that only a tiny minority of individuals actually choose to remain on the dole, it is worth asking your students to look at their own motivation to work. This exercise uses a 'force-field analysis' to examine the pros and cons of going to work.

Form two equally sized groups of not more than eight in size (larger numbers are better divided into four small groups). Invite group 'A' to discuss and agree amongst themselves 'The ten best reasons for going to work'. Invite group 'B' to discuss and agree amongst themselves 'The ten best reasons for *not* going to work'.

Someone from each group should then write these reasons down on prepared 'force-field' sheets, preferably A2 size, as follows:

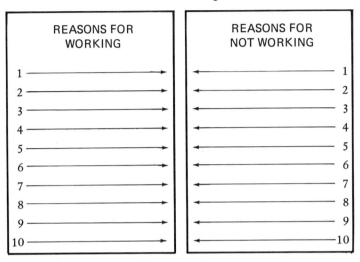

REASONS FOR WORKING	REASONS FOR NOT WORKING
1	1
2	2
3	3
4	4
5	5
6	6
7	7
8	8
9	9
10	10

These should then be displayed alongside each other where everyone can see them. The resulting 'force-field' can be used as a discussion starter in its own right, or it can be added to by having each individual in the two groups rate the two sets of items on a score 1 to 5, where 1 means that that is not thought to be a very strong reason for working or not working; and 5 *is* a very strong reason.

So for example if the first three reasons for 'not working' were:

1. Money's the same.
2. Jobs are boring.
3. People boss you about.

an individual who thought that not getting more money was a very strong reason for not going out to work might give that a score of 5. If he thought that the boring nature of work was quite a strong reason for not going he might score that 3. And if he thought that being bossed about was not a very good reason for avoiding work he might rate that 2.

When all the items on both sides of the force field have been rated, the scores should be added up to give two totals; one on the 'For' side and one on the 'Against' side. The difference between these two scores provides a crude index of motivation to work, and can form the basis of discussion about the individual points on the two sides of the force field, and also about the scores of the individuals in the group. It may help if the average scores for the whole group are calculated and added to the sheets on the wall.

The exercise can be varied by asking individuals to compile their own personal force-fields before the groups generate them; having pre-prepared lists of items which cover points which you want to bring out; getting individuals who have rated the items personally to work in small groups (pairs, trios, or fours) to reach an *agreed* score between them; using the scores for and against work to form debating teams to debate the proposition that 'Going to work is a waste of time' or 'Work is worthwhile'; inviting individuals to add items to each side of the force field until they have exhausted all the possibilities for themselves; arranging the items on both sides as far as possible to cancel each other out — inventing new items where this does not occur — so that every item is matched by an opposite; suggesting that teams produce presentations, tapes or films supporting their side of the argument and then present them to the whole group; using the resulting items as the basis of a questionnaire which members of the group can apply to other people (e.g. parents, friends, occupational groups) to see how representative their own views are.

A final summary of five points in each column may help individuals to look at desirable and undesirable qualities in particular jobs.

Writing job descriptions

One of the things that personnel officers do as part of their work is to write what they call job-descriptions; precise lists of the things which people in certain kinds of job have to do. This helps them to recruit suitable individuals for the jobs in question, and also to decide pay levels.

A job-description for a milk delivery worker might look like this:

Reports for work at 5.30 a.m.
Checks vehicle.
Loads milk and milk products onto float or van.
Confirms load with checker/supervisor.
Drives to start of delivery round.
Delivers milk to customers' doors.
Collects empty milk bottles.
Enters amounts delivered in round record book.
Takes orders for cream and other items.
Signs up new customers.
Collects money on weekly or daily basis.
Balances books.
Returns to depot.
Unloads empty bottles.
Returns undelivered milk to stock.
Pays in takings.
Cleans vehicle.

If someone is interested in a particular job it can be useful to try writing a job description like this to see whether the job is as suitable and as interesting as it appears. Pairs of group members could work together to develop descriptions for jobs they were interested in pursuing. If necessary they could consult sources of job information, careers leaflets, recruitment literature and occupational indices like Signposts and CODOT.

Analysing jobs

Before deciding what kind of job or training course to apply for it can be helpful to look more closely at what is involved in the work; to measure personal strengths and weaknesses against the requirements of the job, and to prepare mentally for interviews and other selection procedures.

The aim of this exercise is to take an individual job and break it down in three ways; into *specific job skills* — the actual tasks entailed in doing it; *general skills* — some of the background abilities that are useful; and *personal qualities* — the kind of person you need to be to do the work successfully. Start by writing the title of a job like NURSE on a wall sheet and asking the group members to brainstorm items to fit in each of the three columns, e.g.:

NURSE		
Job Skills	**General Skills**	**Personal Qualities**
Bedmaking	Talking	Cheerful
Looking after	Getting on with	Kind
patients	people	Tough
Giving medicine	Remembering	Not squeamish
Giving injections	Being organized	Strong
Keeping records	Hygienic	Understanding
Taking temperatures	Being patient	Calm
Dressing wounds		
Knowing symptoms		

Discuss the results of the brainstorm, and if it seems useful, ask the group to rank order some of the items in terms of their importance. Divide the group into smaller groups of three or four and invite them to repeat the process for one job in which each member of the group is interested. The results should be entered in blank JOB ANALYSIS SHEETS which you provide for each person taking part.

Group members then work in pairs helping partners to estimate their strengths and weaknesses in relation to the job requirements they have just produced. The simplest way of recording this is to tick those items which the person thinks he or she does well or could learn to do well. Alternatively, each item can be given a score out of ten, and totals for each of the three areas arrived at.

(The job profiles devised in this exercise could also be used as the basis of the 'ideal job' interviews described on page 116.)

Job prospects survey

This project is designed to gather systematic information about the availability of particular kinds of work in particular areas.

Students can work by themselves, or in groups of two, three, four or more to find out about specific jobs, e.g. engineering, office work, retail, building, service, catering, or highly localised occupations.

The aim of the survey is to identify major employers in these particular areas; to ascertain the level of vacancies; to describe the kinds of jobs they entail, their entry qualifications, pay and prospects, etc; and to outline application procedures.

Each team should plan its project, allocating specific tasks to specific members of the group; one person might look up entries in local telephone directories and trade registers; another might interview a personnel officer to get job descriptions; someone else could ring round firms and offices asking about current and prospective vacancies for school-leavers; someone else can visit the local youth employment office and the job centre. All the members could collaborate in devising a letter or questionnaire to send to employers asking about either job descriptions or vacancies.

Where possible written materials should also be collected; recruitment literature, leaflets, posters, training course descriptions, and in relevant occupations, specimen application forms.

The results of all this endeavour – and they can be considerable – should be organized by the teams for presentation to all their colleagues; this to be done as imaginatively as possible using displays and exhibitions, talks, speakers, films, tape recordings and discussion sessions – all presented by the researchers themselves so that they gain practice in collecting, digesting and presenting occupational information.

Making career decisions

Before making decisions of any sort it is a good idea to gather as much information as possible.

Before making a career decision, two main kinds of information are necessary:

Information about yourself, e.g.:

Basic characteristics
Interests
Experience
Abilities
Personal circumstances etc.

(The categories used in the interview plan on page 115 below could be useful here.)

Information about jobs, e.g.:

Nature of work   Prospects
Training required   Availability
Entry qualifications   Location
Working conditions   Security
Pay

(The questions developed for use in the job prospects survey would be useful here.)

Sometimes just having information like this at your fingertips makes it possible to take a reasonable decision. But on other occasions there is an extra ingredient that is required to make a good decision: some sort of standard, or test, which you can apply to the information; a 'criterion' or 'requirement' in other words. One person's criterion or requirement in choosing a job might be that it would have to be 'exciting' or 'to do with people'. Those would be *positive* requirements. *Negative* requirements might be things like 'Not too far from home' or 'Not involving mental arithmetic'.

Individual members of a group can develop a short list of requirements under the title of 'Most important things I want from a job', in a number of ways. Individuals can compile their own lists on the spot, or after consultation with friends, parents, interested adults, or vocational guidance professionals. For example one individual's list might look like this:

Positive requirements	*Negative requirements*
Working with a small group	Lengthy training on low wages
Making decisions	Too much responsibility
Opportunities for overtime	Too much pressure
Using my hands	Too much travelling
Reputable firm	No opportunities for promotion
Job security	Few young people working there
Chance to acquire new skills	Exhausting
Talking to people	Boring

These requirements can then be applied to possible jobs to see how they measure up. A job might be rejected because it met too few of the standards in the boxes; or because it did not meet a specially important one. One way of making this more clear would be to rank the items in the 'positive' and 'negative' boxes in order of importance: (1) for the most important, (2) for the next most important, (3) for the next and so on. A job might fail to meet several less important requirements but still be worth pursuing because it met one or more of the more important ones.

My job goals

Another way of deciding what to do about jobs is to present people with a list of possible goals, from which they can select those they wish to pursue.

Lists like this should be specially constructed to meet the needs of particular groups; which will vary according to their recruitment and the nature of the local work environment.

Some examples

1. ☐ To find out more about the job of . . . .
2. ☐ To practise writing letters of application.
3. ☐ To get better at filling in forms.
4. ☐ To ring up three firms or other employers every day to ask about job vacancies.
5. ☐ To sign up for an evening class.
6. ☐ To get on a Work Experience Project.
7. ☐ To find out what Industrial Tribunals do.
8. ☐ To ask ten people I know if there are any vacancies where they work.
9. ☐ To imagine what job I will be doing in ten years time.
10. ☐ To think how I will spend my first pay packet.
11. ☐ . . . . . .
12. ☐ . . . . . .
13. ☐ . . . . . .

It is not difficult to produce quite lengthy lists like this one, tailored to the requirements of specific groups of job seekers. The items which an individual ticks off on the checklist can then become targets for action; either as part of a project organized during sessions of a course, or to be pursued in students' own time.

Two main categories of personal goals have been included in the example above: things *to find out* about jobs or training, and things *to do* about them.

Using the telephone to find a job

The ability to use the telephone is a social skill of considerable value to people who are looking for jobs, and can save them a great deal of time and trouble. The exercise described here can form a starting-point for training in telephone use.

Divide the group into trios. Each trio works together to decide what they think are the five or the eight or the ten most important things to look for in a *good* telephone call; excluding the purely mechanical procedures of dialling, inserting money and so on. Each member of the trio should take a copy of the list of items on which they eventually agree. The items of the different groups can be compared at this point, or later; after the telephone calls have been made.

The commonest points which emerge from the work of these trios include:

1. Prepare for the call; make notes; formulate questions, etc.
2. Speak clearly.
3. Identify yourself.
4. Identify who you are speaking to; and that it is the right person.
5. State purpose of call.
6. Adapt tone of voice to purpose of call.
7. Achieve objective; get information; give message, etc.
8. Confirm any agreements made.
9. Round off call.

Armed with these lists, whatever they contain at this point, each member of the group takes turns at acting as caller, receiver and observer.

Sit the caller and the receiver back to back; and the observer at right angles to them so that he can watch and record his impressions of the caller's performance.

Set three possible telephone calls, which may be done in any order. Some possibilities:

Ringing a firm about an advertised job in a newspaper.
Ringing a firm to make an appointment about a job interview.
Ringing a firm to change an appointment for a job interview because of some personal difficulty; or to explain why you missed the interview.

The caller and the receiver require a moment or two to agree between themselves the nature of the firm and the job involved, and to think about the applicant's character if the caller is not intending to be him or herself.

The observer times the calls to last not longer than three minutes; and at the end of that time gives the caller feedback on his or her performance. This should be based on the items on the checklists; the observer should tell the caller how good he or she was at doing them.

Everyone then moves round so that the caller becomes the receiver, the receiver becomes the observer and the observer moves into the caller's chair, where his performance is timed and observed and commented upon by the new observer. The process is repeated a third time so that everyone has rotated through all three positions.

Video tape recordings of conversations can be used to enrich this exercise.

Finally, when all the calls have been made, general group discussion, comparison of checklist items, and feedback on performance strengths and weaknesses rounds off the exercise.

For individuals who emerge as being poor at telephone calls, remedial coaching and modelling exercises may be called for, provided by the tutor or better still by another group member who is more competent at using the phone. Practice, and homework tasks: ringing the railway station to find out about train times; ringing a college to ask about an evening class; or ringing an employer to ask about vacancies, should improve competence in using the telephone.

First impressions

It is not uncommon for people to claim the ability to judge character from appearance. The way other people look is of course the first impression we have of them when we meet them in person. Sometimes, as in interviews, or in more casual encounters, these first impressions can be critical – 'He didn't look right for the job', 'We were looking for someone younger', 'Must be of smart appearance', 'You remind me of my father/mother/teacher/first girl friend', 'I don't like the look of him'.

Everybody admits that these 'first appearances can be deceptive'. And yet they remain influential in forming our judgments and decisions about the people we meet.

Appearance and its consequences is a topic well worth airing in a series of exercises devoted to job search.

One way in which it might be done is to use portrait snapshots of the kind that are produced in booths at railway stations and in shops. If a number of these are taken of individuals who match your students in terms of sex, age and general appearance, they can be used in a variety of ways. To illustrate some of these, look at the six portraits opposite, and see if you can guess the occupations of the people shown.

Photographs like these can be used in several ways.

1. First, you can take each photograph in turn and ask individuals to say what they think is the occupation of the person portrayed, perhaps giving their reasons why in each case. (All the people shown are, in fact, Youth Employment Officers; but their previous occupations are as follows: Photograph 1, hospital admissions officer; 2, local government officer; 3, social worker; 4, postmistress; 5, slater and tiler; and 6, primary school teacher.)

2. Alternatively, the exercise can be made slightly easier by providing participants with a list of occupations and asking them to match them to the photographs. You can do this even using fictitious occupations, so that the ensuing discussion can focus on the *way* impressions have been formed rather than on their accuracy.

3. You can make the exercise more engaging by asking participants to imagine that they are personnel officers who have a short-list of six candidates for a job (e.g. as a bank clerk, youth club leader, tourist guide

1   2   3

4   5   6

in a listed building, babysitter, social and life skills instructor). They then
have to place the candidates in order of preference for each job, on the
basis of their appearance alone (pretending, for example, they they sub-
mitted photographs with their application forms). A series of questions
might then be posed, such as why individuals listed the candidates in a
particular order; how similar their rankings are when various group members are compared; what are the reasons for differences of opinion over
each of the candidates, etc.

There are many variations on themes like these which can be explored using
photographs of this kind. The exercise need not, of course, be restricted to
the question of employment. Individuals can be asked, for example, to pick
out possible friends or partners from a series of pictures; to imagine which
offences the people in the photographs might have committed were they
criminals; to decide which of them would be suitable to lead a Himalayan

expedition, and so on. The decisions individuals make on these and other issues furnish valuable insights into how impressions of others are formed.

Finally, it should be reiterated that any exercise using photographs should if possible depict types of people with whom your students will be familiar. Those used in the exercise here simply illustrate some of the possibilities.

Selection panels

One of the reasons why some people shun interviews is the fear of failure; the feeling that rejection for a job is somehow a rejection of the whole person. The feeling can never be removed entirely, since in some situations at least there is an element of truth in it. But it can be modified by an illustration of the obvious arbitrariness of many decisions that are made in interviews.

This exercise makes the point whilst providing at the same time some opportunities for taking part in interviews both as interviewees and as interviewers.

Ask for five volunteers to be interviewed for a job. The job is not important in itself, but should be something within the competence of the applicants: e.g. clerical assistant, trainee, apprentice, shop worker, labourer, or whatever fits the group you are working with. It may be useful to specify what the job entails, e.g. its hours and conditions, rates of pay, type of work, and prospects.

Divide the remaining members of the group into five equally sized panels, whose task is to interview each of the applicants in turn for not more than five minutes and to make a list in rank order of preference for appointment to the post.

When all the interviews have been completed, i.e. when all the applicants have been seen by all of the panels and rank order lists have been made, a master list of the applicants and their positions in the rankings of the panels can be drawn up as follows:

Applicant

Panel	1	2	3	4	5
A					
B					
C					
D					
E					

Unless there are absolutely outstanding candidates, the normal outcome of this exercise is a spread of positions; which undermines the idea that interviews are an objective method of selection.

The exercise could be varied by giving each panel a different task; concentrating for example on appearance, qualifications, or potential. In addition, the interviewees can form a group of their own and make a rank-order list of the effectiveness of the interview panels.

Interview performance ratings

The only way to become good at being interviewed is to get lots of practice at it. But just repeating a bad performance is no way to improve. The performer must be made aware of his or her strengths and weaknesses so that he or she can correct any faults and work on weak areas.

The most powerful way of providing this sort of feedback on performance is to use videotape recording; or if that is not available then audio tape, although this cannot help individuals look at aspects of their appearance, posture, expression, gesture and so on. If neither form of recording is available then the feedback can be provided by observers.

This can be done by simulating or role-playing interviews of various kinds and appointing observers to watch and record their views of how the person being interviewed has performed.

The feedback can be given in several ways:

1. An individual observer watches the proceedings and then makes general comments.
2. The observer uses a pre-prepared schedule for recording and evaluating an interview performance.
3. Interviewer and interviewee and observer(s) work out in advance what aspects of the performance are important and how the observer shall record them.
4. A number of observers sit round the interview, either using the same rating instruments, or looking at specific aspects of the performance.

Some suggestions for items to include on an INTERVIEW PERFORMANCE RATING SHEET are given below; but they should not be treated as a final version to be used on all occasions. Rating sheets should be tailored to the needs of particular groups and individuals within them.

The interviews to be observed can be of any useful nature, e.g.:

Job interviews	Being interviewed about an HP
Joining a club	agreement
Asking for a special needs grant	Applying for a course

Interviewees can also use something like this to rate their own performance on video tape recordings.

Interview performance rating sheet

Observe the person being interviewed as carefully as you can; and fill in the sections of this form to report your views of his or her performance. Try not to take too long over each question and do not worry about getting the ratings exactly right; it is only your impression in general that counts.

Appearance

1. Describe the clothes of the person being interviewed (e.g. jeans and jumper; three piece suit; plain shirt and tie; blouse and skirt; grey, long sleeved dress, etc.)

   . . . .

2. How suitably dressed is this person for the job in which they are interested?

   Very suitably └─────┴─────┴─────┴─────┘ Not at all suitably

   Mark the point on the scale where you think it best applies.

3. Rate the applicant's clothing for neatness.

   Untidy └─────┴─────┴─────┘ Tidy

Expression

4. Observe the expression or expressions on the person's face throughout the interview and then tick off those words in the following list which apply:

   ☐ Bored   ☐ Scared

   ☐ Always the same ☐ Surly

   ☐ Interested   ☐ Cocky

   ☐ Pleasant   ☐ Intelligent

   ☐ Lively   ☐ Alert

5. Count the number of times the interviewee smiles during the interview and write down the total here. If the person smiles a lot you can record them as you go along by marking bundles of five, one mark for each smile, e.g. ⊬⊦ ///

Scores		Total number

Posture

6. How was the person sitting throughout the interview?

   In the same position?   ☐   Changing a lot?   ☐

7. How would you describe the way they were sitting most of the time?

   . . . .

8. Describe any gestures which the applicant made: e.g. fiddling with nails, or hair, or clothing; touching face or mouth; drumming with fingers; waving hands about whilst speaking.

   . . . .

Speech

9. Look at the items listed below and then tick those which you think apply to the speech of the interviewee.

   ☐ Spoke clearly.

   ☐ Gave a lot of information about him/herself.

   ☐ Answered questions well.

   ☐ Did not speak too loudly or too softly.

   ☐ Changed tone of voice in an interesting way.

   ☐ Used a variety of words and expressions.

10. Count the number of times the applicant said 'Um' or 'Er', and write down the total.

Number of 'Ums' and 'Ers'	
Length of interview in minutes	
'Um' and 'Er' rate per minute	

11. Any general comment about speech; manner and content.

    . . . .

    . . . .

    . . . .

Confidence

12. How confident did the candidate seem to be?

Not at all confident ∟___⌐___⌐___⌐___⌐ Very confident

Summary

13. Write down here any general remarks about this interview performance that are not covered in the above questions.

. . . .

14. Think about each of the areas covered above and give the interviewee a score out of 10 for each one and enter them in the boxes below. If the person was so good in one area that they couldn't be any better you would mark them nine or ten; if they were not very good at all you would give them one; and if they were about average they would score five.

☐ Appearance

☐ Expression

☐ Posture

☐ Speech

☐ Confidence

Now add up all the scores to give a total out of 50.

☐ TOTAL SCORE

How to be an interviewer

Looking at situations from 'the other side' can be interesting and instructive. For those who wish to become adept in the arts of being interviewed, the opportunity to act the part of the interviewer provides an insight into the nature of the experience which can be gained in no other way. This exercise lets people put themselves in the interviewer's chair, and at the same time makes it possible to gather a great deal of information about the person playing the part of the interviewee.

Start the session by dividing group members into pairs; interviewers and their interviewees. (The roles can be reversed during the second part of the exercise, so it doesn't matter who does which first.)

Talk briefly about the qualities of the good interviewer. One way of doing this is to present:

The four 'golden rules' of interviewing

1. *Be prepared* — Have a plan of the points you want to cover during the interview. This doesn't mean conducting the interview by filling in a form with yes/no answers; but it is helpful to have a framework for what you are going to do. (See the interview plan below.)
2. *Ask open-ended questions* — Open-ended questions are ones which invite more than one word answers. For example, don't ask 'Did you enjoy that job?', ask 'What did you enjoy about that job?' Other open-ended questions: 'Why have you applied for this job?', 'Can you tell me something about your spare time interests?', 'What school subjects were you good at?'
3. *Encourage the person to talk* — Look interested. Nod when you agree with things they say. Smile. Encourage the flow of their replies to your questions by saying things like 'yes', 'uh-huh' and 'mmm'.
4. *Sum up* — After a while, sum up the main points of the interview so far to make sure that you have got the facts right.

Preparing an interview plan

This can be done on a 'blank sheet basis' — inviting groups, pairs or individuals to think about what kinds of information they will require from someone who is applying for a job. You can then ask them to decide on headings and on some questions which fit under each heading. Alternatively, some headings and specimen questions can be suggested as in this *interview plan:*

An interview plan

1. *Physical*

Things to look for	*Some questions to ask*
Body build, health,	How fit do you think you are?
strength, eyesight,	What sports do you take part in?
any disabilities.	Have you had any major illnesses?

2. *Skills and Abilities*

Things to look for	*Some questions to ask*
Hobbies	What do you do in your spare time?
Favourite school subjects	What subjects were you best at at
Manual or craft skills	school? What are you good at?
Artistic ability	Do you like making things?
	Are you good with figures?

3. *Interests*

Things to look for	*Some questions to ask*
Spare time activities	Which bits of the newspaper do you
Reading habits	read? What books do you read?
Interests in social or	If you didn't have to go to work
political issues	what would you do all day?

4. *Personality*

Things to look for	*Some questions to ask*
Confidence	What makes you think you can do
Attitude to other people	this job? Do you enjoy mixing with
Warmth	people? What things make you feel
Humour	depressed? How would a good friend
Anxiety	describe your personality to someone
	who had never met you?

5. *Circumstances*

Some things to look for	*Some questions to ask*
Living at home or not?	Are you free to move? How long are
Financial position	you likely to stay in this area?
Commitments to people	What are your main financial com-
or places or activities	mitments?

6. *Achievements*

Qualifications	Have you anv CSEs or O-levels?
Certificates	Which ones? Are you taking
Badges	any exams? Have you any other
Records of achievement	certificates? Have you won
Exam results	prizes/badges for anything?

A format like this can be used in different ways:

1. As the basis of panel interviews (for example in the previous exercise).
2. Peer interviews for jobs chosen by individuals as likely career choices.
3. Peer interviews for an 'ideal job'. Divide the group into pairs. Each person identifies an 'ideal' job, regardless of qualifications or experience. One partner then interviews the other, using the categories in the interview plan above to decide how well equipped he or she is for the job in question. The procedure is then reversed. Follow the interviews, which might last for not longer than ten minutes each, with general group discussion about ideal jobs, qualifications and barriers, and the limits to what is realistically possible for the individuals concerned.

Imaginal rehearsal

Anxiety about future events can sometimes be allayed, not by thinking end-lessly about what might go wrong, but by thinking constructively about how to put right some of the things that are difficult to handle. Worrying about what will happen during an interview is a case in point. This exercise consists of asking group members to think of the 'worst possible thing that could happen during an interview'. This could be anything from finding that they have forgotten to bring a handkerchief when they want to blow their noses during the interview, to being at a loss as to how to answer a tricky question.

Having identified such a 'worst case' situation, group members should then imagine what they would do. They should try to re-enact inside their heads a successful way of dealing with it. And if there is time they should think of more than one way. You can ask some of the group members to describe their 'worst case' and how they have been practising dealing with it.

This exercise could be used to identify some of the fears and difficulties envisaged by students about job and other interviews, and could be followed by role-play, discussion and modelling sessions.

Asking questions

At the end of many interviews, the interviewer gives the person being inter-viewed a chance to ask questions; which sometimes floors the unprepared applicant. Two or three questions in readiness for such a situation are part of the well-prepared job applicant's kit.

Suitable questions can be generated in a number of ways. Brainstorming questions for general use might be one way of starting. Or individuals or small groups could discuss possible questions to ask in relation to jobs which people are interested in applying for; e.g. a group looking at office job appli-cations would think of questions like:

Are there luncheon vouchers?
What sort of typewriters do you use?
Are there any opportunities for further training and/or promotion?

This exercise can be a useful prelude to some of the interviewing role-plays that have been described above.

Problem situations

An obvious way to help people cope with difficult situations in which they might find themselves is to encourage them to think about such encounters in advance and perhaps develop skills for dealing with them more efficiently. Being at work can present a number of problems of this kind and an exercise which directs the attention of young people to them can form a useful component of a social and life skills course.

The situations listed here can be used in different ways:

1. Typed on cards and distributed as discussion starters for pairs, small groups or the whole group.

2. As the basis of brief modelling exercises in which participants show their colleagues how they would cope with the particulation situation.

3. As a basis for development into more *structured* role-plays. (Two examples have been taken from the list and developed in this way; these can be found in the 'structured roleplays' exercise which follows this one.)

It is not difficult to think of further incidents and dilemmas, nor to write structured roleplays of your own.

1. You are a keen football supporter. Your local team has reached the fourth round of the FA cup and the replay is to take place at home on a Wednesday. Your friend who is unemployed has bought two tickets and wants you to go with him to see the match. It will be obvious if you take the afternoon off from work. Your friend suggests that you take the whole day off and ask your mother to ring your employer to say that you are ill. You would like to see the match but wouldn't like to be on the dole again. What do you say to your friend?

2. You have applied to a firm for a job. In your letter of application you said that you knew quite a lot about the sort of work they did, but in fact you only know what a neighbour who works there has told you. You are asked to attend an interview for a job. The interviewer says 'I see you already know quite a bit about this job. Could you tell us what you know?'

3. You are late for work for the third time in two weeks because you have overslept. When you arrive you are given a message to report to your supervisor. What will you say?

4. You have been working in an office doing invoices and general filing work. In the evenings you have been learning typing and shorthand. You would like a better job in the office. What would you say to the person in charge?

5. One of your workmates tells you that another person at work has been telling people that you are no good at your job and ought to be given the sack. You see this person during the lunch break. How do you act towards your critic?

6. The person in charge of your section at work always seems to be picking on you for little things. You think you are doing a good job and don't deserve to be singled out like that. The departmental manager calls you into the office and asks what you think of the section supervisor. You would like to say what you think, but would it get the supervisor into trouble, or even cause you problems for criticising one of your seniors?

7. A friend who works with you says that there are some old bits of material in the store room which no-one wants, and which wouldn't be missed if you shared them between you. Other people take them home, why shouldn't you?

8. After a period of unemployment you find a job which isn't very interesting, but quite well paid; and there aren't that many other jobs going. After a time you find that you are getting more and more bored with it. You feel fed up and irritated and you think it will soon be obvious to the other people at work that you don't like the job. What could you do?

9. A relative rings up to say that there is a good job in a firm he/she works for, but it would mean moving to a place about a hundred miles away. Would you take it?

10. You quite like the job you are doing but find that the amount of work you are expected to get through each day puts a lot of pressure on you because you work a bit more slowly than some of the other people beside you. Is there anything you can do about that?

11. A new union agreement is made where you work, setting up a closed shop. This means that everyone has to join the union to keep their job. You have never belonged to a union. Would you join?

Structured roleplays

Simple structured roleplays with briefings for more than one participant make it possible to look at somewhat more complicated situations and to dictate, to begin with at least, the turn that events are to take in the ensuing drama. Here are two straightforward examples: the first one expands the third of the 'situations' — that of being late for work — and the second looks at pressures to engage in pilfering from work.

Late for work

A   You are late for work for the third morning running. You just find it difficult to wake up and sleep through the alarms. Yesterday the supervisor said that if you were late again you would be 'for the high jump'. You are very keen to keep the job because you have quite a lot of HP payments to keep up and you are saving for a holiday abroad next year. You are on reasonably friendly terms with the supervisor but are not sure how to approach this situation.

B   You are A's supervisor. A has been late three times this week. Yesterday you issued a warning about any further lateness. Today A turns up late again. You quite like A but there are orders to be completed and when people are missing it slows down the rate of production. You are feeling quite angry.

"Other people take it home"

A   A lot of people in your department take home some of the waste material which accumulates in a store room. From time to time you have taken bits home for yourself. Nobody seems to bother about it, although if the boss found out about it there might be a row. You tell your friend about the material and say that it would be all right to take some home.

B   Your friend tells you about some material in the store room which a lot of other people take home with them. Your friend urges you to take some, but you are worried in case you are found out and dismissed.

Job search simulation

Some of the preceding exercises in this job search programme can be usefully, and enjoyably, combined in the shape of a *job search simulation*, which portrays the whole sequence of activities that might be involved in securing work.

Ask the members of the group to constitute themselves as small 'firms' or employers — say three or four in each. The small groups decide on the name of the firm and the nature of its business; manufacture, service, etc. They then decide on two or three job vacancies which they currently have and which are of likely interest to other group members (and likely to be within their competence). They develop brief job descriptions and then advertise the vacancies by writing out job cards which set out the title of the job, the pay and conditions and some instructions about applying.

Collect all the cards and pin them up, noticeboard style.

```
WESTLEY   PRINTERS

Vacancy exists for a trainee
book binder.  Recent school-
leaver with craft or artistic
ability preferred but not
essential.  Printing trade
trainee rates.  Letter of
application to the Personnel
Manager.
```

```
HOYDON   SUPERMARKETS

Storeroom and shelf supply
staff wanted.  Age-related
pay scale.  Forty-two hour
week; including time off
in lieu of Saturday work.
Overalls provided.  Incen-
tive scheme.  Apply to the
Manager.
```

```
Site labourers required by small building
firm.  No experience necessary; training
given.  National salary agreements.
Opportunity to drive site machinery.
Permanent position for right person.  See
site manager or telephone for appointment.
```

All the participants circulate and look at the job adverts and decide which of them they wish to pursue. Letters of application and telephone calls are then made to the appropriate firms or employers, who in turn fix appointments to see their applicants. At any one time no team should be short of more than one member being interviewed elsewhere.

When all the applicants have been interviewed, the panels must decide who they intend to appoint.

Finally, discuss the whole proceedings: who did well, who got jobs, why some people were not accepted.

Although simple in essence this exercise can take two to three hours to play fully, and it allows participants to practise a number of the skills they may have been learning in previous sessions.

DISPUTE . . . a simulation

One of the realities of work is that conflicts occur not just between individuals but between organised and powerful groups; namely managements and trades unions. Industrial disputes raise prickly issues both in the places where they occur and in the social studies classroom.

The aim of this simulation is to reproduce a simplified industrial dispute so that the participants can get the feel of what it would be like to make decisions in such a situation, and to stimulate thought and discussion about some of the many questions it is possible to ask about the state of industrial relations, wages policy and the like.

The simulation can be played with two groups, MANAGEMENT and WORKFORCE, or with these two plus two others, GOVERNMENT and PRESS. The groups may be of equal size but 'management' and 'workforce' should be larger than the others if there is a fairly small number of participants.

Each group receives a briefing; suggested outlines for which are given below. These should, however, be modified by the tutor or group leader to fit the situation either of the group he is teaching or the industrial relations scene at the time.

Management

The BRUMBY ENGINEERING COMPANY employs a workforce of 750 people designing, making and finishing a variety of die-cast components which are used in the car industry, printing machinery, and conveyor belts. Last year was a record turnover for the company, due partly to inflation, but also to the successful completion of export orders for an oil-producing country. The prospects for the next few years, however, are bad; the car industry is in trouble; traditional printing machinery is under threat from computer typesetting; and there is political instability in the Middle East which makes future export orders very difficult. Industrial relations with the workforce have not been bad over the past few years, but the annual wage negotiations have become increasingly difficult in the face of continuing inflation rates around 13—16% per annum. Inflation for the current year is running at around 18% and looks likely to get worse. Although profits were good last year the forecast for this year is that only a small profit will be made, and a large wage settlement with the workforce will mean that prices have to be raised making sales abroad more difficult against lower-priced goods from Europe and elsewhere. Your aim in the wage negotiations is to pay as small an increase as you can.

Workforce/union

You work for the BRUMBY ENGINEERING COMPANY which employs a workforce of 750 people designing, making and finishing a variety of die-cast components which are used in the car industry, printing machinery and conveyor belts. Inflation in the current year is running at 18% and last year the wage settlement fell short of inflation by 3%. Your members are deter-mined to do better this year particularly because you know that the com-pany had a record year last year and has very profitable contracts with an oil-producing country in the Middle East. You will be looking for an increase that is ahead of the current rate of inflation.

Relations with management are not bad but you suspect that *they* have had rises and perks which have kept them ahead of inflation for the past three years. If the negotiations are unsuccessful your members are in a mood for strike action.

Government

You are a recently-elected government which came to power on a promise to bring down the rate of inflation drastically. You think that the answer to inflation lies in the size of wage settlements that are made each year between employers and their workers and you are determined to see that they fall below the rate of inflation this year. You can do this in one of three ways:

1. By imposing a statutory control on the size of settlements. If you decide to do this you will have to decide what percentage you will allow for current settlements.
2. By suggesting a percentage increase and then putting pressure on firms and unions during their negotiations to agree with it.
3. By controlling the money supply, rates of interest and the exchange rate of the pound so that high wage settlements lead to higher unemployment. If you decide to do this you need to tell the parties concerned what pro-portion of their workers would be thrown out of work by high wage agreements.

Press and television

Your job is to report the progress of wage negotiations between the management and workers, and also to tell people about the Government's policy towards wages and inflation. You can do this in a very straightforward way or you can decide to support one or other of the parties in the dispute; Government, Management or Workforce. You can ask any of the parties for statements at any time, but can only sit in on their meetings if they invite you to do so. After each round of the negotiations you prepare and deliver a news bulletin which reports what has been happening and what all the participants think of it.

Playing the simulation

The simplest way to play DISPUTE is to have MANAGEMENT and WORKFORCE only, and this could be done in half an hour or forty minutes.

First period. Allow ten minutes for the members to read their briefings and to decide on their strategy for the forthcoming negotiations. They should also nominate one person to take part in the negotiations.
Second period. Five minutes for the parties to make statements of their opening positions.
Third period. Ten minutes for the groups to meet separately to consider their responses.
Fourth period. Ten minutes of negotiation.
Fifth period. Review of simulation; or if time allows, further periods of negotiation.

Games

Preparing to find a job need not be all hard work; a slightly less earnest exercise or two will leaven the proceedings with a little lightness. Those included here are concerned with identifying sources of information about jobs, identifying jobs themselves, communicating information, using initials to state occupational preferences, and finding out someone else's marketable attributes.

What's My Line?

This game can be used as an ice-breaker or introduction to the business of looking at job skills and activities.
   The basic idea is very simple. Volunteer group members are asked to perform a piece of mime which depicts what people do in a particular job; swinging an axe, typing a letter, or giving an injection are obvious examples. Others are harder: working in a bank, repairing a car, or window dressing —

for example — require more ingenuity and subtlety. The rest of the group, or a panel of four members, then have to work out what the job was by asking not more than ten or fifteen questions.

The game can be made more competitive by splitting the group into two teams, individuals from each team taking it in turns to play the mimic.

Although this is not intended to be a very serious exercise, it could be followed by some discussion about such issues as: which jobs were the easiest or hardest to guess, and why? How did individuals choose which activity in a job to mime? What other actions could they have used? What kinds of questions were found to be most useful in identifying the jobs?

Slave market

Divide the group into pairs. One person is a slavemaster and the other is a slave. The slavemaster must find out what are the good points about the slave so that he can make a good price in a forthcoming slave sale. Allow five to ten minutes for this preparation and then commence the slave auction.

Job whispers

Take a job that is advertised in the local newspaper and give it to one member of the group. Ask him to memorise the essential points about the job and to pass them over verbally (but so that no-one else can hear) to the next person. The next person passes on the details to someone else, and so on until the message has been round the whole group membership. The last person to receive the message repeats it out loud to everyone else.

Initials

Use your name initials, or the letters of your first or second name to think of jobs in which you would be interested. Someone with the initials JR for example might think of Jockey, JCB operator, Jobbing builder, and Removal worker, Receptionist and Repair man. If someone with the surname BARCLAY completed the exercise like this:

B   Bus driver
A   Airline pilot
R   Racing driver
C   Car mechanic
L   Lorry driver
A   Ambulance driver
Y   Yachting instructor

it would be quite clear what occupational preferences were being expressed.

Friends and neighbours

The aim of this exercise is to identify and make use of the job experience and knowledge of people known to members of the group.

Divide the group into project teams, with four, five or six members in each. Invite each group to appoint a 'secretary', someone to write down their findings. The task in the small groups is first of all for each member to think of ten individuals he or she knows who go to work, and who would not mind being asked questions about the jobs they do. The 'secretary' writes down these job titles on a large sheet of paper; so that each team produces maybe forty or sixty job titles, depending on the overlap between individual acquaintances. The first name (or initials) of the individual who volunteered each title should be entered against it; and all the sheets should then be displayed on the wall, constituting a sizeable directory of *potential* information about a variety of jobs.

Time is allowed for all the group members to circulate around this display to select a job or jobs about which they would like to know more.

If someone sees the title of a job in which he is interested, he contacts the group member whose name is beside it. This person's task, in turn, is to take the enquirer's questions to the person who actually does the job. If it is possible and seems appropriate, a meeting could be arranged between the occupant of the job and the individual who wants to find out more about it.

This process of relaying job information can be undertaken on a fairly loose and informal basis. Alternatively, a whole session can be devoted to generating basic questions about jobs so that the information collected is fairly systematic. If desired, a written format for these questions could be prepared and duplicated, so that the results of the ensuing 'survey' can be filed and indexed to form a basic library of job information.

The old boy network

A variation on the 'friends and neighbours' theme would be to identify former pupils of the school or college, or members of the scheme, who would be willing to share their knowledge and experience of the jobs they have done since leaving. They could be used as speakers or panellists for direct questioning by groups of students, or as individual sources of information willing to be interviewed by group members, either in person or over the telephone.

Further sources on 'job search' and on work in general

There is a vast array of learning materials relevant to the topic of work, and for preparing young people to enter the job market. Some of it dates from more prosperous times when full employment was the norm, and the biggest problems faced by careers advisers were those of motivating the unmotivated or of placing more difficult individuals in the right employment niche. Currently, however, although most young people eventually end up in a job of some kind, this may take them a long time, and may be preceded by experience of one or other of the special schemes for the young unemployed. Others, either because of local employment conditions, or because of their unattractiveness to employers, may languish in the dole queue for many years. Either way, young people may be pushed back onto their own resources more than at any other time in their lives; and for many of them these resources are painfully inadequate, since conventional schooling has equipped them, and then only poorly, for the transition to the bottom end of the labour market.

Tutors and teachers should therefore look closely at job search materials and translate them and adapt them to local circumstances and individual needs amongst their students. This does not mean, in areas of high unemployment, that it is not worthwhile teaching job search skills, since many of the elements of successful job search can be transferred to other departments of people's lives.

A number of exercises related to work will be found in the *Life Skills Coaching Manual* which was described in chapter 2; this and a variety of other manuals can be obtained from Information Canada, Publications Satellite, P.O. Box 1565, Prince Albert, Saskatchewan S6V 5T2, Canada. See also J. Ellis and T. Barnes (1979), *Life Skills Training Manual,* published by Community Service Volunteers, 237 Pentonville Road, London N1 9NJ — which also contains a section on 'Job' (and CSV also produce other materials related to job search).

For a comprehensive, but very American, approach to preparing young people for making career choices see: T.W. Friel and R.R. Carkhuff (1974), *The Art of Developing a Career: a Helper's Guide,* Human Resource Development Press, Amherst, Massachusetts.

The Basic Skills Unit of the National Extension College (18 Brooklands Avenue, Cambridge CB2 2HN) has developed a range of materials for use in vocational preparation; e.g., *Starting Work* — a pack of materials which includes a magazine for students containing case studies; a quiz; a cartoon story; an 'instruction-following' exercise on cassette; and 'The Aeroplane Game', a simulated production line. See also *The Jobsearch Tapes* — a tape and transcripts following some young people through the process of finding work and training places; *Working in a shop;* and *Workfacts for Young Workers.*

You may get some ideas for helping individuals to assess their work potential and interests from J. and M. Korving and M. Keeley (1975), *Out of the Rut,* BBC publications.

More quizzes on work can be obtained from CRAC, the Careers Research and Advisory Centre at Bateman Street, Cambridge; see for example the *Job Quiz Books* 1, 2, and 3 written by Tony Crowley. CRAC can also provide a wide range of job-related materials including *Five Simple Business Games; The Interview Programme; The Job Box* which contains 101 job profiles; a useful book by B. Hopson and P. Hough (1973), *Exercises in Personal and Career Development;* plus a number of other directories and guides.

A number of directories of occupational information have been compiled by various agencies; the largest is CODOT — the *Classification of Occupations and Directory of Occupational Titles,* published by HMSO. Perhaps more useful for work with young people are *Signposts,* prepared by the Careers and Occupational Information Centre, Manpower Services Commission, the Pennine Centre, 20-22 Hawley Street, Sheffield S1 3GA (from August 1981: Moorfoot, Sheffield); and *Opportunities for School Leavers,* published by the New Opportunities Press, 76 St James's Lane, London N10 3RD. Both of these are updated annually; *Signposts* is available free to schools.

Additional information connected with work and careers can be obtained from NICEC, the National Institute for Careers Education and Counselling, Bayfordbury House, Lower Hatfield Road, Hertford SG13 8LD; and a comprehensive listing of Life and Social Skills training materials — on work and other topics besides — can be obtained from Cambridgeshire Careers Service, 7 Rose Crescent, Cambridge.

Other useful books and materials are:

The Work Fact Bank, published by Interaction Imprint, 15 Wilkin Street, London NW5 3NX.

Jobhunting Programme Kit, produced by the Scottish Community Education Centre, 4 Queensferry Street, Edinburgh EH2 4PA.

H. Dowson and R. Howden (1979), *School Leavers' Handbook,* Careers Consultants Ltd. and the Home and School Council.

C. Webb (1978), *Talk Yourself into a Job,* Macmillan.

H. Dowding and S. Boyce (1979), *Getting the job you want,* Ward Lock.

J. McMullen (1979), *Rights at Work,* Pluto Press.

P. Kinnersley (1973), *The Hazards of Work,* Pluto Press.

How to prepare your own case for an industrial tribunal — a booklet available from the Equal Opportunities Commission.

LEISURE

If there is one word that encapsulates the subjective experience of many young people it is 'boredom'. They are bored with school, with home, with themselves, with their friends, with everyone and everything. For some of them the use of the word is no more than an expression of passing dissatisfaction; for others it represents one of the symptoms of adolescent depression.

But the prevalence of the feeling is more likely to be a symptom of the social and commercial forces that now dictate the nature of young adulthood, suspended between the more clear-cut roles of childhood on the one hand and full adult status on the other.

The exercises in this programme cannot pretend to provide an answer to the problem of boredom, but they do point in the direction of understanding and doing something active about it. Not that engaging in any of the many available leisure pursuits should be seen simply as an antidote to boredom. They are worthwhile things to do in their own right. But to many young people, used as they are to having their time structured for them by the school timetable, the demands of family life, and even by television programme schedules, the most difficult aspect of their leisure time is having to make their own decisions about what to do, and when and where and how. For young people who have left school but failed to find work, the problem can be an even more pressing one; the hours and days and weeks can hang heavily round the necks of those with few interests or abilities, and with little or no money to spend on other than essentials.

So some of the emphasis in these exercises is on searching the environment for interesting and inexpensive things to do, and on strengthening the determination to *do* something. But in the end, most people's leisure lives revolve, not around expensive and frantic activity of an organized kind, but around the simple and satisfying pleasures of being with family or friends. So anything which equips young people with the ability to get on better with their peers and to contribute in a lively and acceptable way to the communal life of the groups to which they belong can only be helpful.

The exercises here are concerned, first, with assessing how individuals actually use their time; three exercises are included as ways of approaching this — Diary Forms, The Days of the Week, and a leisure checklist.

Given that the kernel of the problem of managing spare time often lies in just finding things to do and gaining access to them, a number of exercises are concerned with generating ideas for leisure activities. These are followed by others which are specifically concerned with the acquisition and exchange of information about leisure facilities and interests: a learning exchange, leisure lectures and related projects, and planning an activity.

Attitudes to leisure — and in particular to the issues of why people engage in particular activities and the importance of informal personal contact — can be explored with two exercises, 'Why do people do it?' and 'Being a friend'.

The skills which individuals might use in solving a number of problems that might arise in relation to leisure — as well as more general social skills — are focussed on in the exercises on 'leisure situations' and 'Here is the news'.

Finally, a few additional suggestions are appended for looking at specific leisure activities like watching television and telling jokes.

Keeping track of time — some uses of diary forms

Diary forms can be used whenever the use of time, either in general or in relation to particular activities is being discussed. If 'leisure time' is being looked at, a leisure time diary form might look like this:

Leisure Diary Form

	Morning	*Afternoon*	*Evening*
MONDAY	///////	///////	
TUESDAY	///////	///////	
WEDNESDAY	///////	///////	
THURSDAY	///////	///////	
FRIDAY	///////	///////	
SATURDAY			
SUNDAY			

If individuals were at school or had jobs, the central portions of weekdays would, of course, be accounted for. If they were unemployed on the other hand, these periods would also be blank and would have to be filled in.

The members of the group can fill this in retrospectively for the week just past, or it can be filled in day by day; as time goes by. The results can be used to stimulate general discussion or as the focus of peer interviews or individual counselling; or all the forms can be collected (anonymously if necessary) and some averages computed concerning the use of time by the group, e.g. percentage of time spent watching the television, talking to friends, doing a hobby, doing absolutely nothing, riding bikes, eating, travelling, etc., and the averages used as above.

The days of the week

Rather than asking group members to map out their pattern of activities over the course of a week, an overall impression of how they see the use of time can be gained as follows.

Ask each individual member of the group to consider each day of the week, starting with Sunday and finishing with Saturday, and to give to each day a boredom rating from 1 to 5; 1 being not at all boring and 5 being extremely boring. The days should then be arranged in a new order, with the most boring at the top and the least boring at the bottom.

Discuss the implications of each person's list, and the similarities and differences between group members and the reasons for them.

Leisure checklist

Another method that can be used to help individuals map out their use of leisure time more clearly is the *leisure checklist* — a simple list of activities in which people might engage during their spare time. It serves three main purposes:

1. To enable individuals to survey their own use of spare time.
2. To present a list of activities as suggestions for their possible use of time.
3. To help them set targets for more effective and/or more enjoyable use of their time.

The checklist can also be used as a starter for group discussion; as a means of generating ideas for the learning exchange described below; or as a forerunner to the setting up of a project in relation to a given spare-time activity. In the form shown here the checklist consists of an inventory of activities, and asks individuals to record how often they take part in each, on a five-point scale, 'never — rarely — occasionally — often — very often'. This could be made more exact by using the categories 'never — once a year — once a month — weekly — daily' or some similar range of possibilities. In addition, however, many other questions could be asked about the use of time and about its effects on other aspects of individuals' lives. The checklist illustrated is a record of frequency only; other questions could be asked about an individual's preferences for different uses of time; the costs of various kinds of pursuits; the role of others (who else was involved); the level of skill if any required; ways in which someone's use of time might change; or their reasons for engaging or not engaging in particular kinds of activity.

Leisure checklist

Using the frequency scale on the right, mark off how often you take part in the various activities listed on the left. Add any others that have been missed out at the end of the checklist.

	Never	Rarely	Occa-sionally	Often	Very Often
Sleeping					
Eating					
Walking					
Talking to people					
Playing games					
Watching TV					
Watching sport					
Listening to records					
Reading					
Visiting friends					
Doing housework					
Crafts					
Gardening					
Collecting					
Playing a musical instrument					
Going to the pictures					
Going to discos					
Listening to the radio					
Looking after a pet					
Evening classes					
Voluntary work					
Part-time job					
Walking the streets					
Doing nothing					

Generating ideas for leisure activities

The exercises below can be used either to help focus the attention of a life skills group on the problems of using spare time, or to help them solve the problem by thinking of different ways in which it can be filled.

Entertainment maps

Apart from trips away on holiday or to football matches, most young people spend their spare time in the area in which they live. It can be interesting, therefore, to ask them to describe — as exhaustively as possible — all their area has to offer by way of leisure amenities. This could be done through a survey, as described later in this section — or through the drawing of a leisure map of the district. This could include all the clubs, pubs, cinemas, cafes, dance halls or discos, sports centres, or any other facilities that exist — and might either make individuals more aware of what their locality has to offer, or suggest to them things which it lacks, and which they think ought to be provided.

Tourist brochure

An obvious extension of drawing a 'leisure map' is to compile an introductory brochure which might help visitors to an area to find things to do. This could be assembled with tourists of all ages in mind — and so include a comprehensive list of places of interest — or might be designed primarily for people of a similar age to the compilers, and reflect their own preferences more. It might be interesting to compare the result with 'official guides' available in the town or district hall. This exercise can also be carried out with an ideal situation in mind — what would the group like to see in the area? What would it have to contain in order to be really good?

Brainstorming

As with solving other kinds of problem, ideas for spare-time activities can be suggested in quantity during a brainstorming session. Apart from directing this at the problem of leisure in general ('Things to do in . . .'), a series of brainstorms could also be carried out, for example, to think of activities that involve different numbers of people; cost different amounts of money; or call for different degrees of skill.

An ABC of things to do . . .

An alternative way of developing a list of activities for leisure or spare time is to take the letters of the alphabet in turn and brainstorm or do project work to list as many things as possible to do that begin with that letter.

A. Angling, archery, art, arranging flowers, archaeology, aqua-gliding, acting . . .

B. Bee-keeping, building, badges, baking, basketwork, bicycling, basketball, baseball, . . .

C. Carpentry, car maintenance, crafts, country walks, cats, cane work, carving, canoeing, . . .

Cards can be made out for each activity under each letter with some information about local facilities, classes, clubs, places that stock materials, etc. These could form the basis of a double indexed catalogue: by alphabet and by types of interests. Such an exercise *might* set individuals off in pursuit of activities they had not heard of or contemplated before.

'Boring'

Another means by which individuals might generate ideas for the use of leisure time is if they are asked to plan activities for someone else.

Divide the group into two roughly equal smaller groups. Both of them have the job of planning a week's programme for a group of foreign students who are coming to this country from the Soviet Union and who wish to see what life is like in this country.

One group is briefed to make the stay of the students as interesting, as lively and enjoyable as possible. The other group is briefed to make the stay of the students as grim and boring and unpleasant as possible. The programme in both cases should fill the whole day from breakfast until bedtime and may include visits, lectures, free time, shopping expeditions, etc. Discuss the resulting itineraries and in particular why they are seen as interesting and boring respectively.

A leisure learning exchange

The idea of a learning exchange, suggested by Ivan Illich (1970), is very simple: in any group of people with a size bigger than about three, it will almost always be the case that some members know things which others do not but would like to. To organize the transfer of this knowledge from one person to another it is only necessary to make two lists: one of the things which individuals are prepared to tell others about; and one of the things which individuals themselves would like to learn.

A simple example is the organization of a 'leisure learning exchange'. Give each participant two sheets of paper. On the first they should write down a list of at least three leisure activities which they know something about and which they are prepared to tell someone else about, even if it only takes two minutes. The items can range from the whereabouts of the nearest judo club to a demonstration of abseiling; from the basics of snooker to the mysteries of darts scoring; from British stamps to racing pigeons; from silly jokes to cave exploration; from first aid to weight-lifting technique; from basic recipes for bed-sitter meals to the fixture list of the local football team. On the second piece of paper they should write another list of the things they would like to know more about.

The lists should be signed or initialled and then displayed under separate signs:

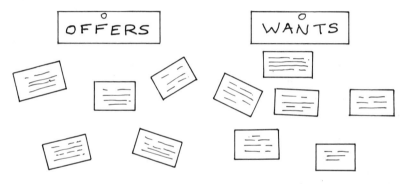

Participants then inspect the two noticeboards, and pair off either to teach or to learn something about leisure pursuits. Unsuited pairs can usually find something *not* on their lists to tell each other about. If the lists warrant it, the procedure can be repeated a number of times until everyone has both imparted and received some information. A group discussion should then take place about what has been learned.

The lists can be left on the walls for future reference or for further additions, or repetitions of the exercise.

Lectures

This exercise could be built onto the leisure learning exchange. Instead of having pairs of individuals talking to each other about their spare time interests, ask each individual to prepare a two, or five, or ten minute talk on one of their interests or pastimes. The length of the talk will depend on the abilities of the group members and on the time allowed for preparation. Large groups may need to be split up into smaller ones so that everyone gets a chance to give a talk in the time available. Alternatively, the talks can be spread out over several sessions so that only a few are heard at a time.

Interests can be grouped together so that one session is devoted to outdoor activities, another to music of various kinds, another to manual and craft hobbies, another to animals and so on.

If the preparation of the talks is spread over a longer period, it may be worth deciding on a format for individuals to work to. This could include the making of some visual display material, the collection of leaflets and other forms of information, and the giving of advice on how to get started.

Besides collecting and disseminating a lot of information about leisure time pursuits, this project can also provide practice in information search and self-presentation skills. (See 'Talking and listening' in the Interaction section.)

A conference

A development of the same idea would be to ask the group or groups to organize a Leisure Conference, inviting experts, professionals and enthusiasts of all sorts to contribute to an afternoon devoted to leisure in the local community. Simply having to decide on topics and find speakers will increase knowledge about the local scene and also give practice in organizing and communicating skills.

A "spare-time" survey

A leisure survey of the local community could range from a simple information search exercise, collecting leaflets and information from local agencies, clubs and commercial facilities, carried out in one morning; to a substantial and lengthy enquiry into local leisure needs and facilities involving questionnaires, samples, interviews and report writing. This might look at the changing leisure requirements of local residents as they grow older and their family situations alter. The end result of such surveys — whether of the simple or the more complex kind — can be made use of in a number of ways.

A register or index of local leisure facilities can be compiled and made available, either to members of the group who compiled it, or to other groups or to advisory agencies or public libraries in the area.

An exhibition might be made with the material and displayed where it can be seen by other people.

Handouts on different aspects of leisure can be prepared and distributed.

Further projects could also be organized, to analyse some of the information that had been gathered in a more systematic way.

One aspect of leisure pursuits which often looms large for young people is the cost of engaging in them. A register of FREE activities in the area may be useful; and the costs of others might usefully be indicated in the information.

Social action projects could also be based on the results of a leisure survey which happened to indicate the absence of facilities for which there is a demonstrable demand in a particular area.

Planning an activity

If the students have identified activities or events which are in short supply in their neighbourhood, it can be useful and educational to get them to fill the gap by organizing such an event or activity themselves. This could lead to anything from an informal disco to an expedition abroad. The students should if possible work in small groups with identified tasks to perform in order to make the venture a success.

Thus in planning a disco one group would concern themselves with the venue and all the arrangements related to the premises and layout of furniture. Another group would organize the music and the entertainment; and another group the food and drink. Others would deal with publicity and marketing, making sure that enough tickets were sold to make the venture viable.

Why do people do it?

It is not always obvious why some people engage in some leisure pursuits, which to the spectator appear to be difficult and dangerous and a great deal of hard work. Why do they do it?

Some ways of finding answers to this question could include use of the following:

Brainstorming. Taking an activity or group of activities, ask the group to think of as many reasons as possible why people might engage in it.

A checklist of words, e.g. interesting, exciting, good fun, meet people, challenge, etc, which can be ticked for each activity in turn and then discussed.

A survey. This could simply mean a canvass of school or college or work mates; or a neighbourhood survey; or a postal enquiry directed to famous exponents of various leisure arts. Or each participant could undertake to interview a pre-selected person about their spare time interest and to bring back a report to the rest of the group.

The results of any of these methods should be used as the basis of a further exercise in which individuals pinpoint the things they look for in an attractive leisure pursuit, and then construct a profile of words which define such an activity. Group members could then work in small groups to suggest possibilities that fit these profiles.

Being a friend

One of the best things about leisure time is just being with friends, spending time with them, talking and laughing, playing the fool, having fun, playing games, doing new things. A lot of the time this sort of activity would be described by many people as just 'hanging about', because it has no clear purpose and no clear structure. It appears — from the outside at least — to be aimless and pointless. And yet, apart from working and sleeping, it is the most common way of passing the time known to mankind. So it is nothing to be ashamed of. Adults 'hang about' in their front rooms watching the television, or in bars drinking alcohol, or in more expensive places like clubs or restaurants. But whatever the setting the aim is identical: to talk to other people in a diverting and amusing environment. The fact that teenagers do their hanging about more visibly on street corners and in cafes and youth clubs does not mean that it is any less worthwhile as a human activity. Good use of leisure should not be seen as the 'organized' use of leisure. The two are not necessarily synonymous.

These exercises are intended to strengthen this informal aspect of leisure time.

Describing a friend

Divide the group into smaller groups; threes and fours; and ask each group to discuss and agree amongst themselves what are the marks of a good friend. You could stimulate them to do this by asking them to complete sentences like:

A friend is a person who . . . .

My friends always . . . .

A good friend would never . . . .

They could also construct a 'friend rating form' with pairs of adjectives such as:

trustworthy	not to be trusted
cold	warm
funny	serious
quiet	talkative

Finally, you should discuss the results in the larger group and construct a composite profile of good and bad friends on a wallsheet or blackboard. It might also be worthwhile considering whether individuals prefer different friends at different times, e.g. when involved in different kinds of activities.

Leisure situations

Like all the other topics dealt with in this book, leisure cannot be seen in isolation; it has to do with attitudes and values, with money, with friends and relatives and relationships, and with conflicts of interest and loyalty. Learning to cope with some of the situations that embody these conflicts and difficulties is an essential part of the process of becoming an independent person. Ten such situations are set out below; they can be used as discussion starters or for role play — and most usefully to help students identify similar situations which they have faced in their own lives.

1. Your sister has to go into hospital for some tests. She asks you to look after her two young children: a girl aged six, and a boy eight, for a Saturday afternoon. She gives you five pounds to spend. How would you spend the afternoon and the money so as to give the two children a really enjoyable time?

2. It is Wednesday night. You have no money. You stay at home to watch the television although there aren't any really interesting programmes on. About eight o'clock your friend comes round and asks if you will come out for a drink. You would like to go, but you can't ask your parents for any more money — you still owe four pounds for last week. What do you do?

3. You are with a group of friends hanging about in the street one evening. You are all bored, there is nothing to do and nobody has any money. One of your friends suggests taking a car and going for a spin. You are not sure if he is serious but he is a bit of a madhead. Three or four of the others say that sounds like a good idea — 'a bit of excitement' — and they set off to look for a likely car to nick. What would you do/say?

4. You are being interviewed for a job that you really want. On the application form you said that one of your hobbies was reading. It wasn't really a hobby but you thought it would look good when they read the form. One of the interviewers says, 'I see that one of your interests is reading. What are you reading at the moment?' You are not reading anything at the moment, apart from the sports page in the Daily Mirror, and you haven't read a book since you left school. What do you say?

5. An old auntie gives you one hundred pounds for your birthday 'to spend on something to do in your spare time'. What would you do with it?

6. You are at a disco with a boy you quite like. Another boy keeps asking you to dance with him. What do you do?

7. You are at a disco with a girl you quite like. Another bloke keeps asking her to dance. What do you do?

8. You have arranged to go out with someone who is not a special friend of yours. You arrange to meet at the cinema at 7 o'clock. At about 6 o'clock your best friend comes round to ask you to go to a party. You would like to go but that would mean letting down the person you have already agreed to spend the evening with. What would you decide to do?

9. You are sitting in a cafe with a group of friends. Two of them start to argue about something trivial, but the argument becomes quite heated and one of them is really rude to the other. Would you say anything? What?

10. Two friends disagree violently about someone else you all know. One friend says this other person is all right, the other says he/she is a liar and a nasty piece of work, and asks you to support this view. You don't have any strong feelings about this other person but feel under pressure to agree or not to disagree, with your friends. What do you think you would say?

'Here is the news'

A simulation

Watching television or listening to the radio occupies a considerable part of many people's lives. This exercise gives some insight into the mechanics of producing a news bulletin for transmission, and also provides practice in handling information, writing, presentation, and working co-operatively against tight deadlines.

The end product of this exercise is a news broadcast which lasts five, seven, or ten minutes, depending on how long is allowed for preparation and on whether the finished result is recorded on audio or video equipment for playback to the participants. Either of these is a bonus but not essential for the success of the project.

The exercise calls for four teams of reporters and presenters: foreign news; home news; local news; and sport. A programme producer is also required to co-ordinate the final transmission. He or she is also responsible for the timing of the programme. Set the limits for the broadcast and when it is to take place. You can then count off the time towards this deadline by calling out at intervals: 'Twenty minutes to on air', 'Ten minutes to on air', and so on.

You will need copies of two or three different national daily newspapers and a copy of the local one. It is most realistic to use that day's papers, but not essential. Cut items from the papers and deliver them to the four production teams at different intervals — sometimes two or three items at a time, sometimes only one — in no particular order of importance. Key stories can arrive at any time, including five minutes before "on air". The teams must sort out these items, decide which ones they are going to use in the broadcast, rewrite them and rehearse their presentation. An additional requirement that might be set is that each team should include in their report one *interview* with someone in the news.

The producer *must* start the programme at the appointed time and *must* finish exactly at the end of the allotted time; five or ten minutes or whatever. If the programme is still going it must be cut off.

If audio or video equipment is used, the finished product can be re-played to the participants but this is not strictly necessary if such equipment is not readily available.

TV programmes

The aim of this exercise is to ask individuals to consider their television viewing preferences and to stimulate small group discussion on the merits and demerits of different programmes.

Divide the group into smaller ones of not more than four. Give to each team a copy of the Radio Times and TV Times; these need not be current ones, nor necessarily the same for each team. Each group has to act as a programme planning team, to plan one ideal evening's viewing, starting at 4 p.m. and continuing till closedown. The items selected should be cut out and pasted on a fresh sheet which should then be displayed and discussed.

Smoking debate

Debates are designed to generate lively and informed discussion, and some topics are virtually guaranteed to bring forth strong opinions. Smoking, for example, is something which almost invariably attracts bad publicity; but many young people still do it. Invite two pro-smokers and two anti-smokers to prepare complementary cases for and against the motion 'Smoking is a good thing' or 'Smoking is a bad thing'. As many people as possible should be encouraged to take part in the debate; it might be useful to have adult supporting speakers primed to weigh in towards the end of the debate with 'for' and 'against' contributions.

A small book of jokes

The skill of telling jokes is one that many people never acquire; partly because they don't know any jokes to tell and secondly because they have never practised telling them. Many of the methods already described in this book could be turned to good advantage in this direction; a joke exchange, a directory of jokes, joke quizzes, joke competitions, and modelling and rehearsal sessions for those who are less well endowed with the joke teller's skills.

Conversation starters

Another skill in convivial companionship is being able to spark off an interesting conversation. Brainstorm suitable topics for this purpose and also practise ways of introducing them into general conversation.

'Leisure': Sources

Although in theory there are numerous ways in which individuals might spend their spare time, in practice few of them are available in most places and accessible to the young at a price they can afford. There are no ready-made solutions and to help young people solve the difficulties posed by their 'spare time', teachers and other workers need to develop new materials of their own. Three topics in particular may merit further attention. The first is 'boredom' in all its expressions and manifestations; the second is the provision of realistic information about local facilities; and the third is the recognition and strengthening of the skills needed to form and sustain friendships.

It is not easy to make precise suggestions about 'boredom', since little is known about the meaning of the term to young people; perhaps teachers and others need to explore with their students what the word signifies for them; this might then lead to concrete action of some kind.

Finding information about local amenities or about leisure pursuits in general is not difficult: town halls or libraries can usually supply it in plenty. But if there are few things to do in your area and young people are dismissive even of those, an alternative strategy might be to undertake a project in which individuals compile information about local facilities or set new ones up. The following books or projects may suggest ways in which this can be done: Clocktower Young Adults Project, Tower Road North, Warmley, Bristol BS15 2XU – a youth project which has produced information packs (written jointly by young people, youth workers, and volunteers) on such topics as accommodation, health, and money. *The Neighbourhood Fact Bank*, developed by the project Education for Neighbourhood Change at Nottingham University, is available from the project at the School of Education, University Park, Nottingham NG7 2RD. See also T. Gibson (1979), *People Power*, published by Penguin Books. J. Ellis and T. Barnes (1979), *Life Skills Training Manual*, published by Community Service Volunteers – see especially the sections on *Leisure* and *Community;* CSV also market a 'community action' kit, *Planning Your Environment*. The programme kits on *Good Health; Drugs, Drink and Tobacco;* and *Carry on Learning*, developed by the Scottish Community Education Centre, are all relevant to 'leisure'. For information on voluntary work, contact the National Council of Voluntary Organisations, 26 Bedford Square, London WC1B 3HU; and see P. Sterret (1979), *Fund Raising Projects: Cash for Good Causes*, Foulsham & Co. Finally, some ideas for fostering friendship skills could be drawn from T. Orlick (1978), *The Cooperative Sports and Games Book*, Pantheon Books.

MONEY

Money is intimately linked to work on the one hand — its source of supply for most people; and to the demands of home and leisure time on the other — which is where most of it is spent. Its importance in people's lives is reflected in the variety and frequency of the difficulties they have with their money; making it go round, paying back debts, resisting pressures to spend more than they can afford, keeping straight with tax and national insurance contributions, saving for holidays, purchasing expensive items like cars and houses and furniture.

In order to manage these and other money problems properly individuals need:

Information about money and the agencies and organizations that deal with it; about their own patterns of income and expenditure; about their consumer rights; and about where to go in case of difficulty for assistance and advice.

Understanding of their attitudes and feelings towards money — and not just their own money — but other people's; together with some grasp of how others feel about these matters.

Skills in gathering relevant information, making decisions, planning, self-control and self-discipline, and assertiveness.

The exercises in this section are designed to introduce some of these issues and to make a start on imparting the necessary information, understanding and skills. They do not however constitute a full programme of activities for achieving all of these goals; that is for the teacher or tutor or group leader to develop in the light of the needs expressed by his particular group of students. Some groups will require more information than others; others will want to practise making decisions; and yet others will be deficient in the ability to resist the many pressures upon them to spend more than they can afford on some of the 'good things' in life which are not only *not* free, but extremely expensive.

The materials in this section are —

1 Some suggestions concerning ways of stimulating thought on money and the problems it presents, using brainstorming, peer interviews, or the giving of information about aspects of money in which group members might be interested.

2 'The way the money goes' — exercises for the self-assessment by individuals of how they spend their money and how they would like to spend it: a 'Weekly Spending Survey'; 'Spending a Windfall'; and 'Lifetime Earnings'.

3 A 'Money Problems' checklist, for self-assessment and discussion sessions.

4 Two exercises for looking at attitudes to money and to earnings in particular — 'A Fair Day's Pay' and the 'Money Satisfaction Scale'.

5   'Making a Balance Sheet' — an exercise that can be used to help individuals make decisions about spending money and improve their decision making skills.

6   Structured roleplays of social encounters in which money may be involved, designed to help individuals develop the skills of dealing with such encounters.

7   'Shopping Around' — a simulation concerned with the skills of budgeting and decision making about money.

8   A money game: 'Win as much as you can'.

Brainstorming and peer interviews

Although money problems are universal, talking about them is sometimes thought to be somehow improper; the secrecy that surrounds the size of people's pay packets is a good example, or the lingering stigma that still attaches to being in debt. Students in school or college, or on a pre-employment scheme, are less likely to be so reticent since their circumstances will be very similar. But a relatively anonymous way of starting to look at some of the issues associated with money, and of stimulating thought about them, might be to conduct a brainstorming session (see page 22 for an outline of brainstorming). Some possible titles for brainstorms related to money are:

Money. Gambling. Debts. Moneylenders. H.P. Spending sprees. Being short. New pound notes. Millionaires. Saving. Banks. Mortgages. Cost of living. Wages. Wage rises. Deductions. Taxes. Inflation. Investment. Stocks and shares. Profits. Exports. Rich people. Poor people. Buying. Selling. Budgeting. Running a car. Rent. Buying a house. Rates. Tallyman. Mail order catalogue. 'On tick'. Credit. Housekeeping money. Beer money. Men's wages. Women's wages. A fortune. A windfall. A 'rainy day'. High cost — low cost. Bargains. Shopping. Gold. Pensions. Pocket money. Perks. Company car. Free gifts. Advertising. Coupons. Green Shield stamps. Discount. Bonus. Overtime. Value. Cheap. Expensive. Dole. Benefit. Winnings. Fines. Sale price. Auctions. Supermarkets. Wholesale. Retail. Salaries. Pay cheque. Post Office savings. Giro. County Court. Special needs payments. Self-made men. 'Rags to riches'.

These titles or others like them could also be used as the basis for peer interviews between individuals in a group of young people, along the lines suggested in the exercise 'Getting to know yourself through others' on page 61.

Information

Another way of focussing the attention of group members on money problems and money management might be to present information on some
aspect of money; or to invite along an 'expert' to give a talk or answer
questions about it. Information will almost certainly be needed by young
people at some stage if they are considering problems related to money.
One way of supplying it might be to incorporate a question-and-answer
session in a life skills course, featuring one or more of the following: bank
managers or bank staff; representatives of stores or shops, of HP companies,
buildings societies, insurance companies, or even the Inland Revenue; or
staff of the local Consumer Advice Centre. Alternatively, a number of organisations can supply information (e.g. in leaflet or booklet form) on different
aspects of money; they include the Consumers' Association; the Office of
Fair Trading; the Advertising Standards Authority; the Building Societies
Association; the Finance Houses Association; the National Federation of
Consumer Groups; and the Mutual Aid Centre. Addresses of these organisations will be found at the end of the book.

The way the money goes

Information about the services offered by banks or about which shops are
cheapest for such-and-such an item is clearly of inestimable value to those
who want to make their money go further. But to make the most of the
money they have available, individuals also need to appreciate their own
preferences for spending it, their own current pattern of expenditure and the
ways in which it might be changed. The exercises below are designed to help
individuals appraise their own spending habits, the extent to which they are
in control of what they spend, and the relative importance to them of the
different things on which they spend their money.

Weekly spending survey

The most obvious starting-point when thinking about money problems —
and an essential first step in helping individuals to manage their money
better — is a review of how someone spends his or her money in the course
of a typical week. Working with a group, you can carry out such a spending
survey by first of all asking members of a group to brainstorm a list of the
things on which they spend their money (wages, grants, benefits, pocket
money or whatever). The list might include items like housekeeping, food,
bus or train fares, clothes, cosmetics and toiletries, magazines and papers,
drink, going to the cinema, records, savings, hobbies, hire purchase repayments, debts, etc.
    If you can then reduce these categories to five or six major ones, you can

invite the members of the group to fill in a weekly expenditure sheet like this one:

Day	Keep	Fares	Clothes	etc	etc	etc
Thursday						
Friday						
Saturday						
Sunday						
Monday						
Tuesday						
Wednesday						
TOTAL						

If these are completed anonymously they can be collected and summarised on a large sheet and then discussed in terms of the differences between individuals; their average patterns of expenditure and so on.

Spending a windfall

This exercise can be an entertaining one and it can help individuals to sort out their priorities for spending money.

Divide the group into pairs. Each person interviews the other about how he or she would spend a windfall of money; this could be a modest one of £100; a somewhat larger amount of £1,000; and a monster pools win of £500,000. Allow five minutes or so each way, and then ask the interviewers to report to the whole group how their partners would spend their windfalls. Discuss the results.

Lifetime earnings

For this exercise it might be useful if the class members were to be equipped with pocket calculators; but if not they can struggle with the multiplications in the traditional manner.

Each person in the group calculates what his or her lifetime earnings are likely to be, based on current rates, but allowing for increases as people become older and command adult wages, and for time off due to unemployment, sickness or for having children. The resulting sums are usually staggeringly large; it is entertaining to add together everybody's answers to arrive at a total group earning power.

The results of the *weekly spending survey* can be superimposed on these lifetime earnings to see how much is going to be spent over the next fifty years on things like cigarettes and drink on the one hand, and on rents or food on the other.

Money problems

A fairly direct way of helping young people to define their money problems or to think about the importance of money to them is to use a checklist like the one shown here. This poses a number of problems in three areas: feelings about money; knowledge of money matters; and behaviour in relation to money. These are intended to act as a baseline for information-giving or group discussion exercises. The list could easily be augmented if there were particular issues or concerns amongst the members of particular groups.

Money in my life

Here are fifteen statements that people make about money. Think about each statement and decide whether you think it is TRUE or FALSE as far as you are concerned. Put a ring round your answer on the right opposite each statement.

1. I am worried about money.	TRUE	FALSE
2. Other people seem to have more money than me.	TRUE	FALSE
3. I am quite mean.	TRUE	FALSE
4. I would like to be really rich.	TRUE	FALSE
5. Poor people are poor because they are lazy.	TRUE	FALSE
6. I understand what 'hire purchase' means.	TRUE	FALSE
7. I know how to open a bank account.	TRUE	FALSE
8. I understand what the 'rate of interest' is.	TRUE	FALSE
9. I don't know what the deductions on wage slips are for.	TRUE	FALSE
10. I can't work out where all my money goes.	TRUE	FALSE
11. I usually spend all my money as soon as I get it.	TRUE	FALSE
12. I try to save some money for a rainy day.	TRUE	FALSE
13. I don't owe anybody anything.	TRUE	FALSE
14. I take a long time repaying what I owe.	TRUE	FALSE
15. I like buying people things.	TRUE	FALSE

A Fair Day's Pay

The aim of this exercise is to explore group members' knowledge of, and attitudes to, the different rates of pay for different kinds of work.

Divide the group into four more-or-less equally sized sub-groups and call them A, B, C, and D. Give each group a copy of the jobs listed below and ask them to:

1. Decide for each job what they think is the current weekly wage, and write down the amount by the side of it.
2. Re-write the list in rank order of the amounts of the weekly wages.
3. Make a second list which rank-orders the jobs in terms of the level of skill or hardness of work they entail.
4. Decide for each job what they think the weekly wage *ought* to be, and list these amounts in rank order.

If the new lists are written on large sheets and displayed on a wall, they can form the basis of a presentation by each group of their findings followed by discussion of the similarities and differences between the lists. A list of current actual earnings for the jobs on the list could add to the realism of the exercise.

Lorry driver	Waitress	Headmaster
Nurse	Doctor	Dustman
Judge	Telephonist	Shop assistant
Policeman	Postman	Builder's labourer
Factory worker	Coalminer	Milkman
DHSS counter clerk	Fashion model	Disc jockey
Bus driver	Primary school teacher	M.P.
TV repair mechanic	Car mechanic	Lathe operator
Computer programmer	Bricklayer	Prime Minister
Film star		

Points for discussion

Why are rates different? What are the differences between men's and women's jobs? Are they fair? What is it about a job that makes it worth more or less? What is a desirable range of wages? etc. etc.

Project

A project which could be built onto this exercise is to have groups fix rates of pay for a number of jobs in a new firm. The nature of the firm can be 'ready-made' and suggested by the group leader, together with a list of jobs, or can be devised from scratch by the participants.

Money satisfaction scale

The aim of the money scale is to examine assumptions about what is a 'fair' wage and the degree of satisfaction associated with amounts above and below it.

The money scale

Satisfaction

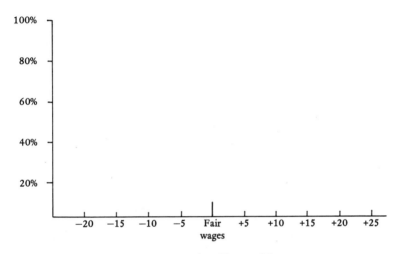

Amount of weekly wage (£)

Distribute a copy of the money scale to each member of the group and ask them to think what would constitute a fair wage for a week's work in a job they might reasonably hope to get. This amount should be entered under the mid-point of the bottom line of the scale. Vertically above this point the degree of satisfaction with such a wage should be marked with a cross, using the percentages on the vertical scale as a guide. Similar ratings should then be made on either side of this mid-point for wages which differ from the 'fair wage' by successive increments or decrements of £5. The resulting points are joined together to form a 'satisfaction curve'.

This can be used as a basis for peer interviews or group discussion on what constitutes a fair wage and what are the upper and lower limits of satisfaction.

A group average curve can be calculated to allow individual members to compare themselves with others.

Making a balance sheet

Most people have a money problem of one kind or another: they may not
have enough; may be in debt; or may have to make an important and expensive purchase. Whatever it is, a 'balance sheet' of the positives and negatives
(or pluses and minuses) that affect the situation can be a useful starting
point for action — for planning expenditure or making decisions.

A balance sheet that could serve this purpose might look like this:

My money problem:	
Credits + + +	Debits − − −
. . . .	. . . .
. . . .	. . . .
. . . .	. . . .
. . . .	. . . .
. . . .	. . . .
. . . .	. . . .
. . . .	. . . .
Action to be taken	

To use the sheet, individuals first of all briefly set out their problem or financial goal in the box at the top, and then itemise the factors which affect them
positively and negatively. This might produce a complete list of their income
and outgoings if they are looking at their money problems in general; or
might generate a more specific list of factors *for* and *against* a particular
course of action they would like to take.

If someone was interested in buying a new and expensive motorbike for
example, the entries in the *credit* column might be things like 'excitement',
'good trade-in price on present bike', 'useful for going on touring holidays',
or 'saves money travelling to work'. The *debit* side might have things in it

like 'mother thinks it's a bad idea to have such a powerful bike', 'HP repayments would need nearly all available cash at the end of each week', 'couldn't afford to buy clothes or records', or 'close friend thinks it would be better to save the money'.

The *action to be taken* would depend on the balance of the pluses and minuses which the completed sheet revealed.

An exercise of this kind could be used to help the members of a group to think in a more orderly way about some of their money problems — by just giving them copies of a blank 'balance sheet' and asking them to think about their financial strengths and weaknesses (e.g. income, savings, good and bad spending habits, etc).

Alternatively, in cases where an existing money problem had already been identified — through the use of a checklist, brainstorm, or group discussion — a 'balance sheet' would be one way of exploring it further and perhaps of deciding what to do about it.

Structured roleplays

Although money is simply a medium of exchange, many of the transactions in which it is involved are personal encounters full of emotional pressures and tensions. Structured roleplay can be used to look at some of these encounters and to explore more effective ways of dealing with them. Three suggestions for structured roleplays are presented below; as with roleplays presented elsewhere, these can be used as the basis of modelling or practice exercises, counselling, or group discussion. The first is concerned with resisting one kind of pressure; that applied by a salesman in trying to persuade a customer to buy something more expensive than he or she has in mind. The other two are to do with the complexities of lending and borrowing: twin rocks on which many a friendship has foundered.

Resisting pressure

Purchaser. You have twenty pounds to spend and you want to buy a cheap cassette recorder. You could probably afford just a pound or two more, but you are already paying out two pounds a week on a clothing club account and couldn't really afford another commitment on HP.

Salesperson. You work in a shop belonging to a chain of radio, hi-fi and television stores. You have a not very high basic wage which you can improve by the commission you earn on each sale. You are anxious to sell as much as possible. One of the things you try to do is to get the customer to buy something which is a bit more expensive than he or she was originally thinking of.

Asking for money back

Alice.   Margaret, who is a good friend, but not your closest one, borrowed two pounds from you three weeks ago to help buy an LP. She promised to pay it back the next week, but didn't. You feel cross because she hasn't offered it back and seems to be avoiding you. You see her in the High Street one morning. You are a bit short of money yourself this week and could do with the money. You decide to ask Margaret for it.

Margaret.   Three weeks ago you borrowed two pounds from Alice to buy an LP. You haven't seen her since to pay it back, and it's slipped your mind. One Saturday morning in the High Street, Alice comes up to you. You are desperately short of money this week because you have just bought a really expensive pair of shoes. She asks for her money back.

Asking for a loan

Tony.   You earn fifty pounds a week on a building site. You pay your mother ten pounds a week for your keep; pay for your own clothes and holidays; and spend the rest in pubs and clubs and on cigarettes. Some weeks you ask your mother for a few pounds to tide you over — like last week when she gave you five pounds which you promised to pay back this week. But this week you are short again and you have promised your friends to go out with them to quite an expensive club. You decide to ask your mother for another five pounds.

Mother.   You are getting fed up with Tony, your son, asking for loans of money back from the ten pounds he pays you each week for his keep. He had five pounds last week to spend going out drinking. This week he not only doesn't pay you back but he comes to ask for another loan of five pounds. You are not pleased.

Shopping around

This exercise is concerned with the skills of 'wise buying' or budgeting, and is in effect a simulation of a shopping expedition. Those taking part are asked to 'buy' a week's groceries and other provisions, to record what they have bought, and then to compare their relative purchases and expenditures.

In advance of the session, you may find it useful to prepare a number of A2 size lists of basic household commodities, together with prices for given quantities or weights, and display them around the room. Most local newspapers contain lists like this, advertising the prevailing prices in rival shops and supermarkets. If these are similar enough in their contents they can be used as they stand; if not, some modifications should be made to make the lists comparable in terms of what they include. Some members of the group should then be invited to act as shopkeepers or sales staff in various shops or markets in different parts of the room.

The rest of the participants then become 'customers' and are each 'given' a notional figure for their housekeeping money over the next week (assuming that rent and other major bills are already taken care of). Their task is to go shopping for a week's supply of food and other necessities; either for a single person living alone; for two people living together; for a family of four; or for some combination of these circumstances.

Allow ten to fifteen minutes for the shoppers to prepare their shopping lists and to go round the shops comparing prices (or not doing so as the case may be). They make their 'purchases' by writing down the names and prices of the items they have bought — until they have used up all their money or obtained everything they need.

When everyone has completed the exercise, discuss how much individuals have spent and on what; how they have allocated the money to different items; and who has shopped most effectively by identifying the cheapest or best-value items in different retail outlets. The discussion can then be widened out to shopping habits in the real world; the problems of budgeting, especially on small incomes; and the virtues of planning what to buy in advance.

To make this exercise as realistic as possible, the prices of goods should of course diverge from one shop to another. There may also be special offers, and some differences in price may be disguised by the quantities on which they are calculated.

The exercise can also be conducted in real shops by asking group members to carry out the same task in the local High Street or shopping centre, and seeing who manages to budget most successfully for one week. In addition, individuals could also be asked to undertake a local price survey, by comparing the prices of the same items in local 'corner shops', quality grocers, and supermarkets.

A money game: 'Win as much as you can'

This game, devised by Pfeiffer and Jones (1970), is designed to explore attitudes towards cooperation and competition — which it does in an amusing and often very revealing way.

The impact of the game derives from the tendency of small groups to compete rather than cooperate with each other. To play the game, you must first of all divide a group into four smaller groups of roughly equal size and ask the groups to sit in different parts of the room. Designate the groups as A, B, C, and D, and give each a copy of the 'Tally sheet' shown on pages 155 and 156.

Next, you should explain that the aim of the game is to 'Win as much as you can'. Over a series of ten rounds, each team must choose an *x* or a *y;* the pattern of wins and losses in each round is determined by the pattern of choices made. The first table on the tally sheet sets out the results when different numbers of *x*s and *y*s are chosen. You should read this out to everyone before play begins. The mechanics of the game are so simple that individuals may be confused to begin with as to what is required. All becomes clear, however, after one or two rounds have been played.

The second table on the tally sheet lists the time allocated for decision-making in each round, and also shows how choices and scores can be recorded by each group. At the beginning of each round you should announce how long it will last; at the end of it, you should collect the choices made by each group and work out the running totals of gains and losses on a board or wall sheet as follows:

	Group A	Group B	Group C	Group D
Round 1	x −£1	x −£1	x −£1	x −£1
Round 2	x −£2	x −£2	x −£2	x −£2
Round 3	x −£1	x −£1	y −£5	x −£1
Round ...				

Each round is played in the same way and the results recorded as in this example. But before rounds 5, 8, and 10, which are bonus rounds, all the groups may confer with one another for two minutes before their one-minute decision-making period. Finally, at the end of ten rounds, you arrive at a grand total for each group.

The most likely outcome is that the group as a whole will end up owing money to the 'bank' — i.e. to you; although one of the sub-groups might well have 'won' in the sense of having accumulated more money or smaller losses than the others. Often all the groups end up owing money to the bank.

Discuss with the group the implications of dividing them into smaller groups which invariably compete with one another for the lion's share of the winnings rather than cooperating with other groups so that the winnings for the total group are maximised. If all the groups vote y all the time they all win £25; £100 in total. But this outcome happens rarely if at all.

Win as much as you can — Tally sheet

Directions: For ten successive rounds you and your partner(s) will choose either an x or a y. The 'pay-off' for each round is dependent upon the pattern of choices made in the group.

4 xs	:	Lose £1.00 each
3 xs	:	Win £1.00 each
1 y	:	Lose £3.00
2 xs	:	Win £2.00 each
2 ys	:	Lose £2.00 each
1 x	:	Win £3.00
3 ys	:	Lose £1.00 each
4 ys	:	Win £1.00 each

Strategy: You are to confer with your partner(s) on each round and make a JOINT DECISION. Before rounds 5, 8, and 10 you confer with the other teams in the group.

		Strategy					
Round	Time allowed	Confer with	Choice	£ won	£ lost	£ balance	
1	2 mins.	partner(s)					
2	1 min.	partner(s)					
3	1 min.	partner(s)					
4	1 min.	partner(s)					
5	2 mins. + 1 min.	group partner(s)					Bonus round: pay-off is multiplied by 3
6	1 min.	partner(s)					
7	1 min.	partner(s)					
8	2 mins. + 1 min.	group partner(s)					Bonus round: pay-off is multiplied by 5
9	1 min.	partner(s)					
10	2 mins. + 1 min.	group partner(s)					Bonus round: pay-off is multiplied by 10

Finding and developing further materials on 'money'

Although there are copious quantities of information in circulation on the subject of money, little of it is cast in a form that makes it suitable for use with young people on the verge of leaving school or recently left. Books on how to fill in your tax returns or maximise your share interests; advice on where to invest in life assurance; consumer information about saloon cars or expensive 'white goods' like split-level cookers or deep freeze chests are all very absorbing for adults, but not very relevant to the average unemployed seventeen-year-old.

The remedy, as in other areas where there may not be sufficient ready-made material to hand, is to invent your own, adapted to the special needs of the groups or individuals with whom you are working.

A Money Simulation: 'Shopping around' on page 153 is a simple money simulation which looks at one aspect of weekly expenditure — buying groceries. It is not however difficult to construct a more complex financial environment which approximates to some other aspect of the real world. We have not included such a simulation here because the specific details need to reflect the needs, circumstances and spending habits of those whom you invite to play it.

The basic ingredients for a money simulation are: (1) a set of characters whose descriptions can range from one word (e.g. shop assistant, factory worker, bus driver, unemployed YOP trainee) to a detailed role briefing setting out a range of domestic circumstances and prior financial commitments; and (2) a number of outlets where participants can spend their money. Each character is credited with so much per week — which can be given out as pieces of paper to imitate banknotes (like Monopoly money). The outlets can include supermarkets, clothes shops, banks, pubs, betting shops or any others which might reflect the spending habits of those taking part. The spenders should keep a note of their income and outgoings and the outlets a record of the sales or transactions they make. You can then see which of the consumers ends up best off at the end.

The number of spenders and outlets in this kind of simulation can be varied to suit the size of group with whom you are working; the amount of time available; the level of incomes provided; and the interests of participants. Rules can also be introduced, e.g. to regulate minimum amounts of spending. This basic format can be elaborated to any desired degree of complexity; and can form a prelude to the use of some business games (such as those provided by the Careers Research and Advisory Centre).

Some useful sources of ideas for exercises concerned with money will be found in: H.M. Dobinson (1976), *Basic Skills You Need,* Nelson. Clocktower Project: *The Money Pack,* obtainable from The Clocktower Young Adults Project, Tower Road North, Warmley, Bristol BS15 2XU. H. Turner (1979), *The Consumers' A—Z. Your Guide to Personal Consumption,* Windward. A. Williams (1975), *Educating the Consumer: a practical guide,* Longmans. Consumers' Association (1979), *Consumer Education, a resource handbook for teachers,* published by the Consumers' Association and Hodder and Stoughton. Both this and the preceding book are very useful sources for work in schools. Scottish Community Education Centre: *Money Matters* Programme Kit, available from the Scottish Community Education Centre, 4 Queensferry Street, Edinburgh EH2 4PA. On consumer rights see: Consumers' Association (1978), *The Buyer's Right,* (compiled by P. Petch and D. Holloway), published by the Consumers' Association and the Open University.

RIGHTS

Introduction

To achieve many goals in present-day society, individuals must act through the medium of large-scale institutions. The laws which govern such institutions and their relations with the public become more and more complex every parliamentary session. To negotiate our way through the maze of modern bureaucracy requires a firm grasp of the laws which affect our lives, and a skill in asserting ourselves in many situations in which the law is irritatingly vague. More and more often, individuals and the institutions which are allegedly there to serve their interests seem to be at odds with one another; and conflict over the status of individual rights has become steadily more common as the law has continued to extend its influence into almost every area of life.

For young people, the difficulties posed by the bureaucratic obstacle-course are exacerbated by the ambivalence of the law towards the age of onset of adulthood. From all sides, the teenager is urged to behave more like an adult: seduced by advertisers into spending, and admonished by parents into acting, always like someone older than he actually is. Although the official 'age of majority' is 18, the acquisition of various kinds of adult freedoms and responsibilities (with their accompanying penalties) takes place in a step-by-step fashion.

At 14,	for example, a young person can go into a bar and play dominoes or cribbage, but not drink; can enter a court to observe a criminal trial; and can go to the cinema to see an AA film;
At 15,	a young person may be given a shotgun as a gift – and may be sent to borstal;
At 16,	young people are free to leave school, leave home, get a job, get married, claim supplementary benefit, and buy wine with a meal in a restaurant;
At 17,	individuals can obtain a driving licence (though not to drive buses), can enter a betting shop (but not bet) – and can be sent to prison;
At 18,	an individual is now free to drink in public houses, vote in elections, open a bank account, buy things on HP, and go to the cinema to see an X-certificate film.

After leaving school, then, the individual is possessed of some rights, but not of others; and, if unemployed, will have to find a path through the jungle of welfare law – and perhaps become an object of interest to the custodians of the criminal law. To keep afloat financially and remain on the right side of the law may not be easy under circumstances such as these. To secure rights and fulfil the associated responsibilities, the individual will need three things.

First, information will be needed on rights, on how the law operates and affects daily life. Second, a set of attitudes will be required which will make the individual inclined to pursue his own rights while at the same time respecting those of others. And third, to apply these facts and attitudes to his own life in an appropriate way, the individual will need a number of life skills, particularly of communication and assertiveness.

The materials which follow are designed to help young people prepare for life after school by equipping themselves with some of the information, attitudes, and skills they will need in the business of obtaining their rights. But the word 'rights' has several meanings; and it is used here with three specific areas in mind. The first is welfare rights, which may be crucially important to the unemployed; the second includes those rights which are affected by the criminal law, which may be of concern to those who have broken the law or who are in danger of doing so; and the third is the area, slightly more difficult to define, of 'everyday rights' — of those implicit yet pervasive moral rules which underpin our everyday dealings with others.

The exercises described here therefore begin with the informational aspect of rights, and include:

1. Rights quiz — for informal assessment of knowledge about rights;
2. A guide to speakers and other sources of information about rights.

Following this, there are two ideas for sessions on the attitudes which young people bring to bear on rights in everyday life:

3. Attitudes questionnaire on rights in some common situations;
4. 'Who's right?' — resolving everyday moral dilemmas.

Next, are a number of exercises for examining and practising the skills involved in negotiating rights issues:

5. Information search — exercises for developing the skills of asking questions and finding information for oneself;
6. Structured roleplays of encounters in which rights are at stake;
7. Putting your case: exercises in self-presentation, communication and assertiveness.

Finally, there are some composite exercises which incorporate aspects of all of the above:

8. Rights projects — large-scale exercises deploying a number of skills;
9. A simulation: 'Parliament'.

Rights quiz

It has been estimated that, every year, approximately £300 million in welfare benefits is left untapped by those who are entitled to claim it. While some individuals recoil from claiming their rights for a variety of personal reasons, there can be no doubt that the prime reason for the failure of most people to take up unclaimed benefit is sheer ignorance of their entitlements; this has been confirmed by a number of surveys (e.g. Casserley and Clark, 1978). Information, then, is a key element in problem-solving in the rights area. This is true not only in relation to welfare rights, but also in dealing with other problems with which we may be confronted — for example if we buy defective goods or are stopped by a policeman in the street. A more thorough knowledge of the law is an invaluable asset in many spheres of life.

It can be useful, then, to help those who are about to leave school, or who have just left, to find out more about the law and how it applies to them. A reasonable starting-point in doing this is to try to establish how much young people know already. If done well, this can in itself provide a strong inducement to remedy their lack of awareness by finding out more. An entertaining way of setting this process in motion is to make use of some kind of quiz.

The running of a quiz allows individuals to assess their own level of knowledge in an informal, game-like way — as far removed from the examination format as possible. Having almost certainly seen quiz programmes on TV, most young people are familiar with the idea; and many who shudder with fear at the thought of an exam will cheerfully participate in a quiz — even though their purposes are almost identical.

Quizzes can therefore be organised along the lines of any of the well-known TV quiz shows. Teams can be formed to compete against each other, as in 'University Challenge'; or individuals can be put in the hot seat on their own, as in 'Mastermind'. One group member can be appointed as quiz-master, another to keep track of the scores. Heats can be organised to discover the overall 'Rights Brain of Britain'.

Three quizzes are presented here: the first a general one covering a wide area of rights; the second dealing specifically with welfare rights; and the third focussing particularly on questions associated with the criminal law. The questions of which they are composed are of two types: some consist of statements which individuals have to describe as true or false; others are 'multiple-choice' items where the correct answer has to be chosen from five possibles. Each quiz is followed by a list of answers, with some additional information on the point being discussed, and a reference is given where further information can be found. The items included here are only a selection from many that could be employed, and users of these exercises would be well encouraged to devise their own questions to supplement, or replace, the ones given here. This is advisable if for no other reason than that the law is in a process of continuous change; the sources used for compiling these items may soon be out of date.

A rights quiz could obviously be used as a straightforward questionnaire; but the TV game approach may be more attractive for groups of young people. Either way, to get the most out of a quiz, it is worthwhile having available a supply of leaflets or pamphlets which illuminate the various points mentioned. For greater impact, an 'expert' could be invited along from one of the many agencies which are concerned with aspects of rights. And a more thorough knowledge of rights could be cultivated by asking young people to undertake some kind of information search or project on rights. Suggestions as to how all these other exercises may be mounted are given in subsequent sections.

You and the law

A quiz on your rights

Part 1 — TRUE or FALSE?

Below are some statements about your rights in a variety of situations. Your job is to decide which of the statements are TRUE and which are FALSE. Put a ring round your answer at the right-hand side.

1. If an employer wants to dismiss you, he can give you wages instead of notice.   TRUE   FALSE

2. You cannot claim redundancy payments unless you are at least 18 years of age.   TRUE   FALSE

3. A shop does not have to give you money back for faulty goods if it displays a sign saying 'No Refunds Given'.   TRUE   FALSE

4. If you look for rented accommodation through an agency they can charge you a fee whether you decide to take the accommodation or not.   TRUE   FALSE

5. If you are under 16, the Education Authority can stop you from working outside school hours if they think it is interfering with your education.   TRUE   FALSE

6. Your Local Education Authority must give you a grant if you obtain a place at a Further Education College.   TRUE   FALSE

7. A policeman who stops you while you are driving a car or motorbike is not allowed to check your licence to see if you have any endorsements.   TRUE   FALSE

8. If you are aged 16 or 17, your parents have a right to any information you give your doctor.   TRUE   FALSE

9. Before you can have a legal abortion, you must have the approval of three doctors.   TRUE   FALSE

10. An employer cannot dismiss you for joining a trade union.   TRUE   FALSE

Part 2 — Which is correct?

The next part of the quiz is different. Here are some statements; you have to decide which of five possible answers is the correct one for each statement. Put a ring round your answer.

1. You cannot sign an HP agreement unless you are aged at least:
   16   17   18   20   21

2. If you had been working in a job for 12 months, an employer who wanted to dismiss you would have to give you notice. The minimum period of notice he would have to give you is:
   24 hours   3 days   one week   two weeks   28 days

3. The gas board can cut off supplies of gas if a bill is not paid within:
   7 days   14 days   21 days   28 days   3 months

4. You can make a small claim in the county court if the amount of money involved is not more than:
   £50   £100   £200   £250   £500

5. If you are sent goods you did not order, you can keep them if they have still not been collected after:
   7 days   28 days   3 months   6 months   1 year

6. Under most circumstances, you cannot get a divorce unless you have been married at least:
   6 months   1 year   2 years   3 years   5 years

7. When you sign an HP agreement you must be given or sent a copy of it within 7 days. After that there is a 'cooling-off' period in which you can change your mind about buying the goods. This period is:
   3 days   7 days   10 days   14 days   28 days

8. The amount of alcohol in your blood is measured in terms of milligrams of alcohol per 100 millilitres of blood (mg%). The upper legal limit of blood alcohol for someone driving a car or motorbike is:
   60 mg%   80 mg%   100 mg%   120 mg%   150 mg%

9. A landlord or landlady who wants you to leave rented accommodation must give you advance notice of at least:
   48 hours   3 days   7 days   two weeks   four weeks

10. It is illegal to sound the horn of a vehicle in a built-up area after a certain time of night. This time is:
    6.00 p.m.   7.30 p.m.   9.00 p.m.   11.30 p.m.   12.00 midnight

Rights quiz answers

You and the law (general rights quiz)

The answers to the general rights quiz 'You and the Law' are given below; answers for the other quizzes on welfare and legal rights are given following each quiz. Where it was thought useful, the answers have been slightly elaborated upon to clarify the points at issue. In compiling the items for these quizzes, several sources were used; and page references following each item indicate where further information on the issue may be found. The abbreviations used in the references are as follows:

(1) NCCL = *Civil Liberty, the NCCL Guide to Your Rights*, Penguin, 1978
(2) SBH   = *Supplementary Benefits Handbook*, HMSO.
(3) CA   = *Dismissal, Redundancy and Job Hunting*, Consumers' Association, 1976 (edited by E. Rudinger).

You and the law Part 1: TRUE or FALSE?

1. *TRUE*   An employer can give you wages and ask you to leave immediately (NCCL, p.199). Further, you cannot draw unemployment benefit until the period of notice is up (CA, p.54).

2. *TRUE*   Under the Redundancy Payments Act there is an age limitation such that you cannot draw redundancy payments unless you have been working for the same employer for at least two years since your 18th birthday (see NCCL, p.201, CA, p.7).

3. *FALSE*   Under the Sale of Goods Act 1893 and the Supply of Goods (Implied Terms) Act 1973 goods that you buy must be of merchantable quality, i.e. suited to the purpose for which they are intended. If they are not you can insist on having your money back and no advertisement in any shop can legally stop you doing so (NCCL, p.214).

4. *FALSE*   An accommodation agency can only charge you a fee for finding you a place to live if you actually decide to live there (NCCL, p.452).

5. *TRUE*   A Local Education Authority can find out from parents or employers about any part-time work being done by someone under 16 and has the right to stop them doing it if they think it may adversely affect the individual's schooling (NCCL, p.435).

6. *FALSE*   An LEA can refuse a grant under various conditions, e.g. if it considers that someone is unfit to receive it (NCCL, p.438).

7. *TRUE*   The police can stop any vehicle and ask to see the driver's licence, insurance and MOT certificates, etc, but are not allowed to check licences to see if there are any endorsements (NCCL, p.163).

8. *FALSE*   Parents have no right to information given to doctors by individuals aged over 16 but under 18. However, a doctor could pass on such information to parents if he thought it was in the individual's best interests (NCCL, p.469).

9. *FALSE*   An abortion can be carried out legally if it is thought necessary by *two* doctors, or by *one* doctor in exceptional circumstances (NCCL, p.174).

10. *TRUE*   Dismissal of an employee because he or she is a member of a trade union is unfair dismissal (Employment Protection Act 1975). However, the onus rests on the employee to show that this was the genuine reason for dismissal (NCCL, p.200; CA, p.15).

Part 2: Which is correct?

1. *18*   Strictly speaking, although someone under 18 can sign a contract, the contract will not be legally binding (NCCL, p.370). Many retailers ask for guarantors even for those aged between 18 and 21.

2. *One week* An employee is entitled to one week's notice if he or she has worked for four weeks or more — and additional amounts of notice if for more than two years (NCCL, p.199).

3. *28 days*   The gas board must however give 7 days' notice (NCCL, p.224).

4. *£200*   You can sue a trader for money you have lost, e.g. through faulty goods, provided the amount lost does not exceed £200. (NCCL, p.228).

5. *6 months* After this period you can keep the goods or sell them (NCCL, p.213).

6. *3 years*   In exceptional cases, people can obtain divorces sooner than this however (NCCL, p.348).

7. *3 days*   If you do change your mind within this period you have to inform the HP company and return the goods (NCCL, p.222).

8. *80 mg%*   (NCCL, p.160). Blood alcohol above this level can be detected using the breathalyser test. Most people's blood alcohol would rise to this level after two or three drinks (whiskies or pints of beer).

9. *4 weeks*   Notice to quit rented accommodation must be in writing and must allow a minimum of four weeks before the tenant is expected to leave. Even then the tenant cannot be forced to leave without a court order (NCCL, p.456).

10. *11.30 pm* (NCCL, p.162).

Survival

A quiz on welfare rights

This quiz is designed to help you find out how much you know about your entitlement to different kinds of benefits. In some of the questions you have to decide whether a statement is true or false; in others you have to find the correct answer from several alternatives that are given. In each case, put a ring round the answer you have chosen.

1. You cannot obtain unemployment benefit unless you register yourself as available for work at your local Job Centre.   TRUE   FALSE

2. If you lose your job through misconduct, or leave it voluntarily without just cause, you will not be entitled to benefit for up to:
   2 weeks   4 weeks   6 weeks   10 weeks   6 months

3. You can draw supplementary benefit from the age of:
   15   16   17   18   21

4. Child benefit can be paid to the parents of those who are in full-time education until they reach the age of:
   15   16   17   18   19

5. If a man and a woman live together, the woman cannot claim supplementary benefit for herself.   TRUE   FALSE

6. The local authority can only help you out with your rent if you live in council accommodation   TRUE   FALSE

7. You can claim supplementary benefit if you are studying part-time, as long as the number of hours per week you study is not more than:
   8 hours   16 hours   21 hours   24 hours   30 hours

8. If you are receiving supplementary benefit you can claim additional allowances for a number of things. Which of the following items can you *not* claim for?

| prescription charges and glasses | down-payments to buy things on HP | clothes for starting work | expenses to attend interviews for jobs | expense of moving to a a job in another area |

9. Once you find a job, you can no longer receive supplementary benefit.   TRUE   FALSE

10. If you disagree with a decision made by your supplementary benefit office you can appeal against it. But you must appeal within a certain time limit. The time limit is:

7 days   10 days   15 days   21 days   28 days

Survival quiz answers

1. *TRUE*   You cannot receive either unemployment benefit or supplementary benefit until you register as available for work (NCCL, p.405, SBH, p.51).

2. *6 weeks*   This is known as the 'six-week rule' (NCCL, p.405-6). It can also apply if you are unemployed and refuse the offer of a job which the Department of Employment thinks it reasonable for you to take.

3. *16*   You can't, however, usually draw benefit if you are still at school, or if you leave school early and claim during term-time (SBH, p.4).

4. *19*   (NCCL, p.411-12). If a child leaves school at 16, however, the benefit is no longer paid.

5. *TRUE*   This is part of what are known as the 'cohabitation rules' (NCCL, p.350). A man and woman living together are treated as if they were married (SBH, p.7).

6. *FALSE*   Just as people who live in council houses can claim rent rebates, those living in privately rented accommodation can claim rent allowances or can have an amount paid towards their rent, depending on their income and other considerations (NCCL, p.418).

7. *21 hours*   As long as you are registered as unemployed and are willing to take a job if one arises, you can study for up to 21 hours a week and still claim supplementary benefit (see leaflet NP/12: School leavers and students: what you pay and what you get, supplied by DHSS).

8. *Down-payments to buy items on HP.*   Supplementary benefit is not usually paid for items which would involve a long-term commitment (SCH, p.31). All the other items on this list could however be claimed.

9. *FALSE*   If someone who is unemployed finds work, they can claim supplementary benefit to cover the period until they receive their first wage packet (Leaflet NP/12).

10. *21 days*   In exceptional circumstances, the chairman of a Supplementary Benefits Appeal Tribunal can accept appeals after 21 days if he sees good reason to do so (SBH, p.62).

Trouble

A quiz on legal rights

This quiz is designed to help you find out how much you know about how to keep out of trouble with the law. In some of the questions you have to decide whether a statement is true or false; in others you have to find the correct answer from a number of alternatives that are given. In each case, put a ring round the answer you have chosen.

1. The police can arrest you if you refuse to give your
   name and address.   TRUE   FALSE

2. You cannot be arrested by a store detective.   TRUE   FALSE

3. A man can be prosecuted for living with a 17-year-old
   girl.   TRUE   FALSE

4. As long as you are aged 17, you can go into a betting
   shop and make bets.   TRUE   FALSE

5. You cannot go to see an X-certificate film until you are:
   16   17   18   20   21

6. The police can stop and search you if they think you
   may be carrying drugs.   TRUE   FALSE

7. If your driving licence is endorsed, endorsements
   usually remain in effect for:
   1 year   3 years   5 years   10 years   the rest of your life

8. When someone aged between 14 and 17 is arrested, they
   can be kept in custody if the police believe they will not
   turn up in court.   TRUE   FALSE

9. People under a certain age cannot be sent to prison.
   This age is:
   17   18   19   20   21

10. An identification parade must contain a minimum
    number of people. This number is:
    6   8   12   15   20

11. You cannot be asked to do jury service until you are
    21 years of age.   TRUE   FALSE

12. In which kind of court are most offences dealt with?
    Juvenile   Magistrate's   Crown   High   County
    Court   Court   Court   Court   Court

Trouble quiz answers

1. *TRUE*   In many situations, the police have the power to arrest you if you refuse to give your name and address; in particular, when they have reasonable grounds that you may have committed some kind of offence. Failure to give your name and address will often make a policeman more suspicious of you (NCCL, pp.22-6).

2. *FALSE*   A detective in a department store can arrest people he suspects of shoplifting, if something has been stolen or he thinks they tried to steal something (NCCL, p.42). This is an example of 'citizen's arrest'.

3. *TRUE*   Although a girl can legally have sex after she is 16, until she is 18 a man who lived with her without her parents' consent would be breaking the law (NCCL, p.172).

4. *FALSE*   Although you can enter a betting shop at the age of 17, you cannot make bets until you are 18 (NCCL, p.371).

5. *18*   This is not actually enforceable by law — i.e. someone under 18 cannot be prosecuted for seeing an X film. Under local byelaws, however, cinema managers could be prosecuted for allowing this to happen (NCCL, p.371).

6. *TRUE*   This can happen under the Misuse of Drugs Act 1971 (NCCL, p.168).

7. *3 years*   You can be disqualified from driving if your licence is endorsed 3 times within 3 years (NCCL, p.162). Some endorsements for more serious traffic offences last for 10 years.

8. *TRUE*   Bail (being allowed to go free until a court appearance) can be refused if the police believe a youth will not come to court (NCCL, p.52).

9. *17*   However, young people between 14 and 21 can be sent to detention centre, and those between 15 and 21 can be sent to Borstal (NCCL, pp.368, 98).

10. *8*   With one suspect, there must be at least 8 people of similar age and size; with two suspects, there should be at least 12 people (NCCL, p.61).

11. *FALSE*   You can be asked to do jury service after the age of 18 (NCCL, p.91).

12. *Magistrates' Court.*   These courts deal with most offences involving people aged 17 and above, and also with such issues as the custody of children when parents are being divorced. *Juvenile Courts* deal with offenders under the age of 17; *Crown Courts* deal with serious offences; *High Courts* deal with civil (non-criminal) cases and with appeals; and *County Courts* also deal with local civil disputes.

Directory of speakers and sources of information

Information is in some ways more important to the solving of rights problems than to the solving of problems in any other area. Many books have been written on rights, and there is also a certain amount of educational material available, though the latter is surprisingly limited at present. Some useful books and materials are listed on page 186.

You can however obtain a lot of information direct from those agencies who are concerned with rights issues (and in fact it is advisable to do so since laws, and amounts given in benefits, frequently change). And a session on rights can be made still more useful by asking along an 'expert' who can answer questions on rights. The guidelines below are divided into three sections: general sources of information that are available nationally; other agencies which may be able to provide speakers or 'experts'; and more specialised sources which can provide information on particular topics but which have few local offices.

1. *General.* A lot of rights information is available in leaflet or booklet form from the local post office, unemployment benefit office, social security office, and town, district, or county hall. The local authority Social Services Department can also be a source of help; many authorities employ Welfare Rights Officers who specialise in helping people with their problems in this field, and whose job it is to disseminate information about rights. On other aspects of rights, the police may be able to help, and may be willing to provide police officers who deal specifically with community issues or with the relationship between the police and young people.

2. To obtain someone who may be willing to talk and be asked questions on particular aspects of rights, there are a number of other possibilities (which are also worth visiting in any case for the information they can provide):

Advice Centres: many areas have community advice centres, sometimes run by the local authority and in other cases run by voluntary organisations. They can give advice on many aspects of the law which affect young people, in relation to social security, accommodation, the police, and so on.

Citizens' Advice Bureaux: there is now a very widespread network of these, with several hundred in operation including some that are mobile. Most are staffed by volunteers but some employ professional workers such as solicitors or social workers. They can provide information of most kinds in relation to rights and can also help people take action on rights problems they are faced with.

Child Poverty Action Group: this is a pressure group which tries to influence government policy on provision for families with children; it has branches in many areas and also operates a Citizens' Rights Office which can supply information (and experts) on welfare benefits and associated problems.

Claimants' Unions: these are also pressure groups, organised on a self-help basis, who advise social security claimants and have branches in many parts of the country.

Consumer Advice Centres: these are run by local authorities in many areas, and aim to supply information and advice on any aspect of the law which affects us as consumers. They can be of help in making complaints about unsatisfactory goods, for example; and are also useful sources for information about local prices, as they conduct their own surveys of these.

Family Planning Association: this is a voluntary organisation which is mainly concerned with giving advice and information about sex education and birth control; but it can also supply information on rights problems which may arise in connection with issues such as abortion (a number of other organisations also do this, and are mentioned in the references following 'Meeting the opposite sex').

Housing Advice Centres: these are run by local authorities in many areas for the purpose of dispensing information and advice on housing problems.

Law Centres: these are jointly funded by the government and local authorities; as yet however there are only twenty-odd in the country. They supply not only information and advice on most aspects of the law, but also actual legal services (there is usually at least one lawyer on the staff).

3. Although it may be more difficult to obtain 'experts' actually to come and talk to a group from the following organisations, nevertheless they can supply a great deal of rights information in the area with which they deal; and some have regional or affiliated offices in various parts of the country. The headquarters addresses of these and other bodies are given at the end of the book.

On rights in general: the National Council of Civil Liberties;
On rights at work: the Equal Opportunities Commission; the Commission for Racial Equality; the Advisory, Conciliation, and Arbitration Service;
On consumer rights: the Consumers' Association; the Office of Fair Trading; the Advertising Standards Authority;
On other 'minority group' problems: Minority Rights Group; Campaign for Homosexual Equality; Release (for information on drugs offences).

Everyday rights

An attitudes questionnaire on the rights of young people

Apart from our legal rights — those rights which are embodied in official statutes or decreed by judges in court — we also have other rights which play an important part in our everyday behaviour. These are the social norms which influence the way we deal with other people and lead us to expect certain things in return. Not surprisingly, however, given that these are vague and ill-defined, they can be a source of conflict between people — since their expectations of each other can often be dramatically different.

The situation with regard to the rights of young people is particularly confused. Not only do different adults and teenagers have divergent views on what is right at different stages of adolescence; but also the attitude of society as a whole to the young changes slowly, but markedly, over time. Yet the attitudes which an individual absorbs during adolescence have an important formative influence on those he or she will adopt during adulthood.

The questionnaire on the next page contains a series of statements which are designed to:

1. help young people assess their views of their rights in some everyday situations;
2. lead to debate and discussion on the issues involved, with the aim of helping individuals to clarify their own attitudes;
3. where necessary, provide a basis for closer examination of attitudes through counselling or other means.

The questions could also be used to carry out an attitude 'survey' — for example by seeking the views of other concerned parties (e.g. friends, parents, relatives) on some of the issues raised.

The questionnaire can be distributed to members of a group and a discussion held after they have all completed it. Alternatively, one question can be taken at a time and used as the basis for group discussion.

Everyday rights

The statements below are about issues on which you might have strong feelings or opinions. On the right-hand side, you are asked to say whether you agree or disagree with each statement, and if so how strongly. Think about each statement in turn, and put a tick or a cross in the box which expresses your viewpoint.

	Strongly agree	Agree slightly	Don't know	Disagree slightly	Strongly disagree
1. Young people should be free to leave home when they want to					
2. Young people should be free to choose whom they mix with.					
3. You are more likely to get your way with people if you're polite to them.					
4. You should always tell your parents where you're going when you go out.					
5. Young people should be *given* pocket money so that they can learn how to handle money.					
6. In return for pocket money, young people should do work for their parents at home.					
7. As soon as they can, young people should bring in wages to help their parents.					
8. Until they are 18, young people should do what adults tell them.					
9. Young people should be able to wear what they like.					
10. You should spend most of your spare time with your family.					
11. Unless it's serious, young people who break the law should be dealt with at home.					
12. Young people should play a part in making decisions which affect the whole family.					
13. People should be told the facts of life before they are 12 years of age.					
14. Your parents have a right to know about your personal problems.					
15. Young people should have a say in what is taught in school or college.					
16. It should be against the law for parents to strike their children.					
17. Young people should be free to stay out as late as they like.					
18. Girls and boys should do the same kind of work at home.					
19. Young people have as much right to privacy as their parents.					
20. You should be free to bring your friends home whenever you like.					

'Who's right?'

Rights and decisions

A questionnaire like that on the previous page can be a useful tool in looking at the views of individuals on their 'rights' in their everyday dealings with others. Another way of approaching the same topic is to present people with a series of problems they have to solve, or decisions they have to make, which touch on their beliefs as to what is right. This is the domain of moral education. One method which has proven very valuable in exploring and developing the moral views of young people is that in which they are asked to resolve some kind of dilemma — to make a decision where two or more factors may be pulling them in different directions.

The exercise below consists of a series of dilemmas of this kind. A set of possible answers is given for each, but the dilemmas can be presented without these.

As with the preceding exercise, the items in this questionnaire can be used singly, as a stimulus to group discussion and decision-making, or used as a complete questionnaire and discussed after everyone has gone through the whole exercise. Either way, an aim of the discussion should be to try to tease out what people consider to be the 'rules' that are operating in any given case. In addition, it might be useful to ask whether the situation presents a simple conflict between one's own interests and someone else's, or whether it is a conflict between different ideas about how you should treat other people.

Dilemmas

The items below describe a number of tricky situations you might have experienced. After each one, there is a list of different things you might do about the problem in question. Think about each one, and try to decide which course of action you would take, and *why*. Put a mark beside the one you would take. If you decide on the last choice "none of these", think about what you *would* do instead.

1. You have lent some money to a couple you know fairly well. They haven't yet paid you back and you know they're quite badly off at the moment. Just the same you could do with the money yourself. Would you —
   (a) Put pressure on them to return the money?
   (b) Drop hints about the money indirectly?
   (c) Avoid mentioning it?
   (d) Ask them when they think they'll be able to pay you?
   (e) None of these?

2. Someone you don't particularly like confided something personal in you. A friend asks you what you were told. Would you —
   (a) Tell your friend?
   (b) Keep it to yourself?
   (c) Tell everybody?
   (d) None of these?

3. You have recently become quite friendly with someone, and you invite him round to your house. You mention this to your mother who has heard about the person and doesn't want him to come. Would you —
   (a) Go and tell your friend you have to change your plans?
   (b) Try to persuade your mother she should be friendly to the person?
   (c) Let the person come and risk some unpleasantness?
   (d) None of these?

4. When you go for a drink in a cafe or a bar, one of your friends never seems to buy though she accepts drinks from everybody else. Do you think you would —
   (a) Stop buying her drinks but say nothing?
   (b) Put it to her that they should pay their share?
   (c) Ask someone else to talk to her about it?
   (d) Start avoiding the person?
   (e) None of these?

5. While a friend of yours is away you see his or her boyfriend (or girlfriend) out with someone else. Would you —
   (a) Go and talk to him/her to make it obvious you knew?
   (b) Tell your friend when they came back?
   (c) Not think twice about it?
   (d) Tell another friend and try to decide what to do?
   (e) None of these?

6. You see a parent hitting a child in the street. The child is wailing but the parent goes on hitting. Would you —
   (a) Look the other way?
   (b) Shout at the parent to stop?
   (c) Fetch a policeman?
   (d) None of these?

7. After you told somebody something in trust, it turns out that she then told someone else. Would you —
   (a) Go and complain to her about it?
   (b) Say nothing but keep away from the person?
   (c) Tell other people not to confide in the person?
   (d) None of these?

8. Sometimes in the evenings you hear loud screams coming from your next door neighbour's house. Would you —
   (a)   Ignore them?
   (b)   Go and knock on the door to see what was happening?
   (c)   Tell the police?
   (d)   Try to get your parents to do something about it?
   (e)   None of these?

9. You lent someone a record and he lost it or broke it. Would you —
   (a)   Insist that he pays for it?
   (b)   Forget about it this time, but never lend him anything else?
   (c)   None of these?

10. You know that a friend of yours recently stole a bicycle. The police come to question you about it. They ask questions about you and your friend. Would you —
   (a)   Tell them your friend did it?
   (b)   Deny all knowledge?
   (c)   Make up a story to put them off?
   (d)   Insist you didn't steal the bicycle and that your friend could speak for himself (or herself)?
   (e)   None of these?

11. A friend of yours wants to do something that you know is completely beyond her. She is talking a lot about it. Would you —
   (a)   Tell her not to be so unrealistic?
   (b)   Let her find out for herself?
   (c)   Try to interest her in something else?
   (d)   None of these?

12 Walking along the street you see your little brother or sister running out of a shop with some sweets. The shopkeeper runs after him/her but gives up. Would you —
   (a)   Tell the shopkeeper you would get the sweets back?
   (b)   Tell your parents about it?
   (c)   Talk to your brother or sister about it?
   (d)   Keep quiet about it?
   (e)   None of these?

Information search

Whether our problem is getting a job, finding a place to live, discovering things to do in our spare time, estimating how much we can save, planning a holiday abroad, or getting married — we will always manage to solve it more easily if we are in possession of the relevant facts. This may be particularly important in coping with problems in which rights are involved; for although it affects nearly every aspect of our lives, most people's knowledge of the law is limited to a few rafts of fact floating on a sea of conjecture.

Not only are most people unaware of the facts, but they are also equally unsure of how they would go about finding them if called upon to do so. But the ability to find things out for oneself is one of the most valuable we can ever learn. Information-search exercises are designed to help foster the development of this ability.

'Information searches' can be organised in a great many ways; but they all have two common and interconnected aims:

1. To help individuals acquire specific items of information they may need for solving a problem; and
2. To help individuals acquire the skill of finding information for themselves.

The simplest kind of information search can be mounted by asking members of a group just to amass as much information as possible, from any available source, that might be relevant to a topic in which they are interested.

If for example young people were interested in collecting facts on welfare rights, an exercise could be launched, lasting perhaps for a half-day, in which they visited all the places where rights information can be obtained — such as the post office, social security office, or citizens' advice bureau. Individuals might split up into pairs or trios and visit one or two places each. Their job would then be to bring back to the classroom, college or youth centre all the material that is available free in leaflet or booklet form. To make this material more accessible, it could then be organised into an information 'bank' on rights, with all the items dealing with one particular topic grouped together.

An exercise like this serves both to collect the information that might be needed for solving one problem on a particular day, and to demonstrate to young people that they can go and find a lot of things out merely by doing a 'round trip' of various information sources. But a great deal of information is not available in this form; it resides in the heads of the 'experts', and has to be elicited from them by asking appropriate questions.

A more elaborate information search can therefore be set up in which individuals have to ask questions of an invited speaker (perhaps drawn from the list on p.169), or to go out and conduct fact-finding interviews with suppliers of information on rights, e.g. in a citizens' advice bureau, advice centre, consumer advice centre, law centre, or housing aid centre. Where possible they might tape-record or video-record these interviews, to show back to others or to keep for future reference. Discussion might focus not only on the actual content of the interviews, i.e. the information itself, but also on how good people were at asking questions, listening, having points elucidated or clarified, and covering all the points they wished to cover. If necessary, the skills of fact-finding could also be practised in additional roleplays or projects.

Roleplay can in fact be used to rehearse situations in which individuals will be asked questions and in which it will be to their advantage to ask questions themselves. For any situation of this kind, a short-list of questions can be drawn up, and then the encounter roleplayed to see whether individuals remember to ask the questions, the way they do so, whether they pursue unclear or evasive replies, and so on.

The skills of information search are applicable in many situations other than those in which rights are involved, and to help people develop these skills, different kinds of exercises can be used. In some cases these need to be linked to instruction, e.g. on how to use a telephone directory, how to use a library, or how to read a map. In other cases they may form part of a more complex project, e.g. where information is gathered for a survey.

Some suggestions for information search exercises, graded roughly from the simpler to the more complex, are given below; these deal principally, though not exclusively, with rights.

Information search exercises

1. Ask students either:
   (a) to bring back some information on a selected topic that is of interest to them, from a book in the local library; or
   (b) to look up a set of numbers in the telephone directory; e.g. of the local DHSS office, Citizens' Advice Bureau, bus or railway station, cinema, etc.

2. Individuals could be asked to make short telephone calls to find information of some sort: e.g. the times of buses or trains to somewhere; whether there are any tickets left for a rock concert; or concerning some aspect of rights (by ringing the DHSS, CAB, Consumer Advice Centre, or other appropriate place).

3. An information search can be organised by asking individuals — working alone or in twos or threes — to go to a list of local sources and collect all the free printed information that is available. This could be tried first on a topic such as leisure (e.g. visiting the town hall to find out about local sports facilities), and then repeated for other areas like work, accommodation, or rights. Alternatively, just plunge straight into one of the latter.

4. The process of finding information by asking others can be practised in some roleplay exercises; these can be organised with varying degrees of structure:

   (a) The group can be divided up into pairs; in each pair, each member has to find out as much as possible about the other on some pre-selected topic, e.g. hobbies, favourite foods, favourite bands etc. — or by asking questions on something the person knows about; individuals then report to the group as a whole.

   (b) This can be given more structure by making one person in each pair an 'expert' on some topic. Give the experts a pre-arranged set of ten points of information on a given subject. Their interviewers have then to try to ask questions on the topic which will elicit all the information the 'experts' possess. This could be made more lively by suggesting that the interviews are part of a TV documentary; and if possible recording them on video. The 'experts' then report on how searching the interviewers were with their questions.

   (c) The same exercise can also be carried out by asking group members themselves to generate points of information, and sets of questions, prior to the interviews — by first of all working separately in 'expert' and 'interviewer' groups.

5. Students can be asked to apply their information-finding skill by carrying out interviews with 'real' experts on rights. Working singly, or in twos or threes, group members have to visit some of the places listed on p.169 and ask a series of questions. The questions to be asked could be formulated by the whole group in advance; and the interview replies could be written down, tape-recorded, or video-taped if a machine is available. The group then re-assembles and individuals report back on what they have found out, playing back any taped materials they have produced. Finally the whole exercise is discussed and the value of different sources of information is appraised.

6. Finally, more ambitious information-search exercises can be conducted which form part of a larger project; a list of suggestions for doing this is given on p.183. As far as information on rights is concerned, topics for projects might include:

   (a) Finding out how a court, tribunal, or other agency works;

   (b) Finding out how the laws of other countries differ from our own, especially in relation to the rights of young people;

   (c) Compiling a report on the statistics of crime, e.g. by using libraries, visiting the local police station, courts, etc.

   (d) Preparing a report on a major issue connected with rights, e.g. torture, official secrets, immigration, drugs, homosexuality, how laws are made, prisons, etc.

Structured roleplays on 'rights'

As with the structured roleplays in other parts of the book, those below on 'rights' are intended to help individuals to:

1. Assess their own skills in dealing with a situation;

2. If necessary, identify different ways in which it can be handled; and

3. Practise the skills involved in dealing with the situation in a more satisfactory manner.

Particularly in an area such as rights, participants in roleplays will be able to act more realistically if they are supplied beforehand with relevant information — e.g. if a 'clerk' at the DHSS is familiar with the kinds of benefit that are available. It might make more sense, therefore, to look at the factual side of rights before moving on to the skills or interactive component; and at the very least, to have leaflets or prepared summaries on hand for players in roleplays to use.

In the Social Security Office (2 players + optional third)

You are Mr Telford, a clerk at the Social Security Office. It's about 3.45 in the afternoon and you will be closing shortly. Which is just as well, because you've had a very tiring day, and you're a bit fed up asking and answering questions. There's one more appointment booked for today. You need to find out the person's name and address, age, previous jobs, how long he or she has been unemployed, whether he or she has signed on as available for work, and whether he or she has any other source of income.

You are Jean Clarkson; you left school two weeks ago and thought you'd get a job right away. But you can't find one and now want to claim social security. You live with your parents and haven't worked before.

(A third person can be introduced to act as Jean's friend if this seems useful.)

Encounter with the police (4 players)

You are PC O'Hare. You have worked in the force for about two years. Your beat takes in a lot of quiet roads in the town where there are warehouses and small factories. There have been a lot of break-ins recently. It is 11.30 and you are walking along with PC Richards when you see two young men coming out of a side alley (which you know is 'blind'). They seem a bit drunk.

You are PC Richards. You have been in the force for six months. You are walking along with PC O'Hare and see the same two youths.

You are David Ingram. You have been drinking with several friends and are on your way home; you're making for a bus stop to catch the last bus. You thought this alley-way was a short-cut to the bus station but it turned out to be a dead end. When you come out you see two police officers approaching.

You are Geoff Smith. You have been drinking with Dave and your other mates, and you're both trying to catch the last bus home. You went up the wrong alley-way and have to come back again, when you see two police officers. You feel a bit worried because you've been in trouble before.

Complaint in a shop (3 players + optional fourth)

You recently bought a pair of shoes which cost quite a lot — in fact they were the dearest shoes you've ever bought. But three weeks after you got them, you twisted your ankle on a kerb and one of the heels came completely off. You go to the shop to get your money back (with a friend if you like).

You are an assistant in a shoe shop. The shop has a good reputation and customers rarely complain. The few who do are usually happy to choose something else. One day, a customer comes in with a pair of shoes. You sell a lot of this make and have never had complaints about them before.

You are the manager/manageress of the shoe shop; and you are proud of the shop's good reputation for quality and service. You are talking to the representative of a shoe company. You have told the staff that if they ever have any difficulties with customers they should summon you.

The Rent Tribunal (7 players)

This roleplay requires three groups of people: (a) the three members of the tribunal (sometimes called a Rent Assessment Committee), (b) the tenant and an adviser (who has been obtained on legal aid), and (c) the landlord/landlady and an adviser to them (probably a solicitor). The tribunal has the power (1) to fix what it considers to be a fair rent; (2) to postpone a notice that the tenant should leave the accommodation for up to six months.

The tribunal: You are the members of the rent tribunal. One of you will be the chairman; you are a lawyer and you are in charge of the hearing. Of the others, one is a councillor and one a businessman; working on the rent tribunal is one of a number of public duties you perform. The job of the tribunal as a whole is to see that a fair rent is fixed on this property. The tenants who live there think it is too high; the landlord disagrees. You have to listen to the case made by both sides and then make your decision.

The landlord: Apart from the house you live in, you also own a four-bedroom town house. The house is in as good a condition as others in the area; you had it painted last year. You think the rent is fair and might even be higher. You have brought along your solicitor. The solicitor knows about the state of the house and the rents of similar houses elsewhere. Together you state your case.

The tenant: You are one of four tenants who think the rent is too high. The house is cold and prone to damp; it could do with re-wiring. Your adviser, from the local Law Centre, helps to make your case for a reduction in rent.

'Putting your case'

Exercises in self-presentation with reference to rights

In many situations in which individuals' rights are at stake, it may be necessary for them to argue their case to others. The more clearly, coherently and forcefully they do this, the more likely it is that they will be able to convince others of the strength of their case. This is not to say that you can persuade others of things they just do not want to believe, or that the content of an argument is itself unimportant: but merely to suggest that there are skills involved in speaking your case which have an effect on its overall impact.

This exercise is designed to help young people look at and practise some of these skills. All they have to do is decide on a case they would like to make and then present it to the rest of their group.

Suggest to the group that they have to deal with some situation involving their rights and have to present a case to the appropriate individual or public body. They can make up a case of their own or choose one from a list provided. Their tasks consists therefore of:

1. Thinking of what to say — the arguments they would use;
2. Deciding on a way to say it that will make it as convincing as possible;
3. Preparing their case (perhaps writing it down, perhaps rehearsing it);
4. Presenting it to the rest of their group.

Some predicaments they might be asked to choose from are:

* You are at work and your wage packet has arrived short for the second week running.
* You are unemployed and your Giro has arrived short for the second week running.
* You are living in rented accommodation and would like to pay less rent; you have to take your case to a rent tribunal.
* 18 months ago, you were banned from driving for 2 years. You have been offered a driving job with your uncle's building firm. You have to persuade a court to restore your driving licence.
* You were dismissed from work for being late four mornings in a row. Each day you were late because buses or trains were delayed for different reasons. You are taking your case to an industrial tribunal.
* You are a solicitor. A mother of five children whose husband has left her has been found guilty of persistent shoplifting. You have to make a case for her not being sent to prison.
* You are a farmer and are speaking at a public inquiry about whether or not a motorway, which would cross part of your land, should be built.
* There is evidence that a particular chemical which is used in food processing can be harmful. You are an MP and want to make a case in parliament for banning the chemical, or for an inquiry into it.
* You have to appeal on TV for the Royal National Lifeboat Institution.
* You are a housewife and mother of two children; you live on an estate near a busy road where there have been two minor accidents to children. You are talking to the councillor for your district and asking for a zebra crossing or overpass.
* You bought a record player which turned out to be faulty, but the firm would not mend it, saying you had done the damage, and refused to give you your money back. You have to make your case in the county court against the shop where you bought the equipment.
* You are a Euro-MP and think that more money should be given to the region in which you live and which contains your constituency.

After each person has put their case to the group, the group as a whole can be asked to decide how good the presentations were. Attention could be focussed on —

Clarity — how clear was the speaker's voice; how clear was the meaning of what they were saying?
Reasonableness — how valid and reasonable were the arguments they made?
Assertiveness — how forceful and firm were they in putting their case?
Conviction — did you get the impression they believed in what they were saying?
General — overall, how convinced were you that the person's case was justified? Would you do what they asked?

These points can if necessary be set out as *rating scales* which listeners could use to judge the talks while they were taking place. If possible, opportunity should be given for individuals to practise their skills in further talks, and to see their own performance on video.

Projects on rights

The idea behind a project is that those undertaking it should carry out some work on their own, find things out for themselves, and if possible in doing so should have to exercise a number of different skills. For example a single project might involve consulting books or leaflets, asking questions, working with others in a group, thinking about the subject-matter, and organising all that has been achieved in a report or in some recommendations for action. Projects can vary in size depending on the time and resources that are available. Here are some suggestions for possible projects associated with rights.

* To write to your MP on a topic of local or national importance.
* To lobby MPs or local councillors over a controversial local issue.
* To join or form a rights pressure group of some kind — or prepare material supporting the group's cause.
* To follow a particular rights issue as it is reported in the press, radio and TV — and compile a dossier on it.
* To propose a change of some kind in the law; and recommend how it could be made.
* To take local community action of some kind (or provide the basis for it), e.g. provision of facilities for the young or old, influence the planning decisions of local authorities.
* To think about a difficult social problem and propose a solution to it.
* To take up a specific case (of one person, or family, or area) and further it in some way.

* To find out how some kind of decision is made, e.g. in local government; in a court or tribunal; in Parliament or the U.N.; and write a report, draw up a chart, or devise a simulation on it that could be used to show people the steps that were involved.

* To carry out a local survey — using questionnaires or interviews with people at home or in the street — pertaining to a rights problem, e.g. the kinds of housing in the area, the number of social security claimants, etc — and write a report or make a documentary on it. The survey could be used to find facts or to explore attitudes; and the report could be in written or videotape form (for ideas on the latter, see Dowmunt, 1980).

A great many projects could be mounted which touched on 'rights' at some stage; some other ideas about project work can be found in the book by Rennie, Lunzer, and Williams (1974).

Simulation: 'Parliament'

A simulation is, in essence, a very complex structured roleplay, with larger numbers of players, and much more activity. The most valuable simulations employ a great deal of prepared material, including comprehensive briefs for the participants, illustrative wall charts, cards describing chance events or changes of circumstances, and back-up information in leaflets. In addition, there may be mock money, simulated telephone calls, letters, or newspapers, and other items that give the simulation a 'real' flavour.

It is not possible to provide all these materials for any one simulation in the present book; and the reader is referred to pages 185-6 for suggestions of places to find ready-made simulations with linked materials. Less formal simulations can, however, be set up with not too much effort, by assigning roles to individuals and presenting them with a problem or event they have to re-enact.

As far as rights is concerned, the 'ultimate' subject for a simulation, in the UK at least, may be the body which actually creates the laws that determine our rights: Parliament. You can set up a miniature Parliament, and ask it to make various kinds of decisions by appointing protagonists for various bills, etc. This may provide participants with some idea of how Parliament works and might encourage them to find out more.

The various groups involved would therefore be:

The Speaker, who presides over debates and enforces the rules.
Members of Parliament, who can be organised in a variety of ways:
— into two or more parties, one in power and one in opposition etc.
— into front and back benches, cabinet and shadow cabinet etc.
— with a third party holding the balance of power; the main parties have then to lobby their members for support.

— incorporating whips, who ensure attendance, communicate with party chiefs, and (in the case of the Government Whip) sort out time for debates;

— perhaps a number of free voters or small parties whose votes are needed by the major parties to win a division (or vote).

Other groups which might be involved could include the press, who report on proceedings, and members of the public, who lobby MPs outside parliament.

The main activity in the simulation would then be:

1. The announcement that a motion of some kind will be debated at a fixed time.

2. A lobbying session, in which the MPs of the major parties have to try to persuade independent MPs or those of smaller parties to support them.

3. A debating session, in which various members give speeches on the motion at stake — as in an ordinary debating society.

4. A division, in which votes are taken on the motion.

There would probably not be time — and little necessity in any case — to have second and third readings of bills as in Westminster; one debate would probably be sufficient. Some of the kinds of debates that could be engendered might take as their starting-point:

(a) a private member's bill, on a particular issue introduced by one MP.

(b) an amendment to an existing act which is a major bone of contention between the two largest parties.

(c) an issue of conscience, on which MPs can vote as they please after listening to speeches.

(d) an issue of major importance such as the secession of one part of the state, or the devolution of power to a region, county, or town.

Briefings could be prepared without too much difficulty to make this a lively and productive exercise. Charts showing the layout of Parliament might help individuals to grasp the nature of the House and its work. Tape-recordings of parliamentary debates or of 'Yesterday in Parliament', copies of Hansard, of parliamentary acts, and so on, could demonstrate more clearly how government decisions are made. A useful booklet is 'The British Parliament' published by HMSO.

A similar kind of simulation could also be mounted for other kinds of decision-making body, e.g. the local council, United Nations, different kinds of committee.

Further sources on 'rights'

General information: a number of handbooks on rights and guides to the law as it affects everyday life are currently available; they include:

L. Grant, P. Hewitt, C. Jackson and H. Levenson (1978). *Civil Liberty: the NCCL Guide to your Rights.* Penguin Books.

N. Berger (1974). *Rights: a handbook for people under age.* Penguin Books.

F. Greenoak and others, *'What Right Have You Got?: Your rights and responsibilities as a citizen.* Part 1 (1976); Part 2 (1977). BBC Publications.

The Family Welfare Association: *Guide to the Social Services* (updated annually).

On social security, see: R. Lister, *National Welfare Benefits Handbook,* published by the Child Poverty Action Group, 1 Macklin Street, London WC2B 5NH.

On accommodation: a variety of teaching materials, including a simulation on housing problems, are available from Shelter, 157 Waterloo Road, London SE1 8UU.
A resource pack, 'Housing Ideas', can be obtained from Tyneside Housing Aid Centre, 33 Groat Market, Newcastle-upon-Tyne.

On consumer rights: useful background information will be found in *The Buyer's Right* (1978), published jointly by the Consumers' Association and the Open University Press. See also: *Consumer Education: a Resources Handbook for Teachers* (1979), published by the Consumers' Association.

On rights at work: see *Dismissal, Redundancy, and Job Hunting* (1976), published by the Consumers' Association; and Jeremy McMullen (1979), *Rights at Work,* Pluto Press.

Sets of materials on different aspects of rights have been prepared by a number of agencies, including:
Community Service Volunteers, 237 Pentonville Road, London N1 9NJ, have produced a series of teaching packs called 'School and Community', which includes *No Bed — No Job,* on accommodation and survival; *Planning Your Environment,* on local politics and community issues; and *Local Government.* Each pack includes information sheets, discussion starters, suggestions for projects, etc.
The Scottish Community Education Centre, 4 Queensferry Street, Edinburgh EH2 4PA, has included a Programme Kit on *Rights and Obligations,* in its Social Education series. (The kit also incorporates a simulation on rights.)
The Basic Skills Unit, 18 Brooklands Avenue, Cambridge CB2 2HN have prepared materials on rights including a *Rights pack* (with simulation) and a game, *Coping with the system* (a guide to helping agencies).

Many other organisations, such as the NCCL and the Consumers' Association, can provide further information and ideas on rights and related topics; their addresses are given at the end of the book.

On moral aspects of rights, see: P. McPhail, J.R. Ungoed-Thomas, and H. Chapman (1972), *Moral Education in the Secondary School,* Longman, and the related series of *Lifeline* materials produced by the Schools Council Project in Moral Education.
See also: D. Wright (1971), *The Psychology of Moral Behaviour,* Penguin Books.

On tactics: for a practical and entertaining guide to the process of securing rights, see C. Ward (1974), *How to complain,* Pan Books.

MEETING THE OPPOSITE SEX

Introduction

Given the significance of sex in human relations in general, and despite the difficulties many people have in forming and maintaining sexual relationships, surprisingly little attention has been paid to how individuals can be helped to cope with this key area of their lives. Relations between the sexes, with or without a specifically sexual element, are the source of a great deal of both happiness and unhappiness. Yet in approaching the phase of their lives when sex will become of greater interest and importance to them, most young people are left to assimilate the myths passed on by their slightly older peers. Their misunderstanding or ignorance of sexual matters may lead to unnecessary anxiety on the one hand, or to careless sexual activity with potentially calamitous results on the other.

Attempts to help young people understand and manage this part of their lives have taken two principal (though overlapping) forms. The first is sex education, which has been concerned mainly with teaching what are usually called 'the facts of life' — about physical growth, reproduction, contraception and related medical problems such as venereal disease. The second is counselling, which is designed to help individuals with the many questions they want to ask about sex, and to give further assistance to those with specific emotional or interpersonal problems.

The materials presented here are not intended to replace either of these approaches but rather to complement them and hopefully increase their range of applicability by focussing on the attitudes and skills which operate in meetings between the sexes.

Given that sex is such an emotionally loaded topic, most discussion of it is conducted in a climate of considerable awkwardness. If included as a topic in a social and life skills course, it needs to be approached with great care. Two pitfalls in particular can present themselves. One is the impression, which some people may have, that sexual worries or 'hang-ups' are indicative of some profound personality defect or disturbance. While a few problems may be of this kind, most of the difficulties young people experience are likely to be due to ignorance, confusion, lack of confidence, or an inability to cope with anxiety and frustration. A rational approach to their problems, giving reassurance that they are not abnormal, may be the best way to help young people in this predicament. A second snare is a tendency, which is fairly widespread, to deal with questions about sex in a moralistic manner — in other words, to consider the topic with the primary aim of imparting a moral standpoint. The worst instances of this are those in which sex education materials or methods have a concealed or built-in moral bias. It is equally indefensible, of course, to create the impression that individuals are somehow deficient if they do not devote themselves to the relentless pursuit of promiscuous sexual encounters without regard to the feelings and views of others. Since discussion of sexual attitudes and behaviour almost inevitably raises moral issues, the best course of action is to make clear your own views; to emphasise that they are *your views;* and to distinguish them as such from other points made in the discussion. The materials below are designed to act as a framework for discussion, roleplay and other exercises concerned with the interpersonal aspects of relations between the sexes. Apart from their specific aims, each of the exercises also reflects two more general, recurring themes: (1) that of helping young people become more aware of the factors which influence their sexual attitudes and behaviour; and (2) partly as a result of this, that of enabling and encouraging young people to think about sex-related topics for themselves, and to arrive at their own decisions about how they can make the best of this area of their lives. The suggestions presented here are:

1. Discussion starters on topics connected with sex;
2. The 'Computer Date' — assessing the basis of sexual attraction;
3. Sex roles: looking at attitudes to sex in relation to work;
4. 'Double Standards': moral expectations of the opposite sex;
5. 'Do you think it's right?' — sexual behaviour and moral values;
6. 'What would you do?' — dealing with personal predicaments;
7. A project — 'Sex and the Media'
8. Structured roleplays of encounters between the sexes.

Starting a discussion on sex

Sexual relationships may be one of the commonest causes of anxiety amongst people in their teens (and probably at other ages as well). Just having a chat with other people about sex can be very helpful in a number of ways — in enabling individuals to sort out ideas they have about others; in helping them to realise that their thoughts and values are similar to other people's, or to understand more clearly how they are different; and to help them find out more about sex through hearing the experiences and insights of others.

Initial reactions to the idea of talking to others about sex range from mild uneasiness, to nervous giggling and laughter or an escape into rude innuendo. But if the topic is dealt with openly and sensitively, discussion of it can be an important ingredient of social education. It might be useful, therefore, to have a number of ideas for starting discussions in this area. Below is a list of possibilities for initiating discussions on various aspects of sex and attitudes to it.

There is a variety of ways in which 'discussion starters' like these can be introduced; for example:

1. Groups can be divided into two teams to debate conflicting points of view on the issues in question.
2. Volunteers with views on particular topics can be asked to give a talk about them to others.
3. A film, cartoon, leaflet, or other stimulus item can be presented to a group and some questions raised about it in discussion.
4. Cards with points of view on given topics written on them can be distributed to a group, and individuals asked to state their views on what is written on their card, to defend it or attack it, etc.
5. The topic or viewpoint can simply be stated and individuals invited to give their views; others then being asked if they agree or disagree, etc.

Newpaper items can also be used as discussion starters. Almost every day most newspapers carry stories or other articles about sex or sexual behaviour. These can be cut out and used to introduce discussions on the aspects of sexual behaviour to which they relate. Individuals might be asked to express their views on the situation; to say what they would do if involved; to say whether any general rules apply to the situation in question, etc. Alternatively, a discussion about the content of various newspaper items can be held in the light of the findings of a project like that described on page 196.

Possible discussion starters on attitudes to sex

* Sex before marriage is wrong.
* People should get married as early in life as possible.
* Marriage is something you should put off as long as you can.
* Men get more out of marriage than women.
* Women get more out of marriage than men.
* It's a girl's responsibility to see she doesn't get pregnant.
* The age of consent should be lowered to 14.
* If a girl gets pregnant, she should get married.
* If a boy gets a girl pregnant, he should marry her.
* It's wrong to have more than one boyfriend/girlfriend at a time.
* Is it possible to fancy/love more than one person at a time?
* How well should you know someone before you sleep with them?
* Girls aged under 16 who get pregnant should be given abortions.
* It's easier for a boy to get a girlfriend than for a girl to get a boyfriend.
* It's easier for a girl to attract a boyfriend than for a boy to attract a girlfriend.
* There's no harm in showing sex on TV.
* X certificates for films should be abolished.
* People should be taught about sex in school.
* People should be taught about sex before they are 12.

* How easy it is to find a boyfriend or girlfriend depends on how good-looking you are.
* Most boys think girls are only good for one thing.
* There is no such thing as 'true love'.
* Should doctors tell parents if their daughters are on the pill?
* Should doctors prescribe the pill for girls under 16?

The computer date

Most people are sexually attracted to members of the opposite sex. But what actually counts as 'attractive' varies a great deal from one person to another. The relative importance of different personal characteristics — and even what exactly each of them is thought to consist of — is different for every individual.

It can be interesting to ask young people to think about the reasons why they feel attracted to some people and not to others — or why they feel *more* attracted to some than to others. One way of helping them to define more clearly what attracts them is to invite them to imagine that they are arranging a date through a computer-matching agency. To do this they have first of all to fill in a form, part of which asks them to describe what attracts them to someone, how important various features of appearance and personality are, and what sort of person they would like to meet — as in the 'computer dating' questionnaire on the next page.

This questionnaire can be used as a whole or in part, or you can add other items as you think fit. If it seems inappropriate to use the items in questionnaire form, they can be used instead as a basis for peer interviews or group discussion. The questions asked here are unlike those that would be asked on a real computer dating form — so if you want to make the exercise more 'realistic' you can use dating forms from magazines. In addition, computer-matching services also ask respondents to supply information about themselves — a dimension which has been discarded for the purpose of the present exercise. This could however be included in the exercise if you wanted to add a 'self-assessment' element to it.

Individuals can be requested to complete this form and then to compare their replies with those of others. Comparisons can be made between the replies of the female and male members of the group. Subsequent discussion might focus on, for example: the importance of looks in attracting people; the importance of personality; how you can improve your appearance if you want to do so; how to meet and approach members of the opposite sex; what kinds of relationships last and what attracts people to each other on a long-term basis.

Dating form

The questions on this form are designed to help you to describe the kind of person you find attractive.

1. Some people feel attracted to others only because they are good-looking. Other people don't care about how someone looks but are much more interested in what sort of person they are.
   What kinds of things are important to you? Here is a list of the reasons people sometimes give for fancying others. Which ones are most important to you? Put a ring round the number opposite each one where
   1 = this is very important, it matters a lot
   2 = this is fairly important
   3 = this doesn't matter much
   4 = this doesn't matter at all

   How important is it to you that someone should:

1. be good-looking in general	1	2	3	4
2. have a handsome or pretty face	1	2	3	4
3. have a nice figure or physique	1	2	3	4
4. dress well	1	2	3	4
5. have polite manners	1	2	3	4
6. have a nice personality	1	2	3	4
7. have the same interests as yourself	1	2	3	4
8. come from the same area as you	1	2	3	4
9. come from the same background as you	1	2	3	4
10. be the kind of person your parents would like	1	2	3	4

2. In the following list of items, underline the choice you would make.

   I would prefer someone to be:
   (a) quite like me / quite different from me
   (b) a bit older than me / the same age as me / a bit younger than me
   (c) happy not to see much of me / wanting to spend most of the time with me

3. Can you describe the person you would like to meet? Put a ring round the point on each scale which describes the kind of person you would prefer.

talkative	1	2	3	4	5	quiet
serious	1	2	3	4	5	humorous
shy	1	2	3	4	5	outgoing
busy & energetic	1	2	3	4	5	relaxed & easy-going
easy to get to know	1	2	3	4	5	takes a while to get to know

Sex roles

Boys and girls are for the most part brought up to take different kinds of roles in life; though attitudes to this are changing, arguments about what sorts of things men and women should or shouldn't do are fairly common in everyday conversation. An individual's views on this issue can be an important aspect of his or her overall attitude to sex and this exercise is designed to help individuals assess their own views on 'sex roles' and compare them with those of others.

Some of the 30 jobs or other activities listed below would be described by most people as exclusively 'male' or 'for men'; others would be associated much more frequently with women. Whether this is because men or women *more often do* particular jobs, or whether individuals think they ideally *ought* to, is an important point of discussion; however for the purpose of the exercise you should ask group members to think of what men and women ought to do.

The exercise consists first of asking individuals to sort these activities into five groups, and then discussing their reasons for sorting them in the way that they do. The jobs or activities can be written on cards and actually grouped into five bundles; or a number from 1 to 5 can be written beside each. The first bundle (or items marked 1) should consist of activities that only men should do; the second should contain things that ought usually (but not always) to be done by men; bundle 3 should contain things that can be done equally by men and women; bundle 4, things that should be done usually (but not always) by women; and bundle 5, things that only women should do.

When individuals or small groups have completed the task, discussions or debates can be held on their results. Comparisons can be made between the views of male and female participants in the exercise. You can even compile a crude score by counting the numbers of things classed in each bundle and comparing the 3s with the 1s and 5s.

Occupations and activities

Looking after children	Digging the garden	Secretary
Coalmining	Decorating the house	Working on a lifeboat
Accountancy	Arranging flowers in a	Working on an oil-rig
Cooking	house	Disc jockey
Changing babies'	Wearing make-up	Deep-sea diving
nappies	Drinking beer	Flying a jet
Washing dishes	Drinking Babycham	Driving a train
Drying dishes	Taking a contraceptive	Collecting refuse
Nursing	pill	Modelling clothes
Cleaning the house	Social work	High court judge
Captain of an oil tanker	Playing in a rock band	Receptionist

'Double standards'

Not only is it widely expected that men and women should engage in different occupations and other activities; a lot of people also believe that different rules apply to the behaviour of men and women in general — and especially when they are dealing with each other in a sexual relationship. Once again, individuals' views on this can influence how they react in a large number of encounters with the opposite sex.

The views of young people on this issue may be particularly important because during their late teens they may make many decisions — such as to get married or not, have children or not — which will affect their lives for many years afterwards. The topic of 'single or double standards' can be introduced by asking young people for their views on a number of points like those suggested below. Taking each item in turn, individuals can be asked to say whether it is all right for them to do it and for others to do it respectively; or whether it is all right for men or for women respectively. Alternatively, a single item or issue can be selected and debated or discussed by itself.

Individuals can be asked whether they think men or women should be able to:

ask someone out
sleep with someone if they're not married
go out with someone else if they are already going steady
have a relationship with someone just for sex
initiate sex
decline sex
talk to friends about what they do in bed
go on holiday with a group of the opposite sex
have a sexual relationship with a member of the same sex

There are many points like these on which some individuals think the behaviour of men and women should be different, and with some thought a much longer list could be produced.

'Do you think it's right?'

Few areas of human behaviour arouse such contradictory sentiments as does sex. While on the one hand it is the subject of both legal and moral precept, and furnishes a main ingredient for many rumours and scandals, on the other it is used as a vehicle for advertising of almost every kind and is probably the focus of a larger number of jokes than just about any other single topic.

It is difficult to discuss sexual attitudes openly and rationally without causing something of a stir. Yet individuals' views on their own and other people's sexual relationships are an important part of their general moral outlook. Central to these views are their opinions on the 'rightness' or 'wrongness' of the sexual activity of different people. For example, some people believe that sexual activity should take place only between men and women within marriage; others think that sex should be (morally) allowed between any two individuals who want to enjoy it, regardless of whether they are married or of any other considerations.

This exercise is concerned with issues such as these and has two specific aims:

1. To provide a basis for discussion and debate on the relationship between sex and morals;
2. To help young people think about and make decisions about their own sexual behaviour.

A number of possible sexual relationships are listed below. These can be typed on a sheet and distributed as a questionnaire; or read out one at a time and used for small group discussion. In each case individuals should be asked to give their views on whether or not they approve or disapprove of the sexual relationship — whether they think it's 'right' or 'not right'. This should lead on to discussion and reflection about sexual behaviour. You can choose to use all of the items or to select some and discard others according to what will be acceptable and valuable to the young people with whom you are working.

Which of the following do you think are right?

Sex between — a man and a woman who are married to each other.
a man and a woman who are each married to different partners.
a single man and a single woman.
a single man and a married woman.
a single woman and a married man.
an engaged couple.
an unmarried couple who have been going out together for:
2 years;   2 months;   2 weeks;   2 days
a woman aged 20 and a man aged 50.
a man aged 20 and a woman aged 50.
complete strangers who have just met.
men only.
women only.
groups of people.

What would you do?

Most individuals are more likely to be able to deal with a difficult situation if they have spent some time thinking about it in advance. The 'predicaments' below, like those included in the sections on job search (page 118) and leisure (page 139), are intended for use in helping young people prepare for awkward encounters in which they might find themselves.

A session incorporating these can be run in several ways. A problem can be presented to an individual or group and they can be asked for suggestions as to how it might be dealt with. Alternatively, a game or group problem-solving exercise (similar to that described on page 93) can be organised in which the predicaments are written out on cards and handed out. Group members are then asked what they would do in the situation on the card they have been given (or, they can be allowed to 'pass the buck' by selecting another group member to say what he or she would do). Whichever strategy is chosen, the session can be developed into discussion, peer interviews, or roleplays as seems appropriate.

(Some of the items below have been written for boys or girls only and can be changed by simply altering the pronouns.)

Predicaments

* There is a girl whom you fancy but you don't know her very well. One Saturday morning you see her walking by herself down the street. What would you do?
* You are in a group of people and one of them is very attractive. You fancy her (him) a lot but nobody tells you who she is and you're not sure whether you'll see her again. What would you do?
* A boy you know well and regard as a close friend asks you out. You can't really think of him other than as a friend. What would you do?
* You are with a boyfriend or girlfriend in a group of people. He/she shows a lot of interest in somebody else in the group. What would you do?
* You are at a party when suddenly you meet face to face with someone you stood up last week. What would you do?
* You come home one evening (or back from holiday) to find that a letter from your boyfriend (or girlfriend) has been opened. What would you do?
* You run into a friend who has just started going out with someone you told him (or her) you fancied. What would you do?
* A friend of yours would really like to go out with somebody he (or she) fancies but is nervous about even talking to girls (or boys). What would you do?
* A group of your friends — including your boyfriend — are going camping for the weekend. Your parents definitely don't want you to go. What would you do?

Project: sex and the media

Sex is a commodity with which the media continually bombard us, chiefly in order to direct our attention towards something in order to sell it or to persuade us of a point of view in relation to it. In many respects, people's attitudes to sex must be under the influence of the way in which sex is represented in the newspapers, in magazines and books, or on television. It can be a useful project then to take a closer look at the way in which sex is presented, reported and manipulated by these forms of communication.

One way of doing this is to carry out what is known as a 'content analysis'. All this means is breaking down the content of written or other material in order to see what proportions of it fall into different pre-arranged categories. In this case, the categories have to do with sex and topics related to it.

The most accessible material for this kind of analysis is the daily press. Buy a selection of the newspapers on one day and ask groups to look at the items they contain, and to sort them into categories. Some of the classifications you use might include:

Items concerned with sex versus those not concerned with sex
(compare different newspapers for example)
Advertisements using sex as a proportion of all advertisements.
Pictures emphasising sex as against those which do not.
Stories about sex. These could be further subdivided into:
Items dealing with marriages, divorces and affairs.
Items dealing with sex and crime.
Items describing or hinting at 'sexual goings-on'.

Different kinds of publication could be compared in the way they use sex; for example daily newspapers; weekly magazines; romance magazines, etc.

The exercise could be extended by looking for examples of the use of sex in other areas, e.g. TV, books, record covers, billboards, advertisements in shops, and so on.

Discussion points might include: the numbers of items dealing directly with sex; the numbers using sex to achieve some other purpose; the ways in which the latter is achieved; the attitudes engendered by the representation of the sexes in particular ways; the reasons why the media employ sex as they do; the attitudes of particular newspapers or programmes towards particular topics, e.g. the sexual behaviour of young people, marriage, divorce, bringing up children, contraception, abortion, homosexuality, etc.

HEARTACHE 'BRIDE' ON THE RUN

Unwed mums shown the door

By MICHAEL EVANS

TEENAGE girls who have sex with boy friends and become pregnant should be refused council accommodation, a housing chief said last night.

Under the controversial Homeless Persons Act, pregnant women are regarded as priority a waiting lis

Council said no to marriage at 16

By FRANK WELSBY

A TEENAGE bride-to-be w on the run last night—becau a council barred her weddin

The heartbroken gir'

PARENTS GET RIGHT IN BILL TO KNOW ABOUT SEX LESSONS

By JOHN IZBICKI, Education Correspondent

PARENTS are to be informed by law exactly what kind of sex education ses to be pub- also likely to y inspect sex-

the Government's d its third reading House of Lords

are no taboo sub-
What people get is
l time to talk openly
quality. It is rather
xtended hour with a
or   analyst."
Hazel Slavin, an
ir
nt visitor was Mrs
y White, newly

Red alert over town's prostitutes

Sex scare man sought

POLICE are searching for a

Secrets of the sleazy riders

By SUN REPORTER

THE WILD sex lives of Hells Angels and other motorbike gangs

JOBLESS GIRLS 'TURN TO VICE'

SOME jobless girls will be driven to vice, a report warns today.

For research shows th some teenagers turn crime to try to keep t with school-leavers luck enough to have found work.

The report predicts tha there will be 360,000 young sters on the dole in January 1981. This would be a 70-fold increase since 1974 when only 5,400 were jobless.

"Perhaps the most damaging consequence of unemployment is its effect on the dignity and self-respect of the individual," says the report

By BRUCE KEMBLE   nev—sh...

Ann Hills visits a course in sex education and personal relationships run by the Family Planning Association

The plain facts of life

A BIOLOGY teacher said she was asked to take sex education classes because she had wallcharts on the reproductive system. She was one of delegates at a multi-dis-

unless these lessons can be transferred back to school — to the staff room as well as the classroom — teachers won't be able to develop an atmosphere conducive to trust. "I doubt whether any teachers would have

timed. A well respected doctor, Elphis Christopher, was abused by a television programme which feature her holding up a sheath i front of a class of 14 to 1 year olds. It was n explained that she had give them several lessons in t

Structured roleplays

Apart from the numberless factors that influence the way people think about sex, and the decisions they make about it, dealing with the opposite sex also requires a number of social skills. Given existing sex roles and stereotypes, the skills required by the two sexes are slightly different. Whatever the case, encounters between the sexes can be looked at more closely, and opportunities given for practising social skills, through the use of structured roleplays. The complexity of the situations which it is possible to roleplay depends a great deal on the sophistication of the group with whom you are working; the examples given below depict fairly simple and common events.

Beginning a relationship

You are John. You have been at a party or disco (or have been spending time at a local youth club) and have been dancing with (or talking to) Anne for about an hour. You'd like to ask her out for next week. You are not sure whether she already has a boyfriend.

You are Anne. You have been at a party or disco (or at the local youth club) and have spent a while dancing with (or talking to) John. You haven't got a boyfriend at the moment. How will you react if he asks you out?

(A roleplay on this theme could also be run in which Anne has a boyfriend who isn't with her that evening.)

Ending a relationship

You are Susie. You have been going out with Tim for six weeks and though you like him, you don't really want to go on seeing him as he wants things to get serious and you don't. You'd like to end the relationship but stay friends, and avoid hurting his feelings too much.

You are Tim. You have been going out with Susie for six weeks and you're really fond of her. You'd like to see more of her and in fact you were thinking of asking her if she'd like to go on holiday with you this year. As far as you can tell she likes you too.

Some further sources on 'meeting the opposite sex'

The emphasis in most sex education and teaching materials associated with it is placed principally upon sexual development and with issues such as birth control. Of the few books which also examine the social or interpersonal side of sex, perhaps the best are: Jane Cousins (1978), *Make it Happy: what sex is all about,* Virago (Penguin edition published 1980) — an excellent book aimed directly at teenagers; and C. Adams and R. Laurikietis (1976), *The Gender Trap,* Virago and Quartet Books. The latter book is in three volumes: 1, *Education and Work;* 2, *Sex and Marriage,* and 3, *Messages and Images;* each contains many ideas that could be used for discussion, roleplays, projects and other work.

See also the *Sex and the Sexes* Programme Kit produced by the Scottish Community Education Centre, which contains quizzes, cartoons, leaflets, and practical advice. As a basis for imparting information about sex, see the book by Cousins cited above, and: B.H. Claesson (197), *Boy, Girl, Man, Woman,* Calder and Boyars; M.V. Lea (1975), *Health and Social Education,* Heinemann Education; W.B. Pomeroy (1968) *Boys and Sex* and (1969) *Girls and Sex,* both published by Penguin Books; and on birth control see H.I. Shapiro (1980), *The Birth Control Book,* Penguin. For books addressed particularly to girls and women, see A. Phillips and J. Rakusen (1978), *Our Bodies Ourselves,* Penguin (a book originally published in the United States by the Boston Women's Health Collective); A. Coote and T. Gill (1977), *Women's Rights: a practical guide,* Penguin; S. Sharpe (1976), *'Just Like a Girl': how girls learn to be women,* Penguin; and *Please Yourself: Sex for Girls,* published by the Coventry Women's Education Group, 12 Westminster Road, Coventry.

For further information and advice on specific issues related to sex, the following organisations will prove helpful (many supply free leaflets and other materials, are willing to send along speakers, and have offices in different parts of the country): The Health Education Council, 78 Oxford Street, London WC1A 1AH; and the Scottish Health Education Unit, 21 Lansdowne Crescent, Edinburgh EH12 5EH. The Family Planning Association, 27-35 Mortimer Street, London W1N 7RJ (has many local clinics, runs an information service jointly with the Health Education Council, and also runs training courses in sex education). British Pregnancy Advisory Service, Austy Manor, Wootton Wawen, Solihull, W. Midlands B95 6DA (has many branches and staff who can give talks on contraception etc.). Brook Advisory Centres, whose head office is at 233 Tottenham Court Road, London W1P 9EA, specialise in giving advice to young people. Equal Opportunities Commission, Overseas House, Quay Street, Manchester M3 3HN. The British Association for Counselling, 26 Bedford Square, London WC1 3HU, and the National Marriage Guidance Council, Herbert Gray College, Little Church Street, Rugby, Warwickshire, will both supply information on counselling services for young people as will Grapevine, 416 St John Street, London EC1V 4NJ. The Albany Trust, 16-20 Strutton Ground, London SW1 and the Campaign for Homosexual Equality, 42a Formosa Street, London W9, can provide information and advice on all aspects of homosexuality.

6 The Social Skills Curriculum

Much current educational thinking is centred on the notion of the 'curriculum'. Formal education has for a long time, of course, taken as one of its basic assumptions the idea that some kind of order must be imposed on the way in which knowledge of a subject is transmitted; and it makes good everyday sense when learning about something to proceed from the simple to the complex, the familiar to the unfamiliar, the safe and certain to the less assured and more questionable areas of any given discipline or topic. At present, however, the study of how courses can be structured and different units of a subject interlinked has almost become a separate enterprise in itself, having adopted such titles as 'Curriculum Studies' or 'Curriculum Design and Development'. But the academic curriculum, around which most of this debate and discussion revolves, is only one of many possible ways in which the transmission of information or skills can be organised. 'Curriculum', in its fuller sense, need mean nothing more than some roughly ordered sequence of learning opportunities; the principles upon which it is based being only that it engages the interest of the learner and thereby proves effective as a means of helping him or her to achieve the appointed learning goals.

The previous chapters of this book have outlined the background to social and life skills training; the problems to which it is addressed; the kinds of methods it employs; and have presented some exercises that can be used directly by anyone working with young people and trying to help them solve problems in the life skills domain. The present chapter has somewhat different aims: to provide users of this book with a framework for developing new materials and exercises of their own; and to make some suggestions as to how these can either be incorporated into existing curricula or assembled into a life skills curriculum that will stand by itself.

In so far as the concept of a curriculum can be applied to the teaching of social and life skills, it must remain a very elastic one. The actual content of any course should be primarily a response to the needs and wishes of those taking part. The topics dealt with, the methods used, the overall pace, and the sheer length of a social skills course are all, therefore, open to modification according to what participants want and what are the available possibilities for action. Learning will obviously occur more readily if it is geared to problems on the minds of learners. Courses therefore need to have as much built-in flexibility as possible; and no exact prescriptions can be made here as to their most suitable size and shape. The object of this chapter, then, is merely to sketch some broad contours — of ways in which exercises can be combined, or new ones devised, for insertion into courses already in progress or for the construction of a separate 'package' on social and life skills.

COMBINING EXERCISES: THE LIFE SKILLS SESSION

The running of social and life skills sessions will in most cases be subject to at least two sorts of constraints. It will be dependent, first of all, on the nature of the location in which the work is being done; on the need, for example, to fit into a school or college timetable or to find some pattern of working that is acceptable to other people whom it might affect. And it will be a product, secondly, of the general willingness of the target group — whether schoolchildren, college students, YOP trainees, or regular users of a youth centre — to take part in the activities being offered; and of the ability of staff to sustain their interest.

Within these limits, however, the number of ways in which life skills sessions can be put together is literally enormous — perhaps distressingly so for the teacher, lecturer or youth worker who is new to these kinds of methods. There are nevertheless some guidelines that can be laid down as hints to the planning of sessions and exercises.

First, it is almost always worthwhile to capitalise on the principle of variety in learning. This is advisable for two main reasons. To begin with, effective learning involves a complex interplay of a number of different mechanisms. There is assimilation of facts and concepts through the medium of the spoken or written word. There is direct, face-to-face experience of situations which helps individuals appreciate them in a way no other learning process can. There is reflection, which may bring individuals to realisations they would not achieve by any other means; and there is practice, on which the proper execution of any skill — mental or motor — is absolutely dependent. In parallel with this, individuals themselves have different cognitive styles — they each may learn best in a different mode, one by reading, another by talking to people, a third by going out and seeing or doing things for himself. Even if this were not the case, most individuals certainly learn more if sessions are broken up in an engaging way with variations of speed and content. Life skills sessions will work best, then, if different teaching methods are balanced against each other — with instruction being given at one stage, action being taken at another, and the whole matter being discussed at the beginning, middle, and end.

Second, as far as the sequence of events is concerned, a life skills session can be seen as being something like a symphony in its overall structure. At the outset there is a statement of the topic of interest; this is followed by development, with occasional digressions; returning at the end to the same general theme but now with much more elaboration. Although there are some exercises — such as simulations or outings — which may last a whole session in themselves, and a fruitful group discussion should be allowed to last for as long as seems beneficial, for the most part a mixture of different exercises can be relied upon to maintain motivation and stimulate learning.

An afternoon's timetable of life skills, then, might contain the following kinds of elements:

(a) a general INTRODUCTION to the topic or problem with which the session is concerned;

(b) a PENCIL-and-PAPER exercise, e.g. questionnaire or rating scale, for helping individuals to explore the topic in more depth;

(c) some INTERVIEWS between group members or GROUP DISCUSSION of their responses to the pencil-and-paper questions;

(d) some ROLEPLAYS which focus on specific situations which have been identified by individuals as posing problems for them;

(e) FEEDBACK of the views of others on how these situations were handled or could be handled — possibly involving further roleplays;

(f) finally, a general DISCUSSION of what has come out of the session, whether problems have been understood more fully, or solved, and what further action might be taken by the individuals involved.

If this series of activities were addressed to such life problems as managing money, or how to interact with a particular group of people like parents, personnel officers or policemen, a final exercise might be appended in which individuals set their own targets for the future. In turn, these might occupy them in finding out about something before the next session, in monitoring their own behaviour in some respect, or in accomplishing a small-scale goal of some kind.

An example of how a full-length session might be organised in one life skills area is given below. The skill examined is performance in job interviews; a frequently quoted example in life skills training which is repeated here because of its wide applicability. The combination of exercises given here might last for a half-day with a break somewhere in the middle.

Session on JOB INTERVIEWS

(a) General introduction to the topic — asking group members about experiences in job interviews.

(b) Group discussions on things to do and not to do in interviews; how to be successful in interviews.

(c) Group generates a short checklist of skills for assessing each other's interview performance.

(d) The group is then divided up into two or more smaller groups; each has to think of a job and of questions that would be asked in interviews for it.

(e) Individuals, posing as applicants, are then interviewed for jobs by members of other groups. The rest of the group as a whole observes the interviews in terms of the checklist devised earlier. If possible the interviews are also tape-recorded or video-taped.

(f) The 'interviewees' are then given reports on how well they performed; and comments are made on how they might (if necessary) improve their skills. These last two steps can be repeated for a number of individuals — or if the group is large, several interviews might be taking place at once.

(g) The session ends with a discussion amongst the whole group.

The value of this kind of session could be further enhanced if it were to act as a prelude to another session in which trained interviewers, for example from local firms or careers offices, are invited along to conduct 'mock' interviews that are made as lifelike as possible. Supplementary sessions might consist entirely of practice exercises for those who wish to become more proficient in job interviewing — culminating perhaps in real interviews at the end of it all.

Here is another possible half-day excursion into another topic, that of welfare rights. In this instance, a speaker or 'expert' — perhaps someone from the local Citizens' Advice Bureau, Advice Centre, or Claimants' Union — is taking part. The session however begins half an hour before the speaker arrives.

Session on WELFARE RIGHTS

(a) An opening discussion might concentrate on the problems individuals have had or might have in claiming welfare rights. A list of questions which group members would like to ask the speaker is drawn up.

(b) Following this, a 'rights quiz' is organised, dealing specifically with welfare rights issues; background information is given on the answers and any moot points discussed.

(c) The invited speaker might then give a short talk on aspects of rights that are of interest to the group; perhaps supplying information leaflets if these appear useful. This in turn would probably lead into

(d) a question-and-answer session based on the list of items drawn up before the speaker's arrival; discussing points raised as fully as possible.
(e) Subsequently, things might be taken a stage further by examining the skills involved in securing rights; probably involving roleplays which depict procedures for making claims, or incidents that might occur, etc.
(f) Once again, it is useful to conclude the session with a discussion which ranges over the major points that have emerged.

The idea behind preparing questions for an outsider in advance is not, of course, that some attempt should be made to catch unsuspecting visitors off-guard, but is rather just an attempt to avoid a situation in which (as sometimes happens) no one can think of anything to say at the right time. Presented with strangers, many young people 'freeze' in this way; having an agenda prepared beforehand can make things a lot easier for the session as a whole.

Finally, the third example below illustrates how a shorter session might be run on one very clearly defined interpersonal skill: that of *resisting persuasion*. This may have been preceded by other sessions in which — through the use of interviews, skill surveys, roleplays or similar methods — some individuals identified resisting persuasion as a skill they would like to acquire or improve. Alternatively, the following could be an extract from a longer session on interactive skills, on aggression, on managing money, on friendship, or on any other aspect of personal relations in which the ability to resist persuasion might be called into play.

Session on RESISTING PERSUASION

(a) a broad discussion or brainstorming session on reasons why it might be necessary to resist persuasion or on circumstances in which it might be advisable.
(b) Individuals are asked to form small groups — pairs or trios — and are invited to pinpoint situations in which group members have failed to resist persuasion against their better judgment, and have e.g. bought something they did not want, done something they did not want to do, given in in arguments, or acceded to opinions with which they disagreed.
(c) Small groups then roleplay the encounters they have been considering, with other groups observing.
(d) The roleplays are discussed (and played back if video-recorded); and suggestions collected as to how to cope better with each situation — things to say, things to avoid, arguments to use, ways of behaving.
(e) In ensuing roleplays, small groups try out the suggestions that have been made; various ways of resisting persuasion are modelled by those

who have used them successfully in the past or who think they could show more assertiveness. For any one encounter, three or four alternative approaches might be tried.

(f) The likely success of different strategies for resisting persuasion is evaluated, leading perhaps to further roleplays, feedback and discussion.

Clearly, the tolerance of young people for successively repeated roleplays of the same basic encounter is strictly limited, and it is for social skills tutors to judge when their interest in a topic is likely to be exhausted. The above cycle of events can usually be run through once or twice however for problems about which teenagers are genuinely concerned. And this particular model of working — of pinning down incidents, roleplaying them, generating alternative courses of action, having a go at these, and so on — can be used as the basis of a session on almost any social skill.

A very much broader basis which we have found useful for designing both sessions and courses in our previous work (Priestley, McGuire, Flegg, Hemsley, Welham, 1978) is to organise exercises into a problem-solving framework. This consists of four stages:

1. ASSESSMENT.   This consists of exercises whose principal aim is the identification and exploration of problems, skills, strengths, weaknesses and preferences of the individual.

2. SETTING OBJECTIVES.   Using this self-appraisal as a starting-point, the individual then tries to specify things he wishes to do in order to solve his problem.

3. LEARNING PROCEDURES.   He then sets out to achieve these targets, by acquiring the information, attitudes, and/or skills that are required. This applies both to the immediate problem and also to the question of developing the ability to solve problems in general.

4. EVALUATION.   Final interviews, discussions, rating scales or other exercises are used to discern the individual's degree of success or failure in solving the problems he wanted to solve.

Thus, a social and life skills session might commence with exercises intended to initiate self-assessment; proceed by helping individuals to set learning goals for themselves; continue with films, talks, interviews, roleplays, discussions, simulations, projects, or whatever other methods are thought to be possible routes to achieving these goals; and conclude with some estimation of how much progress has been made by all concerned. Where exercises in each of these phases cannot be incorporated in a single session, they might be extended over several. Such a problem-solving process, then, can also be instrumental in the manufacture of a social skills curriculum.

Curricula for social and life skills

It should be apparent from the outlines of methods and materials contained in this book that the kind of social skills curriculum envisaged in chapter 1 consists of more than just interaction training. In fact, running a course or planning a curriculum which will help young people become more able to solve their problems means using many different kinds of methods. Drawing these together, we can now chart a rudimentary social skills curriculum which embodies the following elements:

1. Informal information-giving, through the medium of talks, films, leaflets, etc.
2. Visits to places of interest in relation to individuals' problems.
3. Pencil-and-paper exercises, e.g. questionnaires or rating scales, usually designed to structure the process of self-assessment.
4. Interviews and discussions between individuals in social skills groups; structured for some given purpose, or less formal 'chats';
5. Roleplay exercises and variations on them, for assessing and practising social skills.
6. A variety of structured group exercises, e.g. games or simulations, with a wide spectrum of possible aims.
7. Projects for individuals or groups with some kind of end-product, e.g. collecting information, organising an event, etc.

The table on pages 208 and 209 presents a summary of how these elements might be deployed in developing a curriculum or course on the problems to which this book is addressed. This table is designed to act as a kind of schematic outline of the contents of the book — although of course not all the exercises are listed within it. But it is also intended to provide a set of guidelines for balancing different kinds of exercises together in an appropriate way, which can in turn be applied to the planning of courses on areas or problems not covered by the book. If you would like to devise a course on another topic — on family relations; drink, drugs or violence; accommodation; or health and hygiene, for instance — the table should hopefully serve as a framework or checklist for selecting exercises which complement each other in a way which makes learning both more enjoyable, and more effective.

The methods and materials which have been presented in this book are but a small sample of the considerable quantity of exercises that could be included in a social and life skills course. When trying to compile a new curriculum or new exercises for it, it will in many cases be obvious what to include: which kinds of problems individuals are likely to face, what information and skills they might need, and so on. On other occasions, however, the means by which some issue may be approached or by which young people may be assisted in dealing with it may be less easy to see. When this happens, a number of other courses of action are open. One is to look in other sources — cited at the end of each section in chapter 5.

Another is to invent your own methods. Many teachers, lecturers, and youth workers shun this possibility perhaps because they cannot imagine that the end result will be 'good enough'. Being involved in the business of face-to-face teaching or counselling and using tried-and-tested methods is one thing; but trying to devise new things to do in this situation is another — which for some reason, many see as being best left to those who don't actually work face-to-face with young people, such as university lecturers, educationalists, or the authors of social skills books. But counter to this, many individuals *do* concoct new ideas and methods of their own, *and* manage to put them into practice. There is no secret formula as to how exactly this can be achieved, and in a way it is difficult to suggest how to go about producing new ideas because at rock bottom the only way that works is simply to *try*. But there are two routes that may make the invention of new materials somewhat easier.

·The first of these is to try asking the target group: young people themselves. Asked to discuss any topic or problem, and to consider what may be done about it, they will often be a source of inspiration and constructive ideas which conjure up further notions on how an issue may be approached. Also, they will almost always be willing to try a new exercise which is only half-prepared — and to suggest ways in which it can be extended, modified — or started again. A great many exercises of the kind described in this book depend, in any case, on the impetus given to them by interested individuals themselves.

A second avenue to new ideas is to try *brainstorming* on the topic at hand. Make a list of any thoughts, views, images, feelings or whatever that are associated with the central idea. Try doing this in turn with the other ideas which result. Possibilities as to how the problem might be solved, how individuals might learn to cope with it, how such-and-such a skill or piece of information might be imparted, will start to form themselves at least partially. The next step is to seize at least one of them firmly and think of how it might be translated into an exercise for concrete use; and once again, things can only proceed further by trying it out.

But the question of 'how good it is' still provides an effective barrier to creativity for many individuals. In social and life skills training, however, the criteria for deciding upon the value of any exercise are different from those that might be invoked in the teaching of academic subjects. The hurdles to be leapt over are less those of achieving an expected standard than those of being recognised by the consumers — young people — as applicable to their problems; and of effectiveness in helping to solve the problems of real life, in whatever a rough-and-ready sort of way. The most naive idea, therefore, might prove invaluable in sparking off a profitable discussion. The methods

A SOCIAL-AND-LIFE-

Topic/Area	Source of information, speakers, films	Place of interest to visit	Pencil & paper exercise
SELF: self-assessment in general	Individuals, group members		Sentence completion: 'I am . . .'; Self-description; Lifelines; 'Top Tunes'; Problem checklist: Self-and-others chart
INTERACTING WITH OTHERS	Individuals, Counsellors, friends, psychiatrist, psychologist	Social clubs of any kind. Homes e.g. for aged or handicapped	Person-perception scales; social skill survey; questionnaire on relations with specific group
WORK	Job Centre; Occupational Guidance Unit; Careers Officers; local firms; Training Boards	Job Centre, Skill-centre; workplace of any kind; industrial tribunal	Aptitude/Preference tests; work skills survey; 'rights at work' quiz; writing job ads; ads for self; letters of application
LEISURE/ SPARE TIME	Individuals on their hobbies; recreation centres & officers; clubs & societies; town hall	Local leisure facilities, indoor & outdoor; tourist info. offices	'Leisure checklist'; profiles of leisure activities; spare-time diaries; drawing leisure maps
RIGHTS: legal, welfare, everyday	Citizens' Advice Bureaux; Advice Centres; Child Poverty Action Group; Police; legal professions; NCCL	Post Office, DHSS, CAB, Courts, Law Centres, Tribunals	'Rights Quiz' and questionnaires; form-filling exercises; writing letters of complaint
MANAGING MONEY	Banks, Building Societies; Insurance Companies; Office of Fair Trading; Advertising Standards Authority	Banks, Post Office, Shops & stores of any kind	'Consumer Rights' Quiz; budgeting accounts of income & outgoings (for actual & planned budgets)
SEX	Family Planning Association; Brook Advisory Centre; Pregnancy Advice Centres; Marriage Guidance Council	Family Planning Clinic	Questionnaires on sex roles, attitudes to sex, self-perception; 'computer dating' form

SKILLS CURRICULUM

Interview/group discussion topic	Possible roleplay incident	Group exercise: game, simulation, other activity	Group or individual project
Good day/bad day: personal likes/dislikes; worst fears; interests; opinions; plans for the future	Situation someone really enjoyed; most awkward situation he or she has ever been in, etc.	'Personal growth' and 'awareness' games; designing emblem or coat of arms;	Interview others and build up composite picture of self; write autobiography; make long-term plans
Person individuals most admire/hate; 'What's the use of others?'; parents' authority; friends and families, etc.	General social skills in commonplace incidents, eg introductions, asking directions, queue-jumpers, apologising etc.	'Communication' games; mapping personal space; 'Trust' games; recording activity in groups; mimes etc.	Observe others; write reports on some aspect of social behaviour; compare own culture with others
'A job I'd like/hate'; why work?; parents' jobs; trade unions; where to look for jobs; 'my career'	Job interviews; Job centre; late for work; problems at work; tribunal; complaints to supervisors etc.	'To work or not to work' game; simulations eg job search, dispute etc., learning exchange on jobs; forming small firms/coops	Information search: entry to specific jobs; surveys of local job market; what a job entails; how an industry works
How much free time people have; past/planned hobbies; holidays; things to do on your own/in groups etc.	Asking if you can join a group; join a club; invite someone along; make group decisions re outings	Learning exchange on leisure; talks by group members; actual leisure pursuits	Survey local leisure facilities; set up facilities or organise events; make radio or TV programmes
Basic attitudes or views on any issue; law, police, welfare, immigration, age, politics, crime; use of items from newspapers	Claims at DHSS; court procedures; meeting police; coming home late; asking friend to pay for item he borrowed and lost, etc.	Simulations, e.g. accommodation search, courtroom; debates on controversial issues; group decisions on dilemmas etc.	Surveys & reports on aspects of law; follow issue in press & report on it; take community action/run pressure group
The importance of money; ideal wage; how to spend a windfall; wealth & poverty weekly budgeting	Borrowing and lending money; asking for money back; resisting sales pressure; inquiring about prices	Shopping and budgeting simulations; group decisions on how to spend; 'Fair day's pay' game	Surveys of prices; information search on finance e.g. HP, loans, insurance; finding out how a price is made up
Attitudes on any aspect of sex e.g. sex roles, intercourse, age of consent, sex and marriage, jealousy	Asking for a dance; asking for a date; beginning & ending relationships; asking for advice	Debates on aspects of sex; group problem solving	'Sex in the media' analysis of newspapers; information search on biology, contraception, law, other societies

and materials offered simply have to be interesting, and have to make sense to those who will be using them.

The question of developing new materials brings us in a way to the final element in any like skills curriculum: that of evaluation. Attempting to evaluate your own work in social and life skills may be beyond the reach of those who engage in such work. The only immediate form of evaluation is that given by young people as they take part in exercises and try out the skills they have learnt to solve their problems. All of which raises the question: do these methods achieve this purpose in any case? At present, we cannot say with any absolute certainty that they do. Social skills and related methods have been shown to be effective in some settings and for the solving of some kinds of problems. Further, many features of current educational practice, which have acquired respectability through traditional use, have never been evaluated; were they to be, some of them might certainly have to be discontinued. The face value of much life skills training suggests that it is applicable to some problems of contemporary youth which call for action with considerable urgency, and concerning which at the moment, little provision is made. Users of these methods can contribute much by carrying out evaluations of their own; but a full-scale study of the utility of the methods may simply have to wait.

List of addresses

Advertising Standards Authority, 15 Ridgmount Street, London WC1E 7AW.

Advisory, Conciliation, and Arbitration Service (ACAS), Cleland House, Page Street, London SW1P 4ND.

Air Transport and Travel Industry Training Board, Staines House, 158/162 High Street, Staines, Middlesex TW18 4AS.

Albany Trust, 16-20 Strutton Ground, London SW1.

Basic Skills Unit (National Extension College), 18 Brooklands Avenue, Cambridge CB2 2HN.

British Association for Counselling, 26 Bedford Square, London WC1B 3HU.

British Pregnancy Advisory Service, Austy Manor, Wootton Wawen, Solihull, West Midlands B95 6DA.

Brook Advisory Centres, Head Office, 233 Tottenham Court Road, London W1P 9EA.

Building Societies Association, 14 Park Street, London W1Y 4AL.

Cambridgeshire Careers Service, 7 Rose Crescent, Cambridge.

Campaign for Homosexual Equality (CHE), 42a Formosa Street, London W9.

Careers and Occupational Information Centre, Manpower Services Commission, The Pennine Centre, 20-22 Hawley Street, Sheffield S1 3GA (from August 1981: Moorfoot, Sheffield).

Careers Research and Advisory Centre, Bateman Street, Cambridge.

Child Poverty Action Group, 1 Macklin Street, London WC2.

Clocktower Young Adults Project, Tower Road North, Warmley, Bristol BS15 2XU.

Commission for Racial Equality, Elliot House, 10-12 Allington Street, London SW1.

Community Service Volunteers, 237 Pentonville Road, London N1 9NJ.

Consumers' Association, 14 Buckingham Street, London WC2N 6DS.

Coventry Women's Education Group, 12 Westminster Road, Coventry, West Midlands.

'Education for Neighbourhood Change' Project, School of Education, University Park, Nottingham NG7 2RD.

Equal Opportunities Commission, Overseas House, Quay Street, Manchester M3 3HN.

Family Planning Association, 27-35 Mortimer Street, London W1N 7RJ.

Family Welfare Association, 501-3 Kingsland Road, London E8 4AU.

Finance Houses Association, 14 Queen Anne's Gate, London SW1H 9AG.

Further Education Curriculum Review and Development Unit, Elizabeth House, York Road, London SE1.

Grapevine, 416 St John Street, London EC1V 4NJ.

Health Education Council, 78 New Oxford Street, London WC1A 1AH.

Information Canada, Publications Satellite, P.O. Box 1565, Prince Albert, Saskatchewan S6V 5T2.

Inner London Education Authority, Learning Materials Service, Highbury Station Road, London N1 1SB.

Interaction, 15 Wilkin Street, London NW5 3NG.

Minority Rights Group, 36 Craven Street, London WC2.

Mutual Aid Centre, 18 Victoria Park Square, London E2 9PF.

National Association of Citizens' Advice Bureaux, 26 Bedford Square, London WC1B 3HU.

National Audio-Visual Aids Centre (NAVAC), 254 Belsize Road, London NW6.

National Council for Audio-visual Aids in Education, 33 Queen Anne Street, London W1M 9LD.

National Council for Civil Liberties, 186 Kings Cross Road, London WC1.

National Council for Voluntary Organisations, 26 Bedford Square, London WC1B 3HU.

National Federation of Consumer Groups, 70-76 Alcester Road South, Birmingham B14 7PT.

National Foundation for Educational Research, 2 Jennings Buildings, Thames Avenue, Windsor, Berkshire SL14 1QS.

National Institute for Careers Education and Counselling, Bayfordbury House, Lower Hatfield Road, Hertford, Herts, SG13 8LD.

National Marriage Guidance Council, Herbert Gray College, Little Church Street, Rugby, Warwickshire.

National Youth Bureau, 17/23 Albion Street, Leicester LE1 6GD.

New Opportunities Press, 76 St James's Lane, London N10 3RD.

Office of Fair Trading, Field House, 15-25 Bream's Buildings, London EC4A 1PR.

Panmure House, Lochend Close, Canongate, Edinburgh.

Release, 1 Elgin Avenue, London W9.

Saskatchewan Newstart Project — see *Information Canada.*
Schools Council, 160 Great Portland Street, London W1N 6LL.
Scottish Community Education Centre, 4 Queensferry Street, Edinburgh EH2 5EH.
Scottish Health Education Unit, 21 Landsdowne Crescent, Edinburgh EH12 5EH.
Shelter, 157 Waterloo Road, London SE1 8UU.
Small Firms Information Centre, Small Firms Division, Department of Industry, Abell House, John Islip Street, London SW1P 4LN.
Teachers' Advisory Council on Alcohol and Drug Education (TACADE), 2 Mount Street, Manchester M2 5NG.
Tyneside Housing Aid Centre, 33 Groat Market, Newcastle upon Tyne.
Youth Opportunities Development Unit, National Youth Bureau, 17/23 Albion Street, Leicester LE1 6GD.
Youth Service Information Centre, 37 Belvoir Street, Leicester LE1 6SL.

References

Abercrombie, M.L.J. (1969), *The Anatomy of Judgment,* Penguin Books.
Abercrombie, M.L.J. (1970), *Aims and Techniques of Group Teaching,* London: Society for Research in Higher Education.
Adair, J. (1971), *Training for Decisions,* MacDonald and James.
Adams, C. and R. Laurikietis (1976), *The Gender Trap,* Vol.1, *Education and Work;* Vol.2, *Sex and Marriage;* Vol.3, *Messages and Images,* Virago and Quartet Books.
Adkins, W.R. (no date), *Life Skills Syllabus,* Unpublished outline, Teachers College, Columbia University, New York.
Anastasi, A. (1976), *Psychological Testing,* Collier-Macmillan.
Argyle, M. (1969), *Social Interaction,* Tavistock Publications/Methuen.
Argyle, M. (1975), *Bodily Communication,* Methuen.
Argyle, M., B. Bryant, and P. Trower (1974), Social skills training and psychotherapy: a comparative study, *Psychological Medicine,* 4, 435-43.
Argyle, M., P. Trower, and B. Bryant (1974), Explorations in the treatment of personality disorders and neuroses by social skills training, *British Journal of Medical Psychology,* 47, 63-72.
Bandura, A. (1969), *Principles of Behaviour Modification,* Holt, Rinehart and Winston.
Bandura, A. (1971), *Social Learning Theory,* General Learning Press.
Bandura, A. (1973), *Aggression: a social learning analysis,* Prentice-Hall.
Bannister, D. and F. Fransella (1971), *Inquiring man: The Theory of Personal Constructs,* Penguin Books.
Berger, N. (1974), *Rights: a Handbook for People Under Age,* Penguin Books.
Brandes, D. and H. Phillips (1968). *The Gamester's Handbook,* Hutchinson.
Brown, A. (1979), *Groupwork,* Heinemann.
Brown, G. (1975), *Microteaching,* Methuen.

Burgess, T. and E. Adams (1980), *Outcomes of Education,* Macmillan Education.

Burns, R.B. (1979), *The Self Concept: Theory, Measurement, Development and Behaviour,* Longman.

Button, L. (1974), *Developmental Group Work with Adolescents,* University of London Press.

Cartledge, G. and J.F. Milburn (eds) (1980), *Teaching Social Skills to Children: Innovative Approaches,* Pergamon Press.

Casserley, J. and W. Clark (1978), *A Welfare Rights Approach to the Chronically Sick and Disabled,* Strathclyde Regional Council.

Chesler, M. and R. Fox (1966), *Role-Playing Methods in the Classroom,* Science Research Associates Inc, Chicago.

Cheston, M. (1979), *It's Your Life: a personal and social course,* Wheaton.

Claesson, B.H. (1980), *Boy, Girl, Man, Woman,* Penguin Books.

Cohen, L. and L. Manion (1977), *A Guide to Teaching Practice,* Methuen.

Conger, D.S. (ed.) (1973), *Readings in Life Skills,* Training Research and Development Station, Department of Manpower and Immigration, Saskatchewan.

Consumers' Association (1976), *Dismissal, Redundancy, and Job Hunting,* (edited by E. Rudinger).

Consumers' Association (1979), *Consumer Education: a Resources Handbook for Teachers.* Consumers Association/Hodder and Stoughton.

Consumers' Association and the Open University (1978), *The Buyer's Right: A Which? guide for consumers* (compiled by P. Petch and D. Holloway).

Coote, A. and T. Gill (1977), *Women's Rights: a practical guide,* Penguin Books.

Cousins, J. (1978), *Make it Happy: What sex is all about,* Virago.

Coventry Women's Education Group (no date), *Please Yourself: Sex for Girls,* 12 Westerminster Road, Coventry.

Crawford, D. (1976), *A social skills treatment programme with sex offenders.* Mimeo, Department of Psychology, Broadmoor Hospital.

Crowley, T. (1978 and 1979), *The Job Quiz Books (1, 2 and 3),* Careers Research and Advisory Centre, Cambridge.

Curran, J.P. (1975), Social skills training and systematic desensitization in reducing dating anxiety, *Behaviour Research and Therapy,* 13, 65-8.

Curtiss, P. and R. Friedman (1973), Training the Life Skills Coach, in D.S. Conger (ed.) *Readings in Life Skills,* Training Research and Development Station, Department of Manpower and Immigration, Saskatchewan.

Davison, A. and P. Gordon (1978), *Games and Simulations in action,* Woburn Press.

de Bono, E. (1970), *Lateral Thinking,* Ward Lock.

Dobinson, H.M. (1976), *Basic Skills You Need,* Nelson.

Douglas, T. (1976), *Groupwork Practice,* Tavistock Publications.

Dowding, H. and S. Boyce (1979), *Getting the job you want*, Ward Lock.

Dowmunt, T. (1980), *Video with Young People*, Inter-Action Inprint.

Dowson, H. and R. Howden (1979), *School Leavers' Handbook*, Careers Consultants Ltd/Home and School Council.

Eisler, R.M., M. Hersen, and P.M. Miller (1973), Effects of modelling on components of assertive behaviour, *Journal of Behaviour Therapy and Experimental Psychiatry*, 4, 1-6.

Elliott, J. and R. Pring (eds) (1975), *Social Education and Social Understanding*, University of London Press.

Ellis, J. and T. Barnes (1979), *Life Skills Training Manual*, Community Service Volunteers.

Ellis, R. (1980), Simulated social skill training for interpersonal professions, in W.T. Singleton, P. Spurgeon and R.B. Stammers (eds), *The Analysis of Social Skill*, Plenum Publishing Corporation.

Falloon, I., P. Lindley, and R. McDonald (1974), *Social Training: a manual*, Psychological Treatment Section, Maudsley Hospital.

Family Welfare Association (updated annually), *Guide to the Social Services*, MacDonald and Evans.

Flegg, D. (1979), *Training of Bar Staff: a study and some recommendations*, Industrial Training Research Unit, Cambridge.

Flowers, J.V. and C.D. Booraem (1980), Simulation and role-playing methods, in F.H. Kanfer and A.P. Goldstein (eds), *Helping People Change: a textbook of methods*, Pergamon Press.

Frederiksen, L.W., J.O. Jenkins, D.W. Foy and R.M. Eisler (1976), Social-skills training to modify abusive verbal outbursts in adults, *Journal of Applied Behaviour Analysis*, 9, 117-25.

Friel, T.W. and R.R. Carkhuff (1974), *The Art of Developing a Career: a Helper's Guide*, Human Resource Development Press.

Foy, D.W., R.M. Eisler and S.G. Pinkston (1975), Modeled assertion in a case of explosive rages, *Journal of Behaviour Therapy*, 6, 135-7.

Foy, D.W., P.M. Miller, R.M. Eisler and D.H. O'Toole (1976), Social-skills training to teach alcoholics to refuse drinks effectively, *Journal of Studies on Alcohol*, 9, 1340-5.

Gibson, T. (1979), *People Power: community and work groups in action*, Penguin Books.

Goldsmith, J.B. and R.M. McFall (1975), Development and evaluation of an interpersonal skill-training program for psychiatric patients, *Journal of Abnormal Psychology*, 84, 51-8.

Goldstein, A.P. and A.W. Goedhart (1973), The use of Structured Learning for empathy enhancement in paraprofessional psychotherapist training, *Journal of Community Psychology*, 1, 168-73.

Goldstein, A.P., R.P. Sprafkin and N.J. Gershaw (1976), *Skill Training for Community Living*, Pergamon Press.

Goldstein, A.P., R.P. Sprafkin, N.J. Gershaw and P. Klein (1980), The Adolescent: social skills training through structured learning, in: G. Cartledge and J.F. Milburn (eds), *Teaching Social Skills to Children: Innovative Approaches*, Pergamon Press.

Grant, L., P. Hewitt, C. Jackson and H. Levenson (1978), *Civil Liberty: the NCCL Guide to your rights*, Penguin Books.

Greenoak, F. and others (1976 and 1977), *What Right Have You Got?* (parts 1 and 2), BBC Publications.

Gutride, M.E., A.P. Goldstein and G.F. Hunter (1973), The use of modeling and roleplaying to increase social interaction among asocial psychiatric patients, *Journal of Consulting and Clinical Psychology*, 40, 408-15.

Her Majesty's Stationery Office, *The British Parliament*, London, HMSO.

Her Majesty's Stationery Office, *Classification of Occupations and Directory of Occupational Titles*, London, HMSO.

Her Majesty's Stationery Office, *Supplementary Benefits Handbook*, London, HMSO.

Hersen, M., R.M. Eisler and P.M. Miller (1973), Effects of practice, instructions, and modeling on components of assertive behaviour, *Behaviour Research and Therapy*, 11, 443-51.

Himsl, R. (1973), Life Skills: a course in applied problem solving, in: D.S. Conger (ed.) *Readings in Life Skills*, Training Research and Development Station, Department of Manpower and Immigration, Saskatchewan.

Hopkins, A. (1978), *The School Debate*, Penguin Books.

Hopson, B. and P. Hough (1973), *Exercises in Personal and Career Development*, Careers Research and Advisory Centre, Cambridge.

Hopson, B. and M. Scally (1980), *Life Skills Teaching*, McGraw-Hill.

Hudson, L. (1966), *Contrary Imaginations*, Penguin Books.

Hudson, L. (1968), *Frames of Mind*, Penguin Books.

Illich, I.D. (1970), *Deschooling Society*, Penguin Books.

Jackson, K. (1975), *The Art of Solving Problems*, Heinemann.

Jones, A. (1977), *Counselling Adolescents in School*, Kogan Page.

Jones, K. (1980), *Simulations: a handbook for teachers*, Kogan Page.

Kanfer, F.H. and A.P. Goldstein (eds) (1980), *Helping People Change: a textbook of methods*, Pergamon Press.

Kelly, G.A. (1955), *The Psychology of Personal Constructs* (2 vols), Norton.

Kinnersley, P. (1973), *The Hazards of Work*, Pluto Press.

Knapp, M.L. (1980), *Essentials of Nonverbal Communication*, Holt, Rinehart and Winston.

Korving, J., M. Korving, and M. Keeley (1975), *Out of the Rut*, BBC Publications.

Krumboltz, J.D. and C.E. Thoresen (1976), *Counselling Methods*, Holt, Rinehart and Winston.

Lawton, D. and B. Dufour (1973), *The New Social Studies: a handbook for teachers in primary, secondary and further education*, Heinemann.

218   Life after school

Lea, M.V. (1975), *Health and Social Education*, Heinemann.
Lee, R. (1980), *Beyond Coping: Some approaches to social education*, London: Further Education Curriculum Review and Development Unit.
Lewis, R. and J. Mee (1980), *Using Role Play: an introductory guide*, Basic Skills Unit, Cambridge.
Lindsay, W.R., R.S. Symons and T. Sweet (1979), A programme for teaching social skills to socially inept adolescents: description and evaluation, *Journal of Adolescence*, 2, 215-28.
Lister, R., *National Welfare Benefits Handbook*, London: Child Poverty Action Group.
Manpower Services Commission (1979), *Instructional Guide to Social and Life Skills*, London, MSC.
Marzillier, J.S., C. Lambert and J. Kellett (1976), A controlled evaluation of systematic desensitisation and social skills training for socially inadequate psychiatric patients, *Behaviour Research and Therapy*, 14, 225-38.
McFall, R.M. and C.T. Twentyman (1973), Four experiments on the relative contributions of rehearsal, modeling, and coaching to assertion training, *Journal of Abnormal Psychology*, 81, 119-218.
McMullen, J. (1979), *Rights at Work*, Pluto Press.
McPhail, P., J.R. Ungoed-Thomas and H. Chapman (1972), *Moral Education in the Secondary School*, Longman.
Morgan, T., N. Rackham and H. Hudson (1974a, 1974b), *DIS — three years on, Industrial and Commercial Training*, pt 1 — June; pt 2 — July 1974.
Morrison, A. and D. McIntyre (1971), *Schools and Socialisation*, Penguin Books.
Munro, E.A., R.J. Manthei and J.J. Small (1979), *Counselling: a skills approach*, Methuen (New Zealand).
National Audio-Visual Aids Centre (1980), *The Audio-Visual Handbook*, Kogan Page.
New Opportunities Press (updated annually), *Opportunities for School Leavers*, London, NOP.
Novaco, R.W. (1975), *Anger Control: the Development and Evaluation of an Experimental Treatment*, Lexington Books, D.C. Heath & Co.
Orlick, T. (1978), *The Cooperative Sports and Games Book: Challenge without Competition*, Pantheon Books.
Osborn, A. (1953), *Applied Imagination*, Scribner.
Panmure House Staff Team (1979), *So You Think You Can Play Games?*, Panmure House, Edinburgh.
Perry, M.A. and M.J. Furukawa (1980), Modeling methods, in: F.H. Kanfer and A.P. Goldstein (eds), *Helping People Change: a textbook of methods*, Pergamon Press.
Pfeiffer, J.W. and J.E. Jones (1970 onwards), *A handbook of structured experiences for human relations training*, Iowa, University Associates Press.

Phillips, A. and J. Rakusen (1978), *Our Bodies Ourselves*, Penguin Books.

Phillips, E.L. (1978), *The Social Skills Basis of Psychopathology*, Grune and Stratton.

Pomeroy, W.B. (1968), *Boys and Sex*, Penguin Books.

Pomeroy, W.B. (1969), *Girls and Sex*, Penguin Books.

Priestley, P. and J. McGuire (1981a), *Forms and Tests — an introduction*, Basic Skills Unit, Cambridge.

Priestley, P. and J. McGuire (1981b), *Learning to Help: Basic Skills Exercises*, Tavistock Publications.

Priestley, P., J. McGuire, D. Flegg, V. Hemsley and D. Welham (1978), *Social Skills and Personal Problem Solving*, Tavistock Publications.

Priestley, P., J. McGuire, D. Flegg, D. Welham, V. Hemsley and R. Barnitt (1981), *Social Skills for Offenders*, Routledge & Kegan Paul.

Rackham, N. and T. Morgan (1977), *Behaviour Analysis in Training*, McGraw-Hill.

Rathus, S.A. (1973), A 30-item schedule for assessing assertive behavior, *Behavior Therapy*, 4, 398-406.

Rennie, J., E.A. Lunzer and W.T. Williams (1974), *Social Education: an experiment in four secondary schools*, (Schools Council Working Paper 51), Evans/Methuen Educational.

Rimm, D.C. and J.C. Masters (1979), *Behaviour Therapy: Techniques and Empirical Findings*, Academic Press.

Rutter, M., B. Maughan, P. Mortimore and J. Ouston (1979), *Fifteen Thousand Hours*, Open Books.

Sarason, I.G. and V.J. Ganzer (1973), Modeling and group discussion in the rehabilitation of juvenile delinquents, *Journal of Counselling Psychology*, 20, 442-9.

Saskatchewan Newstart (1973), *Life Skills Coaching Manual*, Training Research and Development Station, Department of Manpower and Immigration, Saskatchewan.

Scally, M. and B. Hopson (1979), *Lifeskills Teaching in Schools and Colleges*, Mimeo, Counselling and Career Development Unit, University of Leeds.

Scottish Community Education Centre (1979), *Working with young people — an introductory leaflet to the set of Programme Kits produced by the Scottish Community Education Centre*.

Shapiro, H.I. (1980), *The Birth Control Book*, Penguin Books.

Sharpe, S. (1976), *'Just like a girl': How girls learn to be women*, Penguin Books.

Sidney, E. and M. Argyle (1969), *Training in Selection Interviewing*, Mantra.

Spence, S.H. (1980), *Social Skills Training with Children and Adolescents: a Counsellor's Manual*, National Foundation for Educational Research.

Spivack, G., J.J. Platt and M.B. Shure (1976), *The Problem-solving Approach to Adjustment*, Jossey-Bass.

Stansbury, D. (1980), The Record of Personal Experience, in: T. Burgess and E. Adams (eds), *Outcomes of Education*, Macmillan Education.

Stanton, G., E.P. Clark, R. Stradling and A.G. Watts (1980), *Developing Social and Life Skills: strategies for tutors*, London, Further Education Curriculum Review and Development Unit.

Stein, M.I. (1975), *Stimulating Creativity, Vol.2: Group Procedures*, Academic Press.

Sterret, P. (1979), *Fund-raising Projects: Cash for good causes*, Foulsham & Co.

Taylor, J.L. and R. Walford (1978), *Learning and the Simulation Game*, Open University Press.

Taylor, L.C. (1972), *Resources for Learning*, Penguin Books.

Thelen, M.H., R.A. Fry, S.J. Dollinger and S.G. Paul (1976), Use of video-taped models to improve the interpersonal adjustment of delinquents, *Journal of Consulting and Clinical Psychology*, 44, 492.

Trower, P., B. Bryant and M. Argyle (1978), *Social Skills and Mental Health*, Methuen.

Turner, H. (1979), *The Consumer's A—Z. Your Guide to Personal Consumption*, Windward.

Twentyman, C.T. and R.M. McFall (1975), Behavioral Training of Social Skills in Shy Males, *Journal of Consulting and Clinical Psychology*, 43, 384-95.

Ward, C. (1974), *How to Complain*, Pan Books.

Warren, P.W. and L.A. Lamrock (1973), Evaluation of the Life Skills Course, in: D.S. Conger (ed.), *Readings in Life Skills*, Training Research and Development Station, Department of Manpower and Immigration, Saskatchewan.

Watson, D. and R. Friend (1969), Measurement of social-evaluative anxiety, *Journal of Consulting and Clinical Psychology*, 33, 448-57.

Webb, C. (1978), *Talk Yourself into a Job*, Communications Skills Series, Macmillan Press.

Whitehill, M.B., M. Hersen and A.S. Bellack (1980), Conversation skills training for socially isolated children, *Behaviour Research and Therapy*, 18, 217-25.

Whitfield, P.R. (1975), *Creativity in Industry*, Penguin Books.

Williams, A. (1975), *Educating the Consumer: a practical guide*, Longman.

Wright, D.S. (1971), *The Psychology of Moral Behaviour*, Penguin Books.

Youngman, M.B. (1978), *Designing and Analysing Questionnaires*, University of Nottingham School of Education.

Youth Opportunities Development Unit (1979), *Social education in informal settings: case studies of practice within the Youth Opportunities Programme*, National Youth Bureau, Youth Opportunities Development Unit, Leicester.

Youth Service Information Centre, *Audio-visual Resources in Social Education*, Leicester, YSIC.

Ziller, R.C. (1973), *The Social Self*, Pergamon Press.

Zimbardo, P.G. (1977), *Shyness: what it is, what to do about it*, Addison-Wesley.

Index